Advance Praise

Garments without Guilt? is a scholarly tour de force. Kanchana N. Ruwanpura has challenged prevailing analyses of voluntary ethical governance codes which foreground global and national level standards while ignoring the central role of the state in investing in human capital. Educated workers are central to the struggles for decent working conditions and wages, on which the Sri Lankan garments industry claims to be a world-leading ethical producer. Using rich ethnographic data obtained over more than a decade talking to factory managers and garment workers, she has produced a vivid picture of the agency of the workers and the limitations of voluntary industrial and national regulations, and the dangers posed by ethnic divisions and conflict that could undermine ethical standards.

—**Ruth Pearson**, University of Leeds, UK

Kanchana N. Ruwanpura builds on years of field research to develop a provocative and convincing book, highlighting the role that local labour and social institutions actually played in creating conditions for the apparent success of global ethical governance. The contribution of labour and social development policies goes unacknowledged and is even threatened by the voluntary ethical regime, Ruwanpura argues, a regime which remains highly uneven and unstable in the social gains made by workers on the shop floor. Her book offers a thorough, inspiring reading for scholars concerned with the local developmental outcomes of economic globalization.

—**Florence Palpacuer**, University of Montpellier, France

In *Garments without Guilt?* Kanchana N. Ruwanpura unpacks the global clothing industry's complexities as they play out in her home country, shining a nuanced light on ethical clothing initiatives in practice. Drawing on over 10 years of fieldwork, she highlights how Sri Lanka's better track record complying with health and safety codes compared to its South Asian neighbours is rooted as much in workers' movements and agency as it is in industry-led initiatives. Ruwanpura also makes a compelling case that freedom of association, living wages, and humane treatment on the shop floor are ethical codes that remain a site of ongoing struggle.

—**Annelies Goger**, Brookings Institution, USA

Garments without Guilt?

Sri Lanka's apparel sector holds an enviable place in the imaginary of its competitors for having a niche position amongst global retailers, given its claims of producing 'garments without guilt'. Exploitative labour conditions are not part of the industry's portfolio – ethicality, eco-friendly production and unblemished conditions of work are. Sri Lanka's transition away from a protracted ethnic war has meant that the industry portrays itself as investing in the former war zone to create jobs without reflection on how its vaunted mantle, the deployment of ethical codes effectively, itself may be under duress. This book uses an analytical framing informed by labour and feminist perspectives to explore how labour struggles in the post-1977 period in Sri Lanka provided important resistance to capitalist processes and continue to shape the industry both within and outside of the shop floor. It studies contextual moments in the country's recent history to rupture the dominant narrative and record the centrality of labour in the success of the country's apparel industry.

Kanchana N. Ruwanpura is Professor of Human Geography at the University of Gothenburg, Sweden; and Fellow at the Centre for South Asian Studies, University of Edinburgh, United Kingdom. Her focus areas for both research and teaching cover labour geographies, feminist politics and uneven development. She is the author of *Matrilineal Communities, Patriarchal Realities: A Feminist Nirvana Uncovered* (2006).

Garments without Guilt?

Global Labour Justice and Ethical Codes in Sri Lankan Apparels

Kanchana N. Ruwanpura

CAMBRIDGE
UNIVERSITY PRESS

University Printing House, Cambridge CB2 8BS, United Kingdom

One Liberty Plaza, 20th Floor, New York, NY 10006, USA

477 Williamstown Road, Port Melbourne, vic 3207, Australia

314 to 321, 3rd Floor, Plot No.3, Splendor Forum, Jasola District Centre, New Delhi 110025, India

103 Penang Road, #05–06/07, Visioncrest Commercial, Singapore 238467

Cambridge University Press is part of the University of Cambridge.

It furthers the University's mission by disseminating knowledge in the pursuit of education, learning and research at the highest international levels of excellence.

www.cambridge.org
Information on this title: www.cambridge.org/9781108832014

© Kanchana N. Ruwanpura 2022

First published 2022

Printed in India by Thomson Press India Ltd.

A catalogue record for this publication is available from the British Library

ISBN 978-1-108-83201-4 Hardback

For my feminist parents and grandmother:
Chand de Silva, Anoma de Silva and
Harriet Chandrasekera

My *thaththi* for imparting intellect mixed with humour,
ammi for being my first feminist role model
and *achchi* for schooling us in academic discipline and
codes of *sīla*.

With much gratitude for creating a home, where our emotional
and spiritual comfort was intermingled with high doses of love
for books, political curiosity with a quest for social justice.

It's just as difficult, so they tell us
To run a factory. Without the owner
The walls would fall in and the machines rust, so they say.

—Bertlot Brecht
From *Difficulty of Governing*

Contents

Tables, Figures and Images

Tables

Figures

Images

Preface and Acknowledgements

On a crisp, beautiful autumnal morning in 2007, I attended my first away-day in British academia. Quite a few of us in Southampton's School of Geography, had made the transition from North America to a British university. We were *Cool Britannia* then, and we all felt novelty, excitement and dread in equal measure. Little did I know the collective energy I enjoyed on that first day would generate a humbling journey that has culminated in the pages of this book.

That morning, I was treated to a presentation by one of my senior colleagues, Neil Wrigley, about his work with Alex Hughes and Martin Buttle, on multi-stakeholder initiatives and ethical trading. As I sat listening, a nagging question began rattling around my brain. During the question and answer, I first voiced it: 'What about the workers? What do they think of these ethical trading initiatives? Where is their voice?' I don't recall any discussion, but later, during lunch, Neil and another senior colleague, Peter Sunley, followed up and gave encouragement to this newly formed idea: 'That was an important perspective you flagged; there is something there, you should explore it.' Soon I secured an ESRC (Economic and Social Research Council) grant (061-25-0181), which allowed me to launch this project, where I explore these questions in the context of the Sri Lankan apparel sector.

My question had its roots in work I had done before coming into academia. My time at the International Labour Office (ILO) in Geneva, Switzerland, introduced me to senior colleagues who valued ILO's tripartite spirit: Manuela (Tomei), Auret (van Heerden), Naoko (Otobe), David (Kucera), Clare (Harasty) and Azita (Berar-Awad). The many projects I did there instilled in me the need to pay attention to workers' voices and their quest for justice.

Primed to ask questions, I arrived in Sri Lanka where the generous, committed, feisty garment workers taught me what I needed to know to tell this story and answer the questions I posed on that away-day many years ago. And those workers, in turn, taught me the value of listening.

I brought these tenets to my research and analysis on the apparel sector of Sri Lanka. Then I knew very little of the industry or its workers. However, the connections I made – mostly with the workers and worker rights organizations but also managers – has meant that I have remained interested. My curiosity is partly due to the fact that I now constantly ask myself: what sweat and tears may be behind or how many different stitched pieces have come together in one item of clothing?

During the past decade, it also became evident that the lives and livelihoods of thousands of working women and men in Sri Lanka are subject not just to the vagaries of the global political economy but also to the militarization of Sri Lankan polity, society and economy. The clearest evidence of this is the recent fallout of the CoVID-19 community transmission across Sri Lanka via BRANDIX apparels. A militarized CoVID-19 task force, appointed by the President of Sri Lanka, is adrift due to the virus of corruption that the government and the business community remain enmeshed in. It is not just the governments, of various hues, that are corrupt in Sri Lanka. So too is the corporate sector – including, it seems, the apparel sector.

This book, however, is not about the close and corrupt relations between the governments of Sri Lanka and the corporate world (that is a work for another), but about the *workers* primarily. Hence, my first appreciation is to them for having taken the time to become part of this research – and for sacrificing their precious time to mingle with me both onsite and off-site of the factory floors. The early years of my research was possible only because of their camaraderie and then the years after, the friendship and trust they placed in me. For this, I am grateful.

My knowledge of the industry, its complex layering and access to factories, however, was facilitated by a dense network of friends and family that made initial connections to numerous management personnel. I remain grateful to those that allowed access to factories. As I outline in this book, the apparel sector and its management have a commendable vision in undertaking to ensure largely safe work places. However, the apparel sector cannot afford to rest on its laurels. The absence of living wages in the sector and scarcity of freedom of association and collective bargaining opens the sector to charges of exploitation. The recent and high-profile fallout around health and well-being of workers during CoVID-19 testifies to these risks.

Equally, of course, as I have delineated in the book, in the end, corporate management did not raise the bar on its own: Labour struggles past and present continue to matter on how the apparel sector came to its place and will evolve. Striking a cooperative labour–management ethos may also matters for its long-term strength. I remain hopeful that these are possibilities that we do not turn away from exploring, despite dark political times.

I was also able to continue this research because of some of the early links with labour rights organizations, and particularly the support and help that the Women Centre and Da Bindu provided. Their commitment to social justice and courage is inspiring: Working-class women standing up for themselves – and not for a year or two but decades. Their feminist consciousness is borne of labour struggles and infused with solidarities that intersect class, ethnicity, gender, sex, politics and all other social vectors that make up a complex Sri Lanka. I am indebted to them for keeping the faith, generously sharing information, leaflets and photos.

During the past decade, I was fortunate in bonding with committed state officials, policy planners, union organizations and acquaintances of various hues that helped sustain this study for over a decade. I have kept them anonymous (like the workers and management) because of ethical protocol, but mention (late) Aunty Inez and (late) Uncle Christo for generously housing me.

Our research journeys are never solitary ventures, although writing is. I am lucky that in the year before I decided to write in earnest, I came across particularly bright graduate students that supported me in numerous ways: Loritta Chan, Megan Todd and Peter Rowe were pivotal in too many ways to detail. Their spirit, enthusiasm and insight too coloured my analysis. I want to acknowledge them, as well as those other early junior researchers that helped during various stages of this research and help ensure its viability: Virandi Wettewa, Sarah Parker, Lisa Boorman, Anu Tennekoon, W. D. Wasana and Andi Schubert.

Similarly, there are numerous friends and former colleagues that generously supported my writing at various stages. At the start, Alessandra Mezzadri and Rajesh Venugopal took the time to discuss my imprecise ideas and unhesitatingly shared their book proposals to ensure that I pulled together the best proposal possible. I had books sourced and/or sent across from the United States by James-Henry Holland, Bill Waller, Thushari

Wijesekera and Leanne Roncolato. Others were munificent differently. Through the past decade of writing and presenting, at different stages, Vinay Gidwani, Marion Werner, Jane Wills, Adrian Smith, John Harriss, Keping Wu, Prasenjit Duara, (late) Barney Bates, Alex Hughes, Sanchita Saxena, Rahul Mukherjee, Prema-Chandra Athukorala, Florence Palpaucer, Jeanne Marecek, Kumari Jayawardena, Caitrin Lynch, Tania Murray Li, (late) Qadri Ismail, Radhika Coomaraswamy, YouYenn Teo, Vineeta Sinha, Vidyamali Samarasinghe and Madhumita Dutta have offered valuable comments. Towards the very end, Anushaya Collure, Buddhima Padmasiri, Harshana Rambukwella and Asha Abeysekera fielded various trivial requests.

Geert de Neve, Annelies Goger, Steven Pinch, Doug Miller, Ellie Tighe, Jörg Nowak, Priyanka Srivastava, Ayşe Arslan, Hilal Ahmed, Simon Allen, David Featherstone, Alessandra Mezzadri and Naila Kabeer gave up their precious research time to read chapters – sometimes at short notice and others more than one iteration or chapter. Malathi de Alwis, Ben Selwyn and Roger Jeffery went further and took the time to read the entire manuscript and offered me detailed and insightful observations. While I hope I have done justice and taken on board their comments, I know that they make the best of academia: a community invested in reciprocity, humility and collegiality.

It is these qualities, collegiality and reciprocity that attracted me to academia in the first place as a young undergraduate woman at William Smith College in upstate New York, United States. And through much of my academia journey, I have revelled in this collective spirit in various countries and context. For ensuring this, I have to thank my mentors, colleagues and friends: Jane Humphries, Chris Gunn, Bill Waller, Alain Supiot, (late) Stephan Klasen, David Ruccio, Randy Albelda, Anu Seth, Tony Lawson, George Joseph & Thelma Pinto, David Sneath, James-Henry Holland, Dia da Costa, Lisa Tetrault, Bahar Davary, (late) Pasad Kulatunga & Sara Lagerhölm, Alan & Ronny Frishman, Judith & Scott McKinney, Geoff Gilbert, Eileen & Fred Rogers, (late) Dave Cormier, (late) Chuck Craypo, Olga Vasile, Fatmata Sesay, Antje Schumann, Cindy Caron, Laurence Erussard, Katy Goodrich, Leanne Roncolato, Brad Weinberg, and David Ost. So much so, despite not being trained as a geographer, making the transition to my first community of geographers at Southampton did not seem a daunting prospect because I took for granted the collegiality of academia. To the credit of my former colleagues at Southampton, they made the transition easy and ensured inclusivity and sociability. Of this convivial community, Peter Sunley, Steven Pinch, Neil Wrigley, Nick Clarke, Steve

Darby, (late) Ted & Debbie Milton, Dionysia Lambiri, Pete Langdon, Suzy Reimer, Geoff deVerteuil, John Dearing, Sam Cockings, Denise Pompa, Gemma O'Brien, Mary Edwards and Dave Martin need a special mention. Once in the United Kingdom, Scott Soo, (late) Lawrence Saez, Shirin Rai, James Sidaway, Jamie Gillen, Shirlena Huang, Silke Roth, Ben Selwyn, Harvey Neo, Ian Talbot, Naila Kabeer, October Books-Southampton, Marie-Pierre Gilbert, Kunal Sen, Samanthi Gunawardana, Ruth Pearson, Chris Hearle, Tuna Kuyuçu, Nitya Rao, Siobhan McGrath, Gale Raj-Reichert, Craig Jeffrey, John Zavos, Jayanthi Lingam, Alex Hughes, Jane Wills, Adrian Smith, Tariq Jazeel, Annu Jalais, Atreyee Sen, along with my editorial colleagues at *Geoforum* and *Gender, Place and Culture* were sources of sustenance.

If geographers at Southampton were the best of academia, at the University of Edinburgh, I found this spirit at the Centre for South Asian Studies, the School of Social and Political Science, the University and the city more broadly. Wilfried Swenden, Fiona MacKay, Roger Jeffery, Jo Shaw, Ada Munns, Orla Murray, Pankaj Pankaj, Sjoerd de Ridder, Jiaxi Lui, Daisy Mini-Schnauzer, Jose-Maria Munoz, Sophia Woodman, Nasar Meer, Harish Lokhun, Talat Ahmed, Hugo Gorringe, Hepzibah Israel, Mary Hanlon, Kiera McLean, Meaghan Delahunt, Niranjan Atputhasingam, Asanga Welikala, Radhika Govinda, Crispin Bates, Kirsten & Scott Waugh, Kerrigan Bell, Elaine Henry & TarloShan Gata-Aura and Jane Essex-Little offered consistent support.

We often gloss over the difficulties in academia in writing acknowledgements. Still my political sensibilities and feminist politics move me to register how all academic spaces are not safe havens. And yet, the challenges of working amidst hostility animate the contributions made by those who offer collegial support: Antonis Ioris, Simon Allen, Janet Fisher, Miram Gay-Antaki, Rowan Ellis, Nazli Köseoglu, Simon Shackley, Maggie Creed, Tom Slater, Corinne Baulcomb, Hugh Sinclair, Ian Main, Eliza Calder, Eva Panagiotakopulu, David Wharrie, Jan Penrose, Rachel Chisholm and Natasha Honeybone. Their fellowship provided a much-needed antidote to the hostile climate in my former academic home, the School of Geosciences and the Institute of Geography, where I was reminded how discriminatory and oppressive practices discussed in this book pervade all workspaces, including academia.

Given the trying work context, 2019/20 renewed my faith in the academic community, despite personal losses and emotional drain. I was privileged to secure three fellowships during this academic year: A Humboldt fellowship (CeMIS, University of Göttingen, Germany), Max-Weber Stifting fellowship (declined) and the final one, secured at the last moment and through serendipity: France-ILO Chair fellow (IAS-Nantes, France). These fellowships sustained the preliminary work I began as a Senior Visiting Fellow at ARI, National University of Singapore, in 2014.

What stimulating settings! In these locations, I came across not just incredible and fun-loving scholars but colleagues secure in their skin and humble. And we came from all corners of the world! Lorenzo Vinciguerra, Roar Høstaker, Williams Pokam Kamdem, Michele Szkilnik, John Tolan, Aardra Surendran, Michele Oriol, Wai Yip Ho, Alain Supiot, Priyanka Srivastava, Deepankar Basu, Gayathri Rathore, Micheala Dimmers, Ravi Ahuja, Sebastian Vollmer, Murat Akan, Hilal Ahmed, Pu Wang, Isabelle Roy, Marcelo Borges and Jose-Emilio Burucua showered me with friendship, good food, laughter and frequent chats that spanned from politics to ping-pong.

We also had exceptional support provided, with Zaghira Danibert, Anthony Clavier, Sarah Joksimovic, Bertille Leroux, Isabelle Guin (Residhomee, Nantes), Elizabeth Plaintiv, Iris Karakus, Birgit Priemer and Susanne Buente especially making my stay as a fellow incredible with their smiles, chats and *joie de vivre*. So, despite 2020 being a trying year globally, thank you for this humanity and humility.

Likewise, through the years I came across amazing students that made my academic life fun, fulfilling and sometimes even kept me together. They have been such a privilege to be on a journey of learning and education with, as their presence in my classes and commitment to social struggles are a constant source of inspiration and signal the infinite possibilities available for us to craft a socially just world. Their names would fill too many pages and yet what delight to have come across them: Thank you for being part of my academic journey.

The year 2020 has been tough for most – some more than others, as the global evidence suggests. Too many lives lost and political darkness abounds. I too had my share of emotional pain, although fortunately not due to a contagious virus (CoVID-19). I lost three dear academic mentors and feminist champions – in their 50s, too young to leave. Stephan Klasen's mark on my academic trajectory is boundless: It started with my graduation from Cambridge and remained steadfast until his end. My academic sister, Malathi de Alwis, left us not too long after she had read and provided detailed comments on a draft of this book – as she generously had done even on my first book. A friendship and feminist sisterhood that began with my graduate studies, where she taught ethnography and feminist camaraderie by conducting fieldwork alongside me in eastern Sri Lanka in the late 1990s (a time when no one dared to travel to this war-torn part). Qadri Ismail, another academic I have looked up to from my graduate student days, left unexpectedly, leaving us with a profound sense of loss. Malathi, Qadri and Stephan epitomize the best of intellectuals and feminists, through the humility, generosity, wit and humour they showered those that came after them.

Tearing apart, the *dharma* of life, was also what it is when we lost my beloved *thaththi*, unexpectedly for us, but peacefully for him. Yet he lived a good and long life, filled with fun, laughter, love of music and dance, charm and constant cheek intermingled with unwavering affection and compassion. I feel his absence many moments every single day, and still he travels with me daily with the values and spirit he inculcated: be principled, strong, straightforward and yet kind, have fun, take time to gaze at the moon and always have integrity.

Although *thaththi* will not see this book in print, in June 2020, he knew I had the entire draft together. After asking of its progress in his frequent and yet brief phone calls, in his characteristic fashion he had said, 'Good, good.' However, sadly, his time with us ended on 29 June 2020. And through this difficult emotional trauma, I have had *ammi* (my mother) be steadfast, *nangi* be herself, *malli*, Bri, little Akshi and Havish – plus extended family members (*bappis*, other *ammis*, *nandis*, *mamis*, *nangis*, *mallis*, *akkis* and *aiyyas*), family friends (aunties and uncles) and friends across continents and countries stand by us (and me), gesturing in multiple ways their life-long support.

Very much like my research, writing my acknowledgements did not take a linear path. I finalize it at a new academic home at the University of Göteborg in Sweden, which by all that I have taken in, comes across as relaxed and hospitable. I want to especially thank Kristoffer Jansson and Jennie Ericsson for ensuring that I feel welcome in Sweden; and amongst my friendly new colleagues, special thanks to Mikael Ring, Jonas Lindberg, Robin Biddulph, Swati Parashar, Kevin Cullen, Eva Thulin, Marie Stenseke, Anders Larsson, Sara Falkensjö and Apoorva Rathod for their extra effort in supporting a transition during unusual times.

In the end, finishing the book itself was possible because two anonymous readers provided valuable comments, Liz Hunter did an excellent job in finessing it with her meticulous care in copy-editing, Martha Baker-Woodhouse, Benj Brown and Ross Hunter, former students and budding scholars, in reading through the proofs, Megara Tegal for working on the book cover design, and adapting her creative and politically astute collage work for our purposes; together with the publishing team at Cambridge University Press supporting its delivery. And finally, my gratitude to Anwesha Rana for her patience, good humour and commitment, who waited until I found the energy and time to orient myself away from a wearing work place context, to reflect on our embodied feminist politics, for me to galvanize my energy to acknowledge the uneven practices that continue within academia and then to simply write about a different context.

This is the life of an academic book – never a singular effort. Many thanks to each person and any others I may have left out inadvertently.

Kanchana N. Ruwanpura

Published Works and Funding

I have drawn excerpts from articles I have published in *Journal of Economic Geography* (16, no. 2; 11, no. 6), *Progress in Development Studies* (11, no. 1), *Antipode* (50, no. 2) and *Ethnography* (16, no. 1) – and thank Neil (Wrigley) in particular for generously agreeing to let me use sections of our co-authored article.

Funding and Fellowships

ESRC (Economic and Social Research Council): Grant 061-25-0181: *Labour-Practice Responses to Ethical-Trading Codes of Conduct at Sites of Production: A Case Study of the Sri Lankan Apparel Sector*

Senior Visiting Fellowship: ARI (Asia Research Institute), National University of Singapore, Singapore

Max Weber Stiftung Fellowship: ICAS-MP, Delhi, India (Declined)

Humboldt Fellowship: Awarded by the Humboldt Foundation and held at Centre for Modern Indian Studies, University of Göttingen, Germany

France-ILO Chair Fellowship: Institute of Advanced Studies, Nantes, France

Abbreviations

ALaRM	Action for Labour Rights Movement
BOI	Board of Investment
CEO	chief executive officer
CMT	Cut-Make-Trim
CMU	Ceylon Mercantile Union
EPF	employee provident fund
ETF	Employer Trust Fund
ETI	Ethical Trade Initiative
EU	European Union
FDI	foreign direct investment
FTZ	free trade zone
FTZ&GSEU	Free Trade Zones and General Services Employees Union
GCC	global commodity chain
GPN	global production networks
GVC	global value chain
GWG	Garments without Guilt
HG	Hirdaramani Garments
IDG	International Development Group
IIP	Index of Industrial Production
ILO	International Labour Organization
IMF	International Monetary Fund
JAAF	Joint Apparel Association Forum
JTUA	Joint Trade Union Alliance
MENA	Middle East and North African
MODSIT	Ministry of Development, Strategic Investment and Trade
MFA	Multi-Fibre Agreement
NIC	newly industrialized countries
OBM	own-brand manufacturing
ODM	original design manufacturing
OEM	original equipment manufacturing
PSPRB	Private Sector Pension Reform Bill

SAM	standard allowed minute
SLAE	Sri Lanka Apparel Exporters Association
SLFP	Sri Lanka Freedom Party
SVM	standard vector machine
Tripartite	a governance mechanism involving the state, employers and unions
UNDP	United Nations Development Programme
UNP	United National Party
USA	United States of America
USAID	United States Agency for International Development
WOB	Wages Ordinance Board

1
Introduction
Global Labour Justice via Ethical Codes?

Lovingly, to you

With a big burden in your heart
You smile, ignoring tears and hardships in life
Striving in the factory to attain prosperity for it;
You are a courageous Lankan woman serving the country.

Your heart fills with love for your children always
Daily, you try to provide for your sons
With nimble hands, you stitch clothes
This factory runs with your courage.

Weaving clothes using various patterns
You enhance the looks of beautiful women
For bringing in foreign exchange to Sri Lanka
You are appreciated this way.

—Anu

2008: Global and Local Significance

The year 2008: A benchmark globally and, as it turned out, for distinctly local reasons, for Sri Lanka too. Months after I received news of success with my grant application to enable me to explore how Sri Lankan apparels are at the vanguard of ethical code governance, the world went into a global economic meltdown. This put pressure on apparel producers worldwide, including those in Sri Lanka. Local issues also had an impact on Sri Lanka's apparel sector. The Rajapaksa government had started its steady onslaught to end a protracted ethnic conflict and, by May 2009, through a bloody and gory military war, three decades of violence in the country ostensibly ended. What might these shifts mean for the Sri Lankan apparel sector's trademark Garments without Guilt (GWG)? Anu's poem, which I collected during my fieldwork in 2009, is also a reminder to ask: What about labour?[1]

Around 2006, Sri Lanka's Joint Apparel Association Forum (JAAF) members envisioned GWG as a labelling strategy by which garments produced in the country were to carry a brand label and tag.[2] Although the labelling objective was eventually recognized as unrealistic, GWG offered an effective platform to promote the Sri Lankan apparel sector as a safe place for retailers wanting to conduct their business ethically. Under the aegis of the JAAF, the Sri Lankan apparel sector was branded, packaged and promoted as a niche and ethical producer, which also created added value (Gunawardana 2007; Kelegama 2009; Athukorala and Ekanayake 2018). The effort chimed well with various global multi-stakeholder and other corporate governance initiatives (Hughes, Buttle and Wrigley 2008), which had emerged in response to years of extensive debate on the working conditions and welfare of workers under global capitalism (Jenkins, Pearson and Seyfang 2002; Hale and Wills 2005; McIntyre 2008). The degree to which workers, trade unions, management or national governments have an ability to improve working conditions within global production systems is a key issue. Within these debates, the apparel industry has played a vital role, not only because it has been the centre of notorious examples of exploitation, but also because it is the hub of efforts to achieve ethical production systems.

The Sri Lankan apparel industry is at the forefront of these debates because it claims to be ahead of the curve on ethical production systems. The industry dictum, when one visits the website, for instance, is captivating. The JAAF claims that it aspires to improve the workers' quality of life by adhering to Sri Lanka's strong legislative framework (JAAF 2011). It explicitly draws upon the legal and social institutions that matter for doing business ethically (JAAF 2019). Adopting ethical business credentials was important and played out favourably for the Sri Lankan apparel sector (Kelegama 2009; Goger 2014; Athukorala and Ekanayake 2018). Yet so were the social institutions and legal frameworks within the country, which not only provided an educated labour force, but also helped protect it; the political economy context and social institutions, such as education and health care, also matter. Looking specifically at the country therefore brings into sharp focus the degree of agency key actors have to affect outcomes around global governance. It helps us assess whether economic upgrading corresponds with social upgrading.

The 2008–2009 period was also a catalyst in Sri Lanka because it portended changes that industrialists themselves had not envisioned prior to that time. New economic vistas, the North and the East of the country, were opened up for industrialists and capital investment.[3] Due to the ending of the ethnic war, these regions, which had been previously delinked from what was an otherwise globally integrated economy, were now open for business. Despite global economic challenges, changes in governments and political alliances of the left and right, changes in recent years (2008–2020) offered opportunities for the apparel industry in Sri Lanka, with pro-market policies continuing (Venugopal 2018).[4] For apparel industrialists, it meant United States Agency for International Development (USAID)–funded training programmes, tax incentives and military support to set up their production sites (USAID 2013; Goger and Ruwanpura 2014; Sarvananthan 2015). The apparel sector and employment creation in the North and the East of the country were at the forefront of this shift, especially as the sector had been facing labour shortages. A reservoir of potential workers existed within the territory. Yet the implications of these trends for workers are visible only in a piecemeal fashion and so need further exploration (Hagar 2012; Women's Centre 2013; Sarvananthan 2016). It is hence an opportune time to give a voice to labour vis-à-vis ethical governance in a crucial industrial sector.

These developments raise a key question: How has the Sri Lankan apparel sector navigated the pressures of the global supply chain amidst a tumultuous political topography over nearly three decades, and crafted itself as an ethical sourcing destination? More importantly, what role have those labouring for the garment sector played in assisting the sector to become ethical? I use a poem by Anu, a garment sector worker from one of my field sites, for this introductory chapter, as she expresses poignantly her recognition of their role as labourers – to ensure the prosperity of the factory, sector and country.[5] Even as her words are profoundly gendered, she underlines that it is they, the workers, who provide much-needed succour to the factories, the industry and the country. She captures the centrality of labour within and outside the factory floor. By her very poetic licence and eloquent lines, she is disclosing that she, amongst other social attributes, is also educated and analytical. Her poem is both expressive and reasoned.

An educated labour force and associated social advantages are other features that the Sri Lankan apparel sector draws upon. The ability to produce garments, largely without blemish, then relies upon a social fabric that also deserves investigation. This is particularly the case, because the exceptionalism of the Sri Lankan apparel industry, unlike that of its South Asian neighbours (for instance), requires us to pinpoint the various political economy factors and social institutions that have enabled Sri Lanka's ethical trajectory. Focusing on the interplay of these social structures and conditions makes it possible to craft a research narrative that weaves together these multiple threads. It thereby provides a comprehensive basis to allow us to appreciate the centrality of labour in the success of the Sri Lankan apparel industry and aids comprehension of the structuration of labour power.

Sri Lankan Exceptionalism?

Is the Sri Lankan apparel sector actually an exception? Since 2008, when I started doing research on the apparel sector, there have been numerous incidents related to the sector in South Asia that have caught the media's attention. Factory fires, factory collapses, low wages and exploitative labour have all been of interest to the media and scholars alike. The tragedy of Rana Plaza alone, in which 1,134 Bangladeshi garment workers died due to an eight-storey factory collapsing in 2013 (with the incident recorded as the worst apparel industrial accident to date), seemingly shook the industry (Miller 2014; de Neve and Prentice 2017). Neighbouring countries to Sri Lanka, then, have reeled and rocked under these different shocks. Yet, during this entire timeline, the only exposé that brought the Sri Lankan apparel sector under scrutiny was one highlighting the fact that Sri Lankan workers stitching for Beyoncé's clothing line Ivy Park – a joint venture between the singer and Adidas – were not getting paid a living wage (Ivy Park 2016). There is indeed an irony here. A clothing line which, according to its website, Ivy Park, proclaims that it promotes 'women in leadership, shared ownership, empowerment and collaboration' yet fails to deliver on its promises for the workers doing the sewing requires scrutiny. As Domosh and Seager (2001) revealed, based on the brand promotion activities of Nike almost two decades before, these contradictions are not novel; correspondingly, for activists, campaigners and researchers working on the apparel sector, including in Sri Lanka, this information is not new or news (Sluiter 2009). For the Western media, however, it was. This incongruity of the Sri Lankan apparel sector workers not facing dangerous working conditions but being unable to earn a living wage is one that requires to be critically considered. How is it that a country can provide seemingly stable and safe factory premises and work conditions, and yet not pay a living wage? Equally, and despite this incongruity, how has the sector successfully carved out an image of ethical sourcing? Is it that the global supply chain, which purports to govern ethically through ethical trade regimes, knowingly applies the codes unevenly? It is these contradictions that I hope to draw out in my book. My aim is to facilitate a nuanced appreciation of how and how far labour justice can be attained locally via global governance regimes, the limits to such aspirations and, more importantly, the need for attentiveness to labour voices. In other words, my aim is to show labour as fundamental to the Sri Lankan apparel industry's success – for the factory, sector and country.

To foreground labour throughout this book, I trace how its struggles and interjections have been important for Sri Lanka's political–economic trajectory. I also argue that to grasp the efficacy of global ethical trade regimes, there needs to be greater alertness to local inflections. It would in fact be absurd to assume that globally enforced ethical regimes alone can level the playing field in supplier countries. Where labour laws are unevenly applied, laws are lax and/or socio-economic inequities are rife – as events in Bangladesh around the Rana Plaza and Spectrum Factory collapse, less than a decade ago, so tragically illustrate – the limits to top-down global governance regimes are apparent (Miller 2014; de Neve and Prentice 2017). In other words, the limits to neoliberal governance traced by many contributing to the volume by de Neve and Prentice (2017) underscore the need to go beyond the prosaic. For instance, one of the leading apparel firms in Sri Lanka has embraced and promoted a programme entitled 'Women Go Beyond' that seeks to empower women in the sector through four pillars: 'Career advancement, work–life balance, skills development and rewarding excellence.' Within production sites, two of these pillars should translate, at the least, to limited overtime (work–life balance) and rewarding excellence (a living wage) – spheres that the sector does less well in, as I will argue later in this book. To *go beyond*, in my estimation, requires us to understand the political economy of a country and the social institutions that shape uneven development trajectories. Local labour laws, education provision, healthcare systems and other local institutional circumstances matter in appreciating that process, especially because, as Plankey-Videla (2012: 189) notes, 'local institutions and practices are historically contingent' with the potential to constrain or facilitate change (see also Chang 2003; Tewari 2008; Werner 2016; Silver 2019). To help us understand the labour geographies of Sri Lanka, *Chapter Two* goes into the theoretical considerations that influenced the framing of my research.[6]

The need to attend to labour geographies was brought to the forefront by Herod (2001, 2003), who makes the crucial point that capitalism is also shaped by historical labour struggles and strikes. According to him, labour confrontations from yesteryear continue to reverberate in and shape the contemporary period. From a historical perspective, Kumari Jayawardena (1972) has traced the important role that labour unions, strikes and struggles played during the colonial period in Sri Lanka. She outlines episodes that were the catalyst for the many prevailing labour laws and human development indices that the country continues to draw upon (see A. Sen 1983; Humphries 1993; Klasen 1993). Biyanwila (2011) has pursued this line of inquiry further, by specifically centring on social movements and unions, on both their formation and their struggles (Gunawardana 2007; Nowak 2016a). These are key moments for Sri Lanka's labour geographies, points at which workers are central to shaping the unfolding of capitalism, and need to be registered if we are to recognize and acknowledge the role of labour in shaping Sri Lanka's uneven capitalist development process. These contributions, along with contributions by feminist scholars on the subject, influence my theoretical framing. These theories are reviewed in the next chapter (*Chapter Two*), before I go on in *Chapter Three* to outline the research I conducted and the methods I deployed to gather my data over a decade. Together, these chapters offer the relevant context for how Sri Lanka's apparel industry evolved, transformed, 'upgraded' and cultivated an image of producing GWG.

Academic scholars have already established that Sri Lanka occupies an enviable position, despite the uneven power dynamics associated with global production processes (Knutsen 2004; Sluiter 2009; Perry, Wood and Fernie 2014). The legal framework put in place during the British colonial period, for instance, offers the relevant regulatory framing for industrialists to draw upon and use to protect the industry (Knutsen 2004; Ruwanpura and Wrigley 2011; Perry et al. 2014). Equally, the high level of education amongst Sri Lankan workers has also contributed to maintaining labour standards within the industry (Yatawara 2007; Sluiter 2009; Perry et al. 2014; Ruwanpura 2016).

I probe further in *Chapter Four* the temporal trajectory of Sri Lanka's apparel industry and its evolution, particularly in the past decade. I outline how, in a post-MFA context and despite a global recession that none saw coming, the Sri Lankan apparel sector has successfully managed to cultivate dynamic growth. It has also continued to thrive in the past decade. Athukorala (2018) locates the origins of these accomplishments in a combination of pro-market policies and country-specific (non-policy) factors. The open-market policies started in 1977 continued in various phases and included 'double-taxation relief agreements' and 'attractive tax incentives, access to bank credit and also priority allocation of export quotas' (Athukorala 2018: 198–199). For Athukorala (2018: 225), the country-specific features include a labour regime that helped prepare the industry to adopt ethical work place norms and the benefits of adopting trading with 'speciality retailers and brand marketers, who played a pivotal role in putting Sri Lankan firms on a dynamic learning curve'. The existing literature has tended to look at the apparel sector from the viewpoint of industrial capital (Knutsen 2003; Kelegama 2009; Athukorala 2018; Athukorala and Ekanayake 2018). I use valuable secondary data and descriptive statistics from these works together with management interviews to offer a nuanced take on the ways in which the Sri Lankan apparel sector steered through challenging global conditions. I also investigate other local factors that impelled the sector to strengthen itself during this time; differently from Athukorala (2018), I want to highlight that the country's labour regime is also a favourable policy consideration for the sector. More specifically, I note how we also need to ask: Where is labour in this account?

Chapter Five of this book starts by examining the neglected labour histories and struggles within the apparel sector. I zoom in primarily on the post-1970s period, using oral histories, interviews and published pamphlets to unearth the neglected labour histories of the early agitators and using the works of Kearney (1971), Jayawardena (1972) and Biyanwila (2011) to locate labour struggles specifically within the apparel sector in the post-1977 period. This uncovering is important for two reasons. On the one hand, it has significance for appreciating that the Sri Lankan apparel sector's efficacy in upholding ethical trading and corporate social governance is partly a response to the noise, voice and diligence of its early workers. On the other hand, at this current juncture, the redrafting of investor-friendly employment laws in Sri Lanka has neglected labour as a constituency. Even though the country – as a signatory to many core International Labour

Organization (ILO) conventions – is committed to the tripartite principles of involving the state, employers and unions, I will show in this chapter how the ILO, the relevant line ministry and labour union leaders were ignored. As my research shows, labour movements, both formally and socially formed, were an important element for the Sri Lankan state to respond to, even prior to the introduction of global ethical trading initiatives. In other words, garment workers were in the vanguard in helping to ensure that apparel producers were early and ready adopters of global governance standards. As importantly, the fact that labour has a place within the constitution, given the workers' right to freely associate, at least implies that the voice of labour is important for political cohesion. This chapter argues that to neglect the place of labour in Sri Lanka's economy is to expose its people to the vagaries of the global economy as well as risks perpetuating and accentuating uneven development practices, as the CoVID-19 global pandemic has revealed.[7]

Labouring and Producing Ethical Garments?

Chapters Four and *Five* provide the relevant backdrop for examining more closely the labour geographies of ethical trading initiatives in practice. They do so from the vantage point of industrialists, managers and labour rights organizations. These chapters offer the pertinent setting from which to delve into my located ethnographic data from the production floor and analyse how ethical trade regimes are negotiated on a daily basis. *Chapter Six* asks how workers understand global justice initiatives around ethical codes and what their salient features are. The purpose of this chapter is to discuss how multi-stakeholder initiatives manifest from the viewpoint of labour via local practices on the factory floor. I use evidence from my ethnography, conducted in southern Sri Lanka, with a labour force exclusively from the dominant community, to illustrate these concerns. Labourers highlight the codes that receive prominence and those that get downplayed, and in that process underline the question: What can be said about global initiatives that have labour rights as a concern but may not, in practice, uphold labour justice?

Chapter Six takes its starting point from feminist contributions on the Sri Lankan apparel sector's women workers. Feminist scholars from across the disciplines have intervened and called for acknowledgement of the role of women workers within the rapidly expanding apparel sector and the industrialization processes of globalized production (Elson and Pearson

1981; Ong 1987; Enloe 1989). Within this genre, the locus has primarily been the cultural politics and social lives of labouring women, as well as the ways gendered regimes both shape and are shaped by production (Salzinger 2003; Wright 2006; Lynch 2007; Hewamanne 2008; Kim 2013; Zaki-Chakravarti 2019). These contributions have enriched our understanding of how tropes of masculinity and femininity are mobilized within the context of intersecting material and patriarchal and other ideological vectors. For Sri Lanka, studies by Lynch (2007) and Hewamanne (2008) assess the complex web of political, cultural and socio-economic forces that women workers had to navigate with the advent of an open economy in Sri Lanka, using two different geographical spaces (the free trade zone [FTZ] and rural Sri Lanka).

The mediations by these feminist scholars are a necessary and important backdrop to appreciating the situation of garment sector workers. Yet we also need to understand the key governance agendas shaping the everyday working lives of labourers, as ethical trade regimes are part of the neoliberal global architecture that claim to advance conditions of work and engender labour justice. The economic difficulties, challenges and hardships workers face are also a reflection of the uneven ways in which codes are applied and upheld. Or, to ask which codes are upheld and why – and which are neglected or downplayed – helps us acknowledge how these global initiatives resonate and provide meaning (or not) for current workers. They reveal how ethical codes are deployed and practised, and how workers make sense of them. In evaluating these practices, we learn to understand what upholding some codes and neglecting others mean for the working lives of workers. The material conditions that workers find themselves in are partly a reflection of the uneven application of corporate codes of practice; their experiences puncture the global justice claims that come with ethical and corporate codes of conduct.

Chapter Seven moves to another part of Sri Lanka: The North and the East of the country. The new commercial landscapes were intended by the apparel industrialists to be a lucrative boon, but what of labour experiences? In a geographical setting separated, alienated and physically isolated from the rest of the country because of a three-decade war, the case for capitalists to invest followed a familiar track. Economic opportunities (read: profit) were likely to prevail in a region where young people were waiting for jobs (USAID 2013; Sarvananthan 2015). However, in deploying the category of young people as an empty trope, the post-war policies that were crafted emphasized economic aspects to the total erasure and silencing of the ethnic turbulence that was likely to have shaped their formative years and continue to resonate in their work places and lives. By simply treating a new cohort of workers as an economic resource, the workers were stripped of important markers and identities that have shaped Sri Lanka's polity. In work places where there was a disavowal of Sri Lanka's fractured ethnic past, no space was created for negotiating their trauma, as they shifted from three decades of violence, war and, in some instances, paramilitary rule (Goger and Ruwanpura 2014; Thiranagama 2014; Ruwanpura 2018; Lingam 2019). What resonance do global labour justice initiatives via corporate codes have for this constituency of workers? This chapter will centre on whether it is possible to make claims of ethical sourcing and produce garments without guilt, where workers are drawn from conflict areas, where language barriers colour their experiences and where the military was used initially to recruit workers. It will also explore the appreciation these new workers have for ethical code initiatives and their awareness of them. My penultimate chapter thus takes the reader to the post-war landscape of Sri Lanka, to help us appreciate the spatial specificities of labour geographies.

These chapters together, then, help make the case for the importance of heeding labour politics and their connection to other social determinants (Wood 1981; Gidwani 2004). In my concluding chapter, I draw my main threads together to help make the argument that the sector occupies a formidable place in the global landscape, not necessarily or even only due to the vision of Sri Lanka's apparel industrialists. *Chapter Eight* argues that labour is more than an important constituent of the country's apparel industry's capitalist success and that ignoring and downplaying its role is to repudiate the role and agency of labour within the dominant narrative. My concluding chapter hence makes the case that, while we should champion the role of apparel sector industrialists in the upgrading process (Athukorala and Ekanayake 2018; Athukorala 2019), we also need to make space for the rightful place of labour and their claims for labour justice. Without labour's contributions, past, present and future, the Sri Lankan apparel sector's ability to remain successful within the country and produce garments without guilt may necessarily be limited and limiting. The fact that economic upgrading does not correspond to social upgrading, including provision of the living wage, implies that how the sector acts as a catalyst for development is uneven and fractured. Consequently, the views of labour have to be brought to the forefront (Featherstone and Griffin 2016; Silver 2019; Strauss 2020). Labour voices also have ramifications for whether the Sri Lankan state continues on a path of uneven development, punctured by bloody political violence and turmoil, where inequality has proved persistent and has exacerbated over time.

Continuing to disregard the voices of the great majority of workers on the lack of living wages in the country, whether the workers reside in the south, north, east or west of Sri Lanka, not only reveals the potential political costs to a country with a violent past, but also exposes the limits to neoliberal governance. Despite the rhetoric of labour justice, where global governance regimes do not earnestly ensure that the aspirations of workers in the sector are upheld, they risk at best being framed as a sham, a guise and/or exploitative; at worst, in a country, such as Sri Lanka, with a politically violent past, they offer a breeding ground for a relapse from work place discontent to protracted violence. It is hence an opportune time to give a voice to labour and understand the labour geographies in a crucial industrial sector in the country.

Notes

1. My thanks to Anushaya Collure for translating this poem for me and ensuring I did justice to the Sinhala version (see Appendix for a scanned copy of the original).
2. The formation of the JAAF itself was partly a culmination of the need for industrialists to collectively champion their position, as the Multi-Fibre Agreement (MFA) was lapsing; the JAAF was set up as a body to promote the collective interests of the apparel industry.
3. I seemingly carelessly use 'management' and 'capital' interchangeably throughout this book, because some interviewees were corporate-level managers who were joint partners (owners/capital) in their respective firms. While there are likely to be distinctions between their interests, analysing them is a task for another.
4. Venugopal (2018) captures best the untidy political hues of the two leading political parties in Sri Lanka; suffice to say that pigeonholing them to the right and left, as is conventionally understood in politics, is difficult.
5. My motive in starting with Anu's poem is not to delve into the poetics and theatre of labour for Sri Lanka, which is done elsewhere (Rajasingham-Perera 2016; Perera 2018).

6. In bringing the voice of labour to the forefront, in this book I converse primarily with labour geographers and labour and development studies more broadly, as this is where robust considerations of political economy are given due consideration. Framings of global production networks (GPN), global commodity chain (GCC) and global value chain (GVC) literature is borrowed using a critical lens – to highlight their limits when it comes to placing labour experiences (see also Werner 2012; Pearson 2013; Selwyn 2019).

7. I had completed a draft of my chapters, as CoVID-19 and the associated lockdowns globally began to take effect. I therefore only offer passing and cursory comments on its effects for Sri Lankan apparel in the concluding chapter (*Chapter Eight*).

2

Labouring for Apparels

Labour Geographies and Feminist Inflections

Oba thireyan thamai kamhale behivune.
(Striving in the factory to attain prosperity for it.)

—Anu

Introduction

This line from Anu's poem to me captures the essence of labour geography.
It was a poem pinned against one of the walls in the canteen of a production
site where I was doing fieldwork. The creative wall, as it was called, was
vividly colour-washed in orange and was a strip that everyone encountered
upon entering the canteen. It was an initiative introduced by a recently
recruited HR manager, where workers were invited to post their artwork,
poems, verses, short stories and such. One day, the poem caught my eye. I
learnt that these creative works were rotated on a monthly basis to make
way for others. Later, I approached the worker who penned these verses and
inquired if I might have them to use for my research. I let her know that, if I
were ever to use her poem in my writings, she would be acknowledged. She
was bemused by my request: She was ambivalent about her work's poetic
value and so wondered if I was in earnest. I had to assure her that I did find
the poem powerful and effective. This is how I came to obtain a copy of the
poem, while I encouraged her to retain the original.

I had not used this poem before in my writings. Yet, as I returned to my
field diaries and collections, I was reminded that it remained a poignant and
powerful effort to capture the essence of labour geographies; without the
worker, firms would not exist. Even as her entire poem entitled *Lovingly,
To You*, tenderly captures the challenges and hardships of working in the
apparel sector, she also reminds her co-workers that without them or us,

the factories simply would not exist. They, the workers, make an important contribution to the nation's wealth. Her poem then is a tender call for recognizing their agency.

Through the entirety of the poem, Anu invokes the importance of workers to the country and the firm. Her verses are a stimulating way of combining two important theoretical strands – feminist interventions and labour geographies literature – which are pertinent for thinking about labour geographies within the context of the Sri Lankan apparel sector. This angle also draws attention to the fact that Sri Lanka is making a transition from three decades of war and violence, with peace illusory and political volatility still palpable (Kadirgamar 2013; Thiranagama 2014; Venugopal 2018; Lingam 2019; Ruwanpura et al. 2020). Attention to the political context matters for the Sri Lankan apparel sector, as it has shifted to job creation in previously war-torn areas, and yet it has done so without the cognizance that doing business in the North and the East is also a political decision.

In starting this research, my intention was to understand the legislative and institutional contexts that facilitate the Sri Lankan apparel sector in upholding its ethical codes successfully. What local institutions and practices help the country avoid the negative media spotlight that blights the Global South more generally, and its neighbouring countries more specifically? However, I want to argue that, to appreciate the country's relatively strong social institutions and pro-labour market legislation, we also need to get a sense of the place of labour within it. They are, I contend, co-constitutive of each other.

Labour, particularly its collective struggles, has been pivotal to the positioning of Sri Lanka, although it is a constituency that is often disregarded in policy considerations on value creation and upgrading within the apparel sector (Kelegama 2009; Athukorala 2018; Athukorala and Ekanayake 2018). This neglect, however, also reflects debates on global apparel sectors and global governance regimes. These debates have tended to be instrumentalized and fashioned as top-down universal 'solutions' that are likely to benefit workers in the supply chain, irrespective of local specificities (de Neve 2009; Selwyn 2012a, 2013; Ruwanpura 2016).

Globalizing Garments

A primary motivation for garment production to start moving, initially to East Asia and then to the Global South, is the search for cheap labour.

This was coupled with efforts to reduce the bargaining power of unionized labour under a changing development paradigm (Kabeer 2008; Mclntyre 2008; Werner 2016; Mezzadri 2017; Silver 2019). The traction for these views came from structural adjustment policies, which were implemented in the Global South from the late 1970s. More importantly, by the late 1970s, newly industrialized countries (NICs) had tried and tested the success of industrial garment production. Hence, the development orthodoxy advocated by the World Bank was the same for many other developing countries, including such places as the Caribbean, China, India, Nepal and Sri Lanka (Kim 2013; Werner 2016; Mezzadri 2017; Shakya 2018). For the World Bank, NICs were the 'miracle' cases, underlining the possibilities of capital accumulation via the adoption of open-market policies. Chang (2003), in contrast, has persuasively and through careful examination placed the cause of success elsewhere – in the important role of the state, not just for the NICs, but also for the trajectory of the 'developed' world itself (see also Chang 2014; Chang and Andreoni 2020; Silver 2019; Werner 2020).[1] And so, for Sri Lanka, in the spirit of Chang (2014), the extent to which the state may have played a role in the successes of the apparel sector needs brief consideration.

For the Sri Lankan apparel sector, the initial foray into garment manufacturing took place through foreign direct investment (FDI) that came primarily from East Asian capital (Athukorala and Ekanayake 2018). In *Chapter Four*, I discuss in more detail the evolving landscape of Sri Lanka's apparel sector; here, I make a few observations on how the state also helped to shape Sri Lanka's ethical image over time.

The first is that the Sri Lankan state, following neoliberal edicts, provided the necessary tax and relevant financial incentives for investors to jump-start garment manufacturing in the newly formed FTZ in Katunayake (Athukorala and Ekanayake 2018; Athukorala 2019). It also afforded opportunities for local capitalists to enter the sector and embed themselves in the country (Lynch 2007; Athukorala and Ekanayake 2018). However, shortly after the inception of the FTZ in Katunayake, the state was compelled to step in again, this time in response to various worker agitations. Following this, the state dictated clear conditions of work that factory owners, including those in the apparel sector, had to uphold (Women's Centre 2006; Biyanwila 2011). The third significant moment of state involvement came as the war was coming to an end in 2008. During this transitional time, the Sri Lankan state took an active role in offering various subsidies and tax incentives to the sector, and other light manufacturers, to invest in the previously war-torn regions of the country (Goger and Ruwanpura 2014; Sarvananthan 2015, 2016; Ruwanpura 2018; Athukorala 2019). At each of these moments, the state was heavily involved in shaping both how the market economy would evolve and the market regulation that ensued (Standing 1997; Waller 2006; Pearson 2013; Chang 2014; Silver 2019).

The Sri Lankan state did not always or necessarily ignore the voice of labour. As I show in *Chapter Five*, the state also mediated to ensure that labourers were protected, however partial this may have been (Gunawardana and Biyanwila 2008; Biyanwila 2011; Ruwanpura 2016). The state, at different junctures, had to respond to the voice of labour to facilitate the trajectory of capitalist evolution and accomplishment. As importantly, the intrusion of the state in the early 1990s was a crucial moment for the apparel sector to cultivate and champion an image of ethicality in its garment sector. So, the Sri Lankan apparel sector's exceptionalism had more than a little help from the state, which I will explore in greater detail in *Chapter Four*. For now, however, we must ask, what is the place of labour in the Sri Lankan apparel sector?

There are three distinct strands in the literature on global apparel firms that specifically relate to labour. One thread stems from the feminist scholarship that assessed the role of women workers within apparel production; the second is the GCC literature, which has also morphed into debates on GPN; and the third is the labour geographies literature. While each of these make important contributions to appreciating different angles of the apparel sector, I will argue in this chapter that what I find most productive are the debates in feminist scholarship and labour geographies.[2] These lenses, unlike GVC and GPN framings, not only underline structuration of labour power, but also help us appreciate how social institutions and the political fabric shape the (uneven) power of labour (Pearson 1998; Bedford and Rai 2010; Kumar 2019; Selwyn 2019; Werner 2020). Indeed, feminist and labour geographies are most apt for the purpose of understanding the place of labour within the Sri Lankan apparel sector because they aid us in appreciating local institutional components and are also productive for feminist reflections. As I sketch next, curiously these are two strands that have largely bypassed each other – whether wittingly or not (Bair and Werner 2011; Ruwanpura 2011; Mezzadri 2017).

Why Women Workers? Feminist Interventions across Time

Elson and Pearson (1981: 92), in their call for feminist solidarity with working women in the apparel sector, ask a question: 'Why is it women who overwhelmingly constitute the labour force?' This question, asked almost four decades ago, elicited answers to the effect that, according to management and employers, the 'nimble fingers' of women workers and their visual acuity were important for ensuring high productivity within the sector. Elson and Pearson also highlighted the adverse work conditions, low wages, prolonged hours and the implications of exploitative working conditions faced by women workers. Their work was a catalyst for subsequent feminist contributions and remains foundational for understanding both geographies of labour and labour geographies (Pearson 1998; Kabeer 2000; Wright 2006; Bedford and Rai 2010; Werner 2016; Mezzadri 2017; Zaki-Chakravarti 2019).

The immediate deliberation that arose was whether framing women workers' experiences as exploitative was fair and accurate. Countering the position taken by Elson and Pearson (1981), another early feminist contribution was that made by Lim (1983, 1990).[3] In her estimation, women labouring for garment firms and other light manufacturing were also finding ways of earning an income, and this earning capacity could be a generative movement towards empowerment. For her, concentrating on the exploitation of workers would be to forgo the recognition that an important moment of socio-economic transformation was taking place through the entrance of women workers into industrial labour. More than looking at the newly developed earning capacity of women workers, Lim was interested in examining how this earning capacity impacted the workers' sense of self.

Both these positions were important for detailed research into women labouring for global markets. Lim's (1983, 1990) standpoint, although she did not frame it in this way, was also possibly hinting at the need to consider the agency of labour or labour geographies. However, by placing her views as oppositional to Elson and Pearson's (1981) explanation and assuming that truth has to be one or the other, her work fails to reflect on the important labour geographies of women workers. Or, more specifically, she too was charting geographies of labour, namely how labouring women respond to capitalist processes, rather than how these women workers may be important actors in their own right, shaping capitalist processes, i.e., labour geographies. Nonetheless, both these positions led to a plethora of feminist explorations scrutinizing the place of labouring women, both within and outside factory premises (Safa 1981; Ong 1987; Pearson 1998, 2013; Kabeer 2000; Siddiqi 2000, 2009; Salzinger 2003; Wright 2006; Lynch 2007; Hewamanne 2008; Bedford and Rai 2010; Plankey-Videla 2012; Werner 2016; Mezzadri 2017; Zaki-Chakravarti 2019). These explorations also facilitated centring on socially inflected hierarchies on the shop floor, inclusive of ethnicity and kin (de Neve 2001; Kim 2013; Prentice 2015).

Gender, however, has been seen as a pivotal and ubiquitous trope in global production facilities. Using the example of electronics factories in Mexico, Salzinger (2003) calls for vigilance over the deployment of gender tropes within production facilities. She, along with others, suggests that we are better able to appreciate the structures of meaning-making around gender, so as to attract, retain and control workers. This insight helps evaluate industrial labour processes more effectively and recognizes how 'capital makes ... such workers, and that gender is implicated in that process' (Salzinger 2003: 2; see also Wright 2006; Goger 2013a; Ruwanpura and Hughes 2016). More recent feminist ethnographies on the shop floor have drawn on these circulating intellectual thoughts to give currency to their own findings. By reorienting my focus towards these new contributions, it becomes possible to glean how women workers are negotiating and navigating a changing landscape of toil for global garment firms.

However, I also ask the question: Why do labouring men not feature as much in existing analyses? I flag this observation partly because, while a feminist optic was useful for my research (as I narrate in *Chapter Three*), I also became aware of the increasing presence of men on the factory floor – men who were cutting, trimming, stitching, ironing, and so on. Jobs previously categorized as a 'feminized' activity, such as sewing, were now being carried out by men (Plankey-Videla 2012). The men, then, were not always the supervisors; in fact, in one factory they were more likely to be supervised by women supervisors and middle managers. Likewise, management members were painstakingly trying to say that men as well as women can do these tasks and, given the difficulties they had in recruiting and retaining women workers, they emphasized the centrality of working men. The increasing presence of men on the floor was not an anomaly in the two factories where I was doing my ethnographic research or in those I visited. As the national data I set out in *Chapter Four* confirms, the proportion of men working for apparel firms has been increasing, from 23 per cent in 2006 to 31 per cent by 2016 (Table 4.1 in *Chapter Four*).

Zaki-Chakravarti's (2019) ethnography too remarks on this shift for Egyptian garment firms, with her study exploring the cultural politics of gendered youth. Usually, however, in the existing feminist ethnographies on global garment firms, when men do feature, it is to emphasize the troubled gender relations associated with supervisory and management relationships (Salzinger 2003; Lynch 2007; Hewamanne 2008; Plankey-Videla 2012). In an evolving landscape in global garment production, the temporal specificities have meant an increasing reliance of Sri Lankan apparel firms on and recruitment of men to labour alongside women.

During my research then, and as this book unfolded, labour was the motif rather than gender; this may speak to the temporal dynamics affecting Sri Lankan garment production. At a different time and place from the works of Salzinger (2003) and Wright (2006), it was labour, although interlaced with gender, ethnic and political ideologies, rather than 'cheap, docile and dextrous' women that management members were seeking (see also Goger 2013a; Ruwanpura and Hughes 2016). More on this in the sections to follow. For now, what do contemporary feminist contributions on the place of garment workers in different parts of the world have to say?

An abiding concern of these feminist studies has been to trace how gender identities are moulded and remoulded on and outside the shop floor. Starting with seminal texts on Sri Lankan apparel firms, both Lynch (2007) and Hewamanne (2008) establish that women workers in the garment sector had to navigate complex societal expectations and the stigma that was subsequently attached to their recently acquired identities as working women. Their books, in different and yet related ways, highlight that young women workers in the apparel sector not only have to negotiate and navigate challenging working conditions, but also are deeply enmeshed in the larger sociopolitical landscape – and this too has a bearing on the extent that their identities are mediated. At the time that both Lynch (2007) and Hewamanne (2008) were conducting their research, Sri Lanka was entangled in a protracted ethnic conflict: a period in which the pungency of Sinhala-Buddhist nationalism was palpable. During this time especially, women were expected to be the bearers of the nation and, as such, women workers were both constrained by and contesting appropriate conduct (de Alwis 1999, 2002).

My initial fieldwork began at the tail end of a three-decade ethnic conflict and war. While ethno-nationalism was still rife, the Sri Lankan apparel sector was having to contend with a different challenge. This time, the sector was facing a labour recruitment crisis, which management partly related to the effects of women wanting to avoid an industry and sector associated with stigma (see also Lynch 2007; Ruwanpura 2011). Later, there was a doubling of efforts to remove the stigma from working for apparel firms and, in its place, factory managers were keen to portray how workers were contributing towards the nation's prosperity. Goger (2013a) captures this moment as a shift from disposable to empowered women's labour in Sri Lanka (see also Ruwanpura and Hughes 2016). Cultivating a sanitized image of the apparel sector to make it attractive to labour, rather than just women labourers, and to emphasize its crucial role in post-war nation-building became evident after 2009 (Ruwanpura 2018). Hence, the sector emphasized the value placed on labour generally, rather than women's labour, a theme I will return to in more detail in *Chapter Seven*.

Of importance is that labouring for the global garment industry is shaped and mediated by not just the working conditions within, but also the larger sociopolitical context. Yet, as existing feminist studies show, women workers in turn form and modify both their identities and their work place conditions, although with varying outcomes (Siddiqi 2000, 2009; Plankey-Videla 2012; Kim 2013; Arslan 2019; Zaki-Chakravarti 2019). Using illustrations and ethnographies from various corners of the world – Mexico, China, Trinidad, Turkey and Egypt – they all explore in what ways women workers' identities shift and coalesce as they seek respect, dignity and justice in spatially specific ways.

Yet what may at first glance be seen as the politics of resistance can sometimes also be enmeshed in an ambivalence, suggesting that individualist subjectivity has seeped far into the factory floor (Plankey-Videla 2012; see also Prentice 2015). These investigations show how globalized factory work structures create both individualism and opportunities for collectivism, although not always in the way of a collective consciousness arising out of class solidarity. Shared histories of colonialism, nationalism, gender, religion and even maternal identity are what bind. These studies also offer us fine detail not merely on the way in which factory spaces are inhabited and shaped by global forces, but also on how globalization itself is refracted by local ideologies of work, class, ethnicity and gender. In Plankey-Videla's (2012) study, she outlines how women workers, some of whom were mothers, upended the patriarchal constructs usually mobilized within factory settings to collectively muster against failed patriarchal compacts. Likewise, she shows how corrupt union officials can conspire with management against worker solidarity; and yet, when women workers feel that they are unfairly treated, they protest, underlining the potency of the moral economy (Polanyi 1957; Thompson 1966). The distinct ways in which globalization and the global factory operate are also patent in the case of a Korean multinational company in China (Kim 2013). In his ethnography, Kim weaves together the ethnically charged ways in which global factories are managed by a Korean multinational. In all instances, however, chronological changes shape and affect factory floor dynamics, which tend to be shaped by gender, class, nationality and ethnicity, as much as by global pressures and productivity concerns.

While the Middle East and North African (MENA) countries are equally formidable players in the global apparel sector, ethnographies from that region are sparse. Nebahat Tokatli's numerous early writings delineated the important role played by Turkish apparel manufacturing, its upgrading initiatives and the power dynamics they entailed (Tokatli 2007a, 2007b, 2008). An exploration of factory-floor undercurrents, however, is undertaken by Arslan's (2019) careful study of the apparel sector in Izmir, Turkey, where she directs our gaze towards both larger and smaller scale production facilities within the country. She thus not only supports the existence of the clusters of manufacturing argued for by Mezzadri (2017), but also provides a detailed study of how gender frames labour processes, irrespective of scale – although in differentiated ways. Arslan's emphasis is on the interrelationships between women's labour in the productive and reproductive spheres, wherein it bears upon material conditions on factory floors. Labour regimes at various scales are then enmeshed in sociocultural relations connected to familial and household relations. Her work is valuable in drawing our attention again to how producing for global garment firms is necessarily grounded in local cultures, institutions and understandings of gender, class and ethnicity.

The centrality of these tropes, together with religion, is also explored in a study that looks at Egypt's garment sector (Zaki-Chakravarti 2019). As elsewhere, the proclivity of global factory management to invoke familial and patriarchal tropes resurfaces in Egypt too. However, Zaki-Chakravarti is keen to explicate that it is these familial registers that help recruit, retain and manage workers via kin networks (see also de Neve 2001, 2008; Lynch 2007; Hewamanne 2008; Arslan 2019). She traces for us how the firm as a family was an important analytical lens through which to explore various layers of the shop floor. Management deployed the familial trope to ensure 'the various control mechanisms ... management team[s] seek to deploy in order to meet demanding schedules' (Zaki-Chakravarti 2019: 47). Workers appropriated it to realize their material aspirations, while supervisors had to discipline workers away from hiccups that beset families and, by extension, the shop floor (Plankey-Videla 2012; Arslan 2019).

These scholarly tapestries trace the position in fine detail to ensure that we appreciate the spatial politics of global apparel production as they apply in differentiated and multiple locations. Class, gender, ethnicity, colonial history, nationalism and religion all inflect work politics within factory production sites, where labouring for global brands is refracted by distinctly local practices. These studies outline how globalization processes resonate locally and have their distinct permutations within various countries, regions and even clusters (Raj-Reichert 2015; Dutta 2016; Nowak 2016b; Tighe 2016; Mezzadri 2017). The local variations of globalization need consideration too. Or, as Werner (2016: 15) remarks, we need to 'place production as a process that articulates with a shifting, heterogeneous, yet structured global economy'. Feminist approaches, past and present, have then represented women workers both as responding to global capital and as labouring women shaping global capital in their moments of interaction and intersection. It is this latter factor that also implicitly contributes towards recognizing labour agency, while also conceding the constraints within which labourers exert their agency. The wider social and material conditions that shape how labouring women toil also matter. Consequently, global projects that aspire towards universal harmonization, such as ethical codes, need to be understood from worker experiences at sites of production.

Yet almost all these ethnographies are silent to varying degrees on global governance regimes and how these may be shaping management–labour relations on the shop floor. This lacuna is one that needs to be addressed. De Neve (2009) notes that, according to the managers he interviewed, this is a new imperialism that adds to global competitive pressures, because these global corporate codes also shape labour–management processes. Or, to put it differently, there are local inflections of ethical code practices too (Tighe 2016; Raj-Reichert 2019). Hence, to be alert to a global initiative around bettering labour conditions, one must start by grasping how local social institutions are likely to matter in this instance too. Before I try to address this theme via my research, I turn to the scholarship on labour geographies. Why does this nuance matter for understanding the relationship between ethical codes and labour voice?

Potency of Labour? Labour Geographies, Agency and Power

Our present moment is one where labour power has rapidly mutated, with the widely held view that integration into the global economy has tended to weaken labour power (Kabeer 2000; Biyanwila 2011; Hensman 2011; Dutta 2016; Werner 2016; Silver 2019). A closer look at labour politics, however, reveals that workers continually exert their agency – even within a constrained and uneven political-economic terrain. As Featherstone and Griffin (2016: 381) remark, constraints too are 'constantly renegotiated, reworked and politized'; heeding Marx's insistence that wo/men 'make their own history' (Marx 1972 [1852]: 10; Wood 1981). Equally, Hensman (2011) notes, it is important to recognize that the ability of globalization to worsen the place and position of labour is also defined by previous historical and institutional trajectories (see also Dutta 2016, 2019; Neethi 2016; Strauss 2020).

When looking at labour's relationship with the path of uneven development in India, Hensman's (2011) careful argument is that we need to consider both history and the evolution of labour policy. For her, the place of weakened labourers in India is best understood as related both to historically segmented labour markets and to policy reforms in the 1970s, which pushed workers into the informal sector. Against this backdrop, she finds little value in corporate codes of conduct as a mechanism through which to ameliorate work conditions. Since ethical codes only apply to those with formal contracts within registered factory premises, there is limited purchase for workers who labour for global apparel firms, for instance, but find themselves in differentiated informalized clusters (see also Plankey-Videla 2012; Mezzadri 2017; Shakya 2018; Arslan 2019). All these writers imply or state that given the various permutations of industrial clusters, it is unlikely that codes will make any tangible difference to garment workers outside of the factory floor.

To be observant of the historical and institutional backdrop, then, is also necessary. Wood (1981) and Hensman (2011) accentuate the need to understand the potency of labour power as it negotiates uneven layers of the development processes and reflect on Marx's 'insistence that a productive system is made up of its specific social determinations – specific social relations ... legal and political forms' (Wood 1981: 69). Similarly, others emphasize the need for attention to a subjective agency that emanates from structuration, although often the core of these explorations are capital–labour relations to the neglect of scalar-level politics and institutions (Selwyn 2012b; Kumar 2019). In this regard, Herod (2003, 2012) offers an important theoretical lens to understand the place of labour within capitalism, arguing for the need to comprehend not simply from the viewpoint of capital, but also from that of labour. The case he makes is that for a long time, we have looked at labour as it responds to capital but without enough care being taken to examine and analyse how labour too is a vital player in shaping the evolution of capitalism. Herod's call resonates with E. P. Thompson's (1966) landmark contribution, where he argues for the need to recognize labourers as making their own history and the class process (see also Selwyn 2012b; Featherstone and Griffin 2016). By underscoring how labourers collaborated and combined their work with political action, Thompson makes an early argument for appreciating labour agency and also for the ways in which labour structured legislative interventions (see also Humphries 2010).

A similar intervention for Sri Lanka is made by Jayawardena (1972), in which she stresses not just the centrality of labour in agitating against colonial capital intrusion and erosion of working lives, but also how these struggles were important catalysts for subsequent labour regulations – and indeed the anti-colonial struggle (see also Kearney 1971; Wood 1981). The legislative framework that the country's apparel sector boasts of in its web portal provides the relevant protective mechanisms to uphold labour rights. In other words, the apparel sector continues to benefit from these labour laws and uses them as an important prop for giving credibility to its ethical credentials.

The way JAAF positions itself is illustrative of a generative moment of labour geographies and how, as Herod (2001: 30) articulates, 'workers may also be actively involved in the uneven development of capitalism as part of their own social and spatial praxis designed to facilitate their own self-reproduction'. In the heyday of labour potency in the industrial landscape of the United States of America (USA), which Herod considers, giving weight to how labour defined the capitalist landscape was perhaps feasible. Jayawardena's (1972) work for Sri Lanka, positioned elsewhere on the development trajectory, showed how, through colonialism and the immediate post-colonial period, Sri Lankan workers did not hesitate to agitate and were unafraid to flex their muscles. She illustrates how capital and the colonial state did respond to labour agitation, even where the odds might have been seen as against the workers. By restating the need to heed labour voice, the possibility of acknowledging its constrained and varied manifestations is brought to the forefront of debates on uneven development and labour geographies (Featherstone and Griffin 2016; Werner 2016, 2020). Hence, at the current juncture, to appreciate labour struggles and workers' ability to exert power, giving due consideration to the institutional fabric within countries is also important, a point I will return to in *Chapters Four* and *Five*. For now, the context of recognizing and giving centrality to labour voice and agency offers a broad setting within which we can motivate and probe relevant questions – namely, where is labour's voice within ethical code regimes?

From Academic Interventions to Labour Activism

The architecture of global governance regimes was partly a response to the early feminist studies that alerted the world to labour exploitation in global production. These feminist interruptions were important for engaging labour rights activists and consumer pressure groups and for solidarity-building across different scales. They provided the necessary groundswell to precipitate brand retailers and corporates into acting and responding to campaigners' calls for action against labour exploitation (Jenkins et al. 2002; Hale and Wills 2005; Sluiter 2009; Tighe 2016; Raj-Reichert 2019). Consumer campaigners were often located in Western Europe and North America, which required retailers to react – although not without denial at the inception. Brand retailers were restructuring so as to 'increase the power of retailers and newly emerging brand names, and (yet) at the same time exposed them more to public scrutiny' (Shaw and Hale 2002: 102). Yet there was initial denial, which McIntyre (2008: 35) observes was due to the distancing that came with subcontracting arrangements in the supply chain and that thwarted employment relations – in other words, 'the entity for which the productive activity is ultimately performed' (see also Gidwani and Chari 2004; Supiot 2006). So, here, consumer campaign groups have had to step in to negotiate these distant labour relationships, borne out of unregulated labour markets, sweating systems and sweatshop regimes (Kim 2013; Supiot 2013; Werner 2016; Mezzadri 2017).

This denial from brand and corporate retailers came to a head when, as Shaw and Hale (2002) noted, the *Washington Post* published a news item that gave coverage to the use of Chinese prison labour in producing Levi jeans. This negative media attention and publicity led to Levi Strauss adopting codes of conduct for its global suppliers, with other companies following suit – as more consumer campaigns revealed sweatshop conditions (Jenkins et al. 2002; Hale and Wills 2005; Sluiter 2009). Yet, as Jenkins (2002) remarks, the nub of the early codes was on protecting retailers from sensitive concerns, such as child and forced labour, rather than on freedom of association (unionization) and collective bargaining. These telling gaps in the coverage of corporate codes are what propelled consumer pressure groups, such as the Clean Clothes Campaign, to call for the establishment of codes consonant with the ILO's core conventions (Sluiter 2009; see also Jenkins et al. 2002; Hale and Wills 2005).

It is in this vein that the Ethical Trade Initiative (ETI) came to be set up in the United Kingdom by 1998 as a multi-stakeholder endeavour, involving tripartite constituencies. Similar initiatives gained hold elsewhere: The Fair Wear Foundation came into being in the Netherlands in 1999, for instance (Hughes et al. 2008; Sluiter 2009; Hensman 2011). Yet, as Hensman (2011: 293) observes, 'while codes of conduct were becoming popular ... most of the workers they were supposed to protect were not even aware of their existence' (see also Jenkins et al. 2002; Hale and Willis 2005; Plankey-Videla 2012). Her observation underlines the absence of worker awareness of, let alone involvement in, a mechanism that was supposed to have a tripartite element as its guiding principle. However, voluntary corporate codes and multi-stakeholder initiatives still sought to determine and shape the global garment industry.

The concern around the lack of labour voice in multi-stakeholder initiatives, whether in their realization or implementation, has been repeatedly raised. These critical appraisals have accentuated variations in ethical trade strategies and their bearing on auditing practices and working conditions (Blowfield 1999, 2007; Hale and Wills 2005; Hughes 2006; Barrientos and Smith 2007; Raj-Reichert 2019; Selwyn 2019). Debates by these scholars on the efficacy of the initiatives have attempted to come to a judgement over the difference ethical codes may have made on production facilities that were previously non-compliant. The challenging of suppliers' compliance and of how workers navigate ethical and corporate codes of conduct tend to be inadequate, with this failing hampering our ability to appreciate the complex and uneven ways in which ethical codes travel across differentiated international, national and regional spaces (Hughes 2006; Hughes and Reimer 2006; Tighe 2016; Raj-Reichert 2019). While there has been an attempt to redress this gap, a careful and detailed study of how labourers negotiate ethical codes within the apparel sector is tellingly missing (see, for instance, de Neve 2009, 2014; Mezzadri 2012; Ruwanpura 2014a, 2016). It is to fill this gap that I turned my attention, via research extending over nearly a decade; in the next chapter, I trace the main methods I used to gather data over this time period.

Notes

1. Ha-Joon Chang's work takes its cue from institutionalism and Keynes, with infusions from Marxist elements, to investigate the political economy of development, the need for industrial policy and the centrality of the state in several places in the world. I had the good fortune of being taught by him; while I cite some key texts, I am not doing justice to his rich and impressive body of literature, which most employers should be reading – but sadly are not.

2. The GCC, GVC and GPN frameworks have until recently neglected uneven power dynamics, the state and labour in their analysis (Smith et al. 2002, 2015a; Sunley 2008; Coe and Jordhus-Leir 2011; Selwyn 2012a, 2013, 2019). As mostly academic men, they often ignored feminist scholars who had been contributing on the place of gendered labour within global production. Within economic geography, it was feminist scholars who had started to speak about gendered regimes of labour that shaped global production regimes and uneven development processes (Wright 2006; Bair and Werner 2011; Werner 2012, 2020).

3. Ruwanpura (2011), Bair (2010) and Bedford and Rai (2010) offer reviews and positions taken by many early feminist scholars on the subject. Here, I present a necessarily condensed and brief overview.

3

Fieldwork

Prolonged Phases and Multiple Moments

Introduction

Towards the latter part of 2008, when I travelled to Sri Lanka to start this research, I did not envisage that I would be continuing this work for almost a decade. My initial approach was to a large degree dictated by the methods I had outlined for an Economic and Social Research Council–funded research project. Hence, like many others before me, I too followed the well-trodden track of carrying out interviews and located ethnography in a way that fell well within the project timeline. However, for a variety of factors recounted later, I also returned to do further research on the topic, maintaining connections with a number of workers, labour rights activists and managers. In this chapter, I try to capture the unbounded nature of field research and provide a sense of the processual nature of my research over the past decade.

I also aim to discuss the various methods that I deployed, especially as the fieldwork was not conducted during a singular research trip but, in the end, was a prolonged process carried out over several visits and years. This extended timeline was not one that I had anticipated at the start of my three-year project but one that ensued nonetheless. Partly, my motivation for continuing to have an association with a select number of workers had some connection with my feminist and solidarity politics and an upbringing infused with Buddhist empathy. Recurrent visits also involved using and deploying multiple methods at various stages, as the extended field research necessitated an evolving research design schema. In this chapter, therefore, I will detail the progress of my research methods over time. An extended field-research schedule meant that I was able to gather and reflect upon unanticipated changes and different embodied tempos, methods and processes.

Multiple Belongings: Doing Fieldwork Back 'Home'

The year 2008 was the starting point of my fieldwork and, like the experiences of countless others, my initial time in Sri Lanka had its ups and downs. The cyclical process of doing research back 'home' was undoubtedly linked to my shifting subject position as an insider (Sri Lankan born and bred) and outsider (residing and working in the United Kingdom). Like Mullings (1999: 341), I too found 'a constant shift of the multiple axes upon which my identity rested' (see also Hewamanne 2008). It was not only that I needed to acknowledge my gender, class, language and ethnicity but, as I found out during my fieldwork, my marital status and sexuality too were up for discussion and contestation. Foreknowing the challenges was impossible. As a single (i.e., unmarried) woman in my late thirties embarking on fieldwork in garment factories that employed mostly women of various ages (from their late teenage years to their fifties), the issues were difficult to anticipate. Indeed, I found myself having to negotiate the field setting regularly and differently at the two factories where I was based.

When I had envisaged this project, and prior to travelling to Sri Lanka for my initial fieldwork phase, I had hoped to access one of Sri Lanka's leading apparel production factories for my long-term stay, where a neighbour of my parents was the chief executive officer (CEO). I also had numerous and varied other contacts and networks that were likely to facilitate this fieldwork. These were contacts that I thought might have eased access to the factory floor, because I knew that gaining entrance to production facilities would be key to the success of my research. Hence, I started tapping or renewing connections that ranged from neighbours to relatives, friends (men and women), siblings of friends and friends from my teenage years. My purpose was to deploy the connections I already had – across communities of interlocutors. I had assumed that I would most likely succeed in accessing factory sites through one of these connections, thinking that my class position, being English-speaking, educated and middle class, was likely to be a boon in gaining access. As it turned out, my class status was a bonus but not the main reason for success.

Unlike others who have described the difficulties they encountered in accessing the factory floor as a long and arduous process (Lynch 2007; Prentice 2015; Zaki-Chakravarti 2019), my long-term entry to two production facilities was achieved easily and unpredictably. I started my initial fieldwork phase in December–January of 2008–2009 and had almost met the interview target of 25 managers that I had set for myself. Almost all the interviewees had met me at their Colombo offices, over lunch at five-star hotels, at their homes or at various coffee houses. I always indicated my willingness to meet at any research location that was suggested by them. At no point did I find their request to meet at these varied locations awkward. The interviewees who suggested meetings over lunch were old friends, and these meetings represented a moment both to rekindle old friendships and to conduct interviews. A request for the interview to be conducted at the interviewee's home in the early evening hours was usually because there already existed a degree of familiarity or the interviewee had a hectic schedule. I initially interviewed 25 managers of different ranks from various organization types, sizes and locations during this first phase of research, as represented in Table 3.1.

Towards the tail end of my preliminary fieldwork, my last two management interviewees asked whether I was open to meeting them at their factory locations. In retrospect, the suggested locations for a meeting

Table 3.1 Characteristics of management interviewees

Typology	Key characteristics	Numbers
Management rank:	Senior management (CEOs, country directors, managing and group directors)	13
	Middle management (general managers, factory managers, corporate social responsibility managers, compliance managers)	12
Organization type:	Buying offices based in Sri Lanka (of USA and United Kingdom retail brands)	4
	Foreign-owned factories in Sri Lanka	3
	Locally owned factories in Sri Lanka	18
Size:	Large suppliers	5
	Middle-sized suppliers	15
	Small suppliers	5
Factory locations:	All-island	18
	Rural only	5
	FTZ only	2

Source: Author's fieldwork.

were possibly because we met well into January. The new year of 2009 had begun, and their new production cycles too. I had excitedly responded positively to the first such proposition, because, even by this late stage, the opportunity to visit a factory had not yet arisen. I had already mentioned to three interviewees with close family connections how I would like to gain access to a factory for the longer period of fieldwork; they had all agreed in principle but left the discussion of firm details for later.

At the end of the interviews, these two interviewees separately and independently of each other asked me questions regarding the next stage of my research; this was not unusual, as offering context, follow-up clarifications and answering queries are standard during interviews. I explained again the outline of the larger project to them. Both these interviewees, coincidentally on the same day, serendipitously offered their production sites as possible research locations. Since both managers were unknown to me beforehand, this willingness to open their factory settings took me off guard. Yet I was able to seize the moment. In one factory, where access was granted on the same day, a senior manager said that this would be important for the factory because it signalled to multi-stakeholder initiatives the firm's openness to independent reviews.[1] Unknown to both of us, we had studied in sister/brother schools in Sri Lanka, probably as cohorts a few years apart, had common contacts and had studied in the United Kingdom. All these commonalities undoubtedly helped develop the familiarity and ease necessary to grant this access.[2]

At the second factory, the initial manager I interviewed mentioned that they had had previous experiences of long-term researchers in their other factories but not at the factory in which we had met. He shared the view that they usually found the presence of researchers useful, as they continuously learned through the findings of the researcher. Hence, he suggested that I contact his superior and seek consent. He shared his boss's mobile number, said I could use his name and also gave me the tip that I should use other known contacts of his senior manager. I used the knowledge he provided and started asking around my aunts, uncles and cousins – the first port of call in establishing connections. Fortunately for me, a close member of my family knew him very well and agreed to mediate for me. In contacting the senior manager, I used both names. He acknowledged that he had been informed by his junior colleague and my maternal uncle that I would be calling. In our brief telephone chat, he suggested that I visit the factory again, on a day when he would be present.

During the next factory call, a few days later, he and the factory manager, my initial interviewee, spoke to me at some length about the research I was hoping to conduct. This conversation went fairly well. He then inquired whether I would be open to visiting again when one of the family board members was there, because, while he himself was open to the suggestion, it was important that the board members were aware and briefed too. Hence, I yet again visited the same factory. On this visit, I was taken to the board room in the office section within the factory premises, where the senior manager, a family board member and the manager I had interviewed previously were present. I was not entirely prepared for the formality of this meeting. We had an elaborate discussion and conversation on my research, the nature of it and its purpose, alongside subtle queries on my background and the web of my connections in the country (see also Plankey-Videla 2012; Kim 2013; Shakya 2018; Zaki-Chakravarti 2019). This conversation took longer than I had anticipated, and it was evident from the line of questioning that their interest was not just in the research, but also in my reliability – and, for them, my class (i.e., which schools I had attended in Sri Lanka, my educational trajectory outside the country, and so on). I was conscious that I was drawing on my class and my insider/ outsider status to make my research viable (Mullings 1999). I recognized then that, in the next phase of the fieldwork, my social location would need to be navigated differently. Yet my mutliple belongings kept emerging in distinctive ways throughout my fieldwork. After an elaborate and detailed discussion, in the end, I had a positive decision, with two caveats. The first was that I share my findings with the local management team at the end of the fieldwork period and make available any publications that came out. Second, they emphasized the need for discretion and requested that I do no filming within the factory or be involved in media propoganda. I gave assurances that this would be the case, both on my part and on that of the local researcher I was hoping to do this work with.

To ease my entry to the factory setting itself, I requested Wasana, a research assistant on the project in Sri Lanka, to access the facilities prior to me starting my located ethnography. She started visiting these factories from April 2009 on a weekly basis until I arrived in the country in July 2009. By the time I started my located research, some workers had already heard my name or of me and would always associate me with Wasana. The decision to approach the longer spell of research in this way was advantageous, as it eased my presence in the factory in many ways.

For seven and a half months, I visited each factory on alternate days and was on the shop floor on an almost daily basis. This helped me develop rapport and familiarity with the workers. Unlike in other located ethnographies, however, I never worked alongside them (Salzinger 2003; Wright 2006; Lynch 2007; Hewamanne 2008; Plankey-Videla 2012; Prentice 2015; Zaki-Chakravarti 2019). On reading and rereading these texts, I reflected upon my possible rationale for not pursuing the option of labouring with others. I do not have a ready answer, other than that I was possibly trying to ensure that it was my access to the factory premises that was more important rather than whether I necessarily laboured or not. There were, however, a few occasions when workers did seek my help when their work had piled up, and I stepped in when possible – usually when it was the trimmers or packers who sought this assistance. This involvement was noticed by the managers at the two factories. The factory which had had researchers before tended to be most open towards my involvement in helping workers with their various tasks. The other factory gently made it known that this was inadvisable, although a few managers reluctantly acknowledged that, when workers requested my backing, the expectation would be for me to step up. Other than on these occasions, in a similar way to the various supervisory staff, work-study office staff and production floor managers, I was either walking around the shop floor, talking to workers when their schedule permitted, or was seated at a side desk, writing my observations. On a regular basis, however, I ate with the workers and different groups of workers at the canteen during the lunch hour. Sometimes, my lunch period extended for more than an hour, sitting and talking with different groups of workers that came through for their meal at different times.

If, despite my class, I was able to develop a camaraderie with workers, men and women, I had more difficulties with the management at one factory and had to constantly reaffirm my status as a researcher. As with the experiences of other feminist researchers, rumour, gossip and suspicion appeared and disappeared with staggering frequency (Salzinger 2003; Zaki-Chakravarti 2019). In the factory where production floor dynamics seemed congenial, I had multiple avatars ascribed to me. At various points, I was quizzed about my life or it was made known that I might be doing a study for Marks and Spencer, was a reporter for the *Financial Times* newspaper (United Kingdom), a journalist, an auditor for the ETI and even a lesbian, as I seemed too close to women workers. Sometimes, I found these unexpected questions bemusing. For instance, the question on my association with the

Financial Times newspaper took me by surprise, both because I rarely read this broadsheet and because, in semi-rural Sri Lanka, British newspapers were far from my mind. At other times, I found the insinuations hurtful: the one about being a lesbian, for instance, which was conveyed to me via Wasana (she was younger than me but married). Yet it was also, at the same time, amusing: the idea that someone usually residing in the United Kingdom would need to travel to semi-rural Sri Lanka to explore her sexual self. To have to explain to my research constituents my marital status, sexuality, and my friendships and relationships with men was not something that I had necessarily anticipated. My gender, class, ethnicity, marital status and sexuality were all up for grabs during the initial fieldwork – and in this regard, I look back at this research phase as taxing at times.[3]

Away from the FTZ and Colombo

Neither factory fell within an FTZ, and both were located in semi-rural areas outside Colombo. While it was serendipity that led me to these particular production sites, I also knew from the inception that I wanted to avoid traversing previous research locations where detailed ethnographies had already been undertaken, namely in the FTZs of Colombo and Kandy, the capital and a major city in the hill country of Sri Lanka (Lynch 2007; Hewamanne 2008). While Lynch's (2007) research was at a factory based in the small village of Udakande, its five-mile proximity to Kandy, a well-known city in Sri Lanka, meant that its geographical location was likely to have shaped its production facilities through a confluence of factors that may have required vigilance to work conditions. I wanted to avoid proximity to any of the main cities of Sri Lanka.

This aspiration fortuitously worked out; the two factories that became my research sites by happenchance were in semi-rural areas of Sri Lanka in a district adjacent to Colombo District. A geographical location that is ideal for research, however, requires flexibility and adaptability in accessing the space over time. Initially, it meant driving from Colombo for anything between an hour to one and a half hours on a daily basis until such time as I found a local place to stay. These initial drives in a small Kelisa car were quite exhausting. A combination of traffic, pedestrians, avoiding street dogs and potholes, thinning tarmacs and gravel roads required constant alertness. I was relieved of this need for vigilance only once I turned into a B road that would take me to one of the factories, when I would drive through the lush and verdant greenery of paddy fields and occassionally rubber estates (depending on which route I chose). On this stretch of my drive, the beauty and greenery of the landscape never ceased to amaze me (see Image 3.1). It was a picturesque rural and semi-rural Sri Lanka; I felt this way, despite

Image 3.1 Scenery from the area in which the two factories were located

Source: Author's own photos.

still having to navigate treacherously narrow roads, observe domesticated elephants walking on them, pick up abandoned pups to find them homes and continue to avoid pedestrians – for whom pavements were not built.

During these drives, I would sometimes pick up Wasana – whose home was on the way – and then continue to the factories. Over the years I drove to that area, given post-war Sri Lanka's infrastructural boom, the A roads were dramatically upgraded, in some parts even with pavements for pedestrians. Driving the same distance became smoother and relatively effortlesss, although, once I reached the B roads, there was minimal change.[4]

After about two to three weeks of this daily grind, I found lodgings in the area – from where I could walk to one factory and take a short drive in the Kelisa to the other. My accommodation was simple and yet comfortable and, yet again, reflected both chance and class connections. One of my management interviewees introduced me to a couple who had recently taken up residence in the area, after retiring from years of working in the United Kingdom. They had built a separate cottage, with a small room and bathroom, adjacent to their bungalow – and, after preliminary introductions, it transpired that there was a web of personal and family connections with (late) *Uncle Christo* and *Aunty Inez* that made my time there and the revisits incredibly pleasant. I would have my dinner with them and, as the daughter and son of one of their aides worked at the nearby factory, we would ruminate about politics, society and the factory floor. Undoubtedly, my insights were also shaped by these discussions.

Residing in the area during my phase of located ethnography also led to close affinities, as I met contacts both on and off site, at their homes and/ or boarding houses. I got to know their families, took them to hospital with unexpected illnesses, dropped them off in town, attended wedding celebrations, helped take elderly parents for medical appointments, and so on. These moments were often meaningful. To illustrate, on one occasion, my support was sought by a security officer at one of the factories, as his wife – who was a migrant worker to the Middle East – had had to leave her employer hastily due to abuse. By my contacting colleagues and friends at the relevant ministry, it became possible to assist her to be repatriated to Sri Lanka.

Yet this web of connections sometimes also caused awkwardness or tears (see also Plankey-Videla 2012). I would get calls from unknown men from the area or other factories making suggestive propositions; in a couple of instances, spouses of women workers acted likewise. I had to find ways to extricate myself from these uncomfortable situations and came to recognize that the power dynamics between the researcher and the researched are never static but frequently shifting. Yet, by emotionally investing during my initial fieldwork phase, some contacts have endured, and I have met these workers on revisits to the area or their original homes. While initially our contact was also maintained through monthly or quarterly phone calls, more recently I have relied much more on visits, almost every time I am in Sri Lanka, which is at least annually. These prolonged contacts have helped me to capture the individuals' evolving work experiences, as they have moved in and out of the sector, and how in their estimation their work and factory conditions have changed.

During this time, to gain an appreciation for the industry, I made visits to other factories, which were located within and outside the FTZ. Often, these visits were for the entire day. Thus, I had the chance to get a feel of factories of various sizes and scales, from the high end to the low end, as well as the variation in facilities provided for workers. It also helped me better locate my research sites within the landscape of Sri Lankan apparel firms and become aware of the differentiated conditions as factories in the North and the East were set up in post-war Sri Lanka. However, I was never located within factories in the north and the east regions for an extended period of time; hence, my fieldwork involved different methods over an extended period of time, including ethnography.

Sketching the Setting: Factory Profiles

Within the sector, the two factories I was based at were considered large production facilities, employing 800 and 1,500 workers – although the smaller one saw itself as falling somewhere between a medium and a large production facility. Both production sites were involved in original design manufacturing (ODM), also known as full-package manufacturing, with the one at the top end merging into own-brand manufacturing (OBM). Their long-term client bases were high-, middle- and low-end global retailers, based primarily in the United Kingdom or the United States. While I was already familiar with some brands – Marks and Spencer, Next, Levi's, Abercombie and Fitch, Debenhams, Eddie Bauer, Matalan and Tesco – I also became acquainted with Lily Pulitzer and its colourful prints that dotted the factory floor. Despite their different scales, both factories prided themselves on being harbingers of upholding ethical production practices across various global code governance regimes, whether multi-stakeholder initiatives or individual corporate codes of conduct. In their estimation, this also aided their businesses, because, by commiting to the most rigorous code standards, their ethical responsibility towards all buyers would be covered.

During the past decade, then, I used multiple methods to gather my data as my research design evolved over time. The research began as an ethnography: I lived in the area and embedded myself as a participant-observer at both factories over a year and continued to visit and reside in the area until June 2011. By embedding myself in the two factories, I was able to gather meticulous details about the everyday workspaces and how ethical codes were deployed, keeping a fieldwork diary with daily observations of events, incidents and conversations. These details consisted of my observations combined with code issues workers shared with me through their relating of unrecorded incidents or simply chit-chat.[5]

Initially 90 workers were interviewed, with 60 coming from the two factories we were based at and the other 30 from other factories. They were contacted through a snowballing technique. All interviewee contacts were random to some extent, but their willingness to be interviewed already indicated an interest and openness to sharing their views. This reflects to some degree that, even within seeming haphazardness, the interviewees had particular dispositions and interests in sharing their views. The location for our interviews was always at their homes or boarding houses; the interviews were conducted in Sinhala and often recorded, with our discussion honing in on each dimension of the ethical codes.

As Sri Lankans have high literarcy rates (91.3 per cent), 25 workers were asked to keep a weekly journal; yet, by the end of the timeline, only 20 workers had done so. Those who decided against keeping diaries told us that it was because they had a sense of foreboding about notebooks falling into the wrong hands or they found the exercise dull. Encouraging diary-keeping required us to nurture close and continuing relations with this group. For example, occasionally during our ongoing conversations, it transpired that recurrent incidents that workers considered 'normal' had gone unrecorded. In cases where writing was a habitual practice for workers – i.e., they kept diaries, did creative writing or wrote short stories – they wrote copious and rich accounts. It was also providential that, at one point, because of growing disenchantment with the HR team, a secretary of a worker council unexpectedly shared extensive meeting notes with me. These methods allowed access to a wide range of primary data, including the views of management, although, unlike Kim (2013), I was neither sought nor given access to management memos, spreadsheets or reports.

Once the located ethnography was completed, the research continued formally until the end of June 2011. During this time, I returned to Sri Lanka every four to six months and conducted fieldwork for two- to three-month periods. In this way, I got an evolving sense of factory-based politics over a two-year period, through my direct information-gathering and the discussions that Wasana and I would have. I also had other able junior researchers support me during various phases; their conversations also have left an imprint on this research. During the initial project life (until 2012), I was also supported by Andi Schubert, Anu Tennekoon, Virandi Wettawa and Sarah Parker for smaller components of research. In the past year (2019–2020), I was also assisted at various stages by Loritta Chan, Peter Rowe and Megan Todd in updating, gathering and analysing newspaper archival data, with Peter especially offering a gifted and willing hand with the statistical data – and thus enriching my grasp of issues.

After the initial period of research, I kept in touch with those workers who had not changed their mobile phone numbers and with a number of labour rights groups, related contacts and management interviewees. At various times during the past decade, I have undertaken intensive return research stints, because of the evolving labour politics in Sri Lanka, including most recently in July 2019. I draw on all of these different phases in my various chapters.

Elongated Research and Mingling Methods

My data sources for the North and the East, in comparison, are primarily open-ended interviews with garment sector workers, reportage from newspaper archival research, dialogues with labour rights organizations present in the region and additional management interviews conducted in 2014. The initial impetus for seeking these management interviews and revisiting them was joint research done with Annelies Goger, which she subsequently generously and collegially shared with me (Goger and Ruwanpura 2014; Ruwanpura 2018).

In conducting interviews with workers in the region, it was often necessary to draw upon the work of translators, and there are likely to be lapses in the data gathered. Accessing workers in the north and the east areas occurred through the connections I kept with a handful of labour rights organizations, in particular the Women's Centre and Da Bindu. The Women's Centre generously shared an early report on the status of Tamil women workers in FTZs in the south who hailed from post-war Sri Lanka. It was also with their support that interviews were done in late 2019, with a local researcher aiding the process, translating the interviews from Tamil into Sinhala, while the English translation was done by me.[6]

I am hence acutely conscious that the information gathered is likely to be fragmented for at least two reasons. Firstly, as a researcher, I lost richness from not being able to pick up the nuances of the Tamil language. Secondly, the language impediment meant that I had to rely on translation, not from one language to another but from Tamil to Sinhala and then to English. I am acutely aware of the misplacements that translations can bring and that I am guilty of not challenging 'the translation of subordinated language(s) into a dominant tongue' (Visweswaran 1994: 133). Consequently, the data not only was necessarily fragmented, but also may not have confronted the politics of reception. Notwithstanding my inability to speak and represent in several tongues, I am taking sides because I am aware that 'identities are determined by political exigencies of history' (Visweswaran 1994: 132), and, in the case of Sri Lanka, ongoing violent histories. My attempt to overcome these limitations meant drawing on newspaper archival research, video documentaries, secondary sources and various related reports. Given that my data for *Chapter Seven* in particular is fragmented and incomplete, any inferences I make are tentative. Different from Lingam's (2019) rich narrative voices, although only of three Tamil women workers, the responses I received were short and, in some instances, circumspect. Nonetheless, by drawing upon a number of sources, I was able to examine ethical codes in post-war Sri Lankan apparel firms to help capture the distinctly uneven application of codes within the same country.

Prominent women labour activists from the late 1970s and 1980s started the Women's Centre and Da Bindu; analogous to activists' struggles elsewhere, 'how well they all cohered was an ongoing struggle' (Tetrault 2014: 79). Interviews, conversations with several leading women's rights activists over many rounds and published testimonials are the basis for *Chapter Five*, where I explore the neglected labour histories of post-1977 Sri Lanka. Again, this chapter is complemented by fieldwork at the tail end of my project, when approximately 25,000 workers took to the streets of Sri Lanka to agitate and strike against possible pension sector reforms.

From the viewpoint of a researcher, it was a fortutious time to be in Sri Lanka, because, through large-scale labour protests, workers were able to bring the state to heel – although not without the loss of workers' lives (Women's Centre 2011). The perspective of the household economy of garment sector workers became vital at this moment, signalling that social reproduction matters for workers (Ruwanpura 2013b; Rai, Brown and Ruwanpura 2019). In this chapter on unearthing labour histories, I write from the viewpoint of collective mobilization. Labour geographies, in essence, shape the evolution of capitalism.

Yet, as delineated in my book, labour and its crucial role in making capitalist success within the apparel sector possible are not always at the forefront of state policy or employer renditions. Consequently, I reflect on the limits to corporatized neoliberal governance, as ethical trade governance regimes themselves also structure the uneven development path of Sri Lanka, with tenous prospects for the labouring classes. To get to this analytical point, I explore in the next chapter how the apparel sector's successful evolution in the post-2008 decade alone shows that neither the state nor the capitalist sector has made labour a central plank in its platform for progress.

Notes

1. His foresight was rewarded years later because this factory used a working paper that I had produced to gain a higher-level global corporate social responsibility certification (Ruwanpura 2012). At his request, in early 2015 (circa March 2015) I shared an electronic copy of this report and sent a confirmation letter saying that the factory had been one of my research sites.
2. It transpired that these connections helped subsequently, because a newly recruited human resources (HR) manager did not always make my stay at this factory easy and I had to negotiate through many trying moments while doing the fieldwork. However, the fact that this HR manager then caused a commotion that led to worker agitation meant that I was able to maintain my initial relationship with the senior manager with the necessary tact (Ruwanpura 2015).
3. This was my third period of long-term fieldwork in Sri Lanka. My earlier work in eastern Sri Lanka, war-torn at the time (1998–1999), was by contrast far less personally challenging (Ruwanpura 2004), as was the fieldwork I did against the backdrop of post-tsunami Sri Lanka (Ruwanpura 2006).

4. Where some sections of these B roads that connect rural communities to other villages and towns were improved, the fact that most rural citizens are pedestrians was still overlooked. The selective view of citizenship around the road bonanza in post-war Sri Lanka and other parts of South Asia has already been written about, although more work needs to be done on the views of commuting workers, roads and infrastructure (Ruwanpura et al. 2020).

5. See Ruwanpura (2012, 2013a, 2014b, 2016) for more details on the practical details around coding, ethical challenges and issues around bias and positionality.

6. I had planned on meeting and interviewing these same workers again for a month in April 2020, but these fieldwork plans were brought to a grinding halt by CoVID-19 – with the airline cancelling the flight and the borders closing.

4

Clothing the World – Guilt Free?

Sri Lanka's Apparel Landscape

Introduction

When travelling out of Katunayake Airport, visitors to Sri Lanka meet a large billboard – greeting tourists, retailers, buyers and investors with 'Welcome to the world's first ethical apparel sourcing destination' (Image 4.1). The sign incorporates a logo with a shopping cart – located above the slogan

Image 4.1 Billboard on the way out of Katunayake Airport

Source: Author's own photo.

'Made in Sri Lanka' and topped by a halo, no doubt a subliminal message of sanctified sourcing. This bold, confident sign reflects the success of the Sri Lankan apparel sector in recent decades. The advent of free market policies led to the establishment of the first FTZ in the late 1970s and initially attracted FDI. Alongside these rudimentary beginnings was the birth of nascent local capital within the sector. The industry now claims to produce GWG and sees itself in the vanguard of the global value chain. For instance, Sri Lanka was one of the initial countries in the region and the world to go into partnership with Marks and Spencer's Plan A and set up eco-friendly production sites. It also envisages becoming a regional hub and has already set itself up as a centre of fashion design.

This sign raises an obvious question: How has the Sri Lankan apparel industry gone so successfully from strength to strength in the past four decades that its apparel association can make such claims without appearing hubristic or attracting condemnation? In this chapter, I attempt to answer this question with an outline of Sri Lanka's apparel landscape and its evolution over the past 40 years. Taking 1977 as the beginning of the burgeoning of a local apparel sector, I provide the foundation from which to understand the post-2008 years. Drawing on and interweaving my fieldwork, I also examine the impact of the onset of a global recession and the ending of 30 years of ethnic war and violence. Alongside this, I briefly sketch the industry through a combination of management perspectives and secondary data.[1] The chapter provides some historical context to enable an appreciation of how the Sri Lankan apparel industry has successfully navigated various challenges, a success that stands in stark contrast to the death of the industry in neighbouring Nepal (Shakya 2018). I also want to highlight how the dominant narratives of management and policymakers tend to leave labour out of their account of the apparel sector's successes.[2] Before we get to the voice of labour, however, it is important to incorporate management perspectives into recognizing how Sri Lankan apparel firms became front runners in ethical sourcing and how the sector went about cultivating this position.

Benefits of Going Small? The Early Years to 2008

For many years before 1977, the Sri Lankan apparel industry was shaped by an interventionist trade policy based on woven textiles for local use, but the industry remained nascent (Athukorala and Ekanayake 2018). All of that changed with the open economic policies that came with subsidies and tax incentives, orienting the industry away from woven textiles and towards clothing manufacture for exports (or garments). It was a shift that initially attracted FDI to Sri Lanka's first FTZ. Yet the backdrop of an ethnic war compounded by quota restrictions proved unattractive for mass-scale manufacturing of basic types of clothing (Knutsen 2003; Kelegama 2009).[3] These incentives and subsidies also attracted local industrial capital, however, which held fast, in contrast to quota-hopping East Asian investors, despite the unstable sociopolitical backdrop (Athukorala 2018). According to Athukorala and Ekanayake (2018), it was the second wave of reforms in the early 1990s that boosted the growth track of local capital. The pivot for this phase was 'abolishing import duties on textiles and yarn, freeing up exchange control on current transactions, and extending FTZ privileges to export-oriented ventures in all parts of the country' (Athukorala and Ekanayake 2018: 250).

As is the case for many countries in the South Asian region, the early growth of the Sri Lankan apparel sector is closely associated with the MFA (Knutsen 2003; Kelegama 2009; Mezzadri 2017; Shakya 2018). Trading via East Asian intermediaries characterized the first phase for Sri Lankan apparel firms. By the mid-1980s, this reliance on intermediaries receded, as international buying offices, often with direct links to retailers, moved to the country to create a permanent presence (Kelegama 2009; Athukorala and Ekanayake 2018). Together with these transformations, a number of local firms also set up production facilities. Some initiatives started as collaborative joint venture operations, while others matured from being local brands to having a global presence.

MAS, Brandix and Hirdaramani are the three big names in Sri Lanka's apparel sector. While Hirdaramani Garments (HG) has a history that predates 1977, Sri Lanka's two other largest apparel manufacturers, Brandix and MAS, took off as small start-ups that now not only are formidable producers in Sri Lanka, but also have a regional and global presence.[4] Brandix began as a joint venture; MAS began with three enterprising brothers in 1987, starting off exclusively manufacturing lingerie. In both cases, the support from Mast Industries, a subsidiary of USA-based Limited Inc., was crucial (Athukorala and Ekanayake 2018). HG was different. Its early beginning was as a retailing clothing store in the early 1900s in Fort, Colombo, which I recall occasionally visiting with my mother as a little girl on her shopping expeditions in the early 1980s. HG's transition from the clothing shop I visited has focused on apparel production and expanding the reach of its brand name, both regionally and globally.

These three big names, MAS, HG and Brandix, are largely owned by ethnically varied local capital, capturing the multifaceted and hybrid ethnic diversity of Sri Lanka.[5] Hence, according to a senior manager, the leading producers 'were here to stay'. I was also told that they were different from the initial foreign investors, who were there to make a quick buck: *staying* meant doing business differently. It meant not only shifting from Cut-Make-Trim (CMT) to ODM by the late 1990s, but also investing in production facilities and people. These transformations were possible because the sector established itself as a niche supplier. By positioning itself as an ethical producer in the global production process, it eschewed the mass production of basics and instead specialized in fashion-basics (Knutsen 2003; Kelegama 2009; Athukorala and Ekanayake 2018). Those writing on the apparel sector have identified the success of this supplier strategy, although Knutsen (2003), writing early on about this period, notes her ambivalence about the viability of upgrading. Others have outlined factors that contributed to Sri Lankan apparel firms' success, for example, the targeting of high-value-added products and having an educated labour force capable of timely delivery (Kelegama 2009; Athukorala and Ekanayake 2018). A number of my management respondents echoed these findings and remarked that there was also symbolic value embedded in local capital making it big, as that offered the necessary boost for other smaller producers to emerge.

The culmination of this strategic ascendance was the ability of these three leading producers to shift to eco-friendly production sites and become part of Marks and Spencer's Plan A (Goger 2013b; Fernando et al. 2019). Other apparel producers too had moved from CMT to at least original equipment manufacturing (OEM). The former, a feature of second-tier exporting countries, including those neighbouring Sri Lanka, is basic manufacturing where designs, fabric and accessories were all provided by the buyer (Mezzadri 2017; Shakya 2018). The latter allows suppliers to source fabrics and inputs by designated suppliers, provided that they meet customer specifications. ODM is a further step up and involved Sri Lankan suppliers offering product development, pattern-making, finishing, sourcing, manufacturing and delivery.

Athukorala and Ekanayake (2018: 252) note that almost 60 per cent of export value comes from ODM, with the rest largely coming from OEM and with CMT becoming a 'relic of the past'. During my fieldwork, I was based at two production facilities that largely did ODM (full package production), but one of my sites had production lines that also did CMT and others that did OBM. I also visited factories that had ongoing CMT operations alongside ODM, with the newly set up factories in the North and the East of Sri Lanka starting with basics or CMT. Hence, it would be fair to say that while the industry leaders were likely to be creating more value, including through developing their brands, the industry as a whole also relied upon CMT, resulting in a more diversified production portfolio. This resonates with Kim's (2013) observation in a South Korean factory in China. He notes that the pressures of the global supply chain meant top-tier factories would not only subcontract, but also take up subcontracting themselves to ensure viability over slow periods. Management interviewees shared similar views with me, and/or I observed the same, both at factories that I visited and where I was doing my located ethnography.

Sri Lankan apparel firms' ability to make this transition and have a varied range of manufacturing was partly a reflection of buyer profile and the fact that the customer base was long-standing. My respondents constantly spoke of the sector's ability to assure *quality* and *timely delivery,* noting that these two facets were key to the strength of Sri Lanka's apparel industry. As I have already noted in *Chapter Two,* the retailers that sought Sri Lanka's production were established brand names, which was the case not just for the two production sites I was based at, but also for the country more generally. Those writing on the successes of the Sri Lankan garment sector have already noted that its customers ranged from high-street retailers, such as Marks and Spencer, GAP and NEXT, to high-end brands, such as Ralph Lauren, Lily Pulitzer and Pierre Cardin (Knutsen 2003; Kelegama 2009; Goger 2014; Athukorala and Ekanayake 2018). For them, it was this speciality retail customer base that facilitated the upgrading of the Sri Lankan apparel sector, as it required close cooperation and partnership, with the sharing of technical, managerial and marketing knowledge imprinted into the relationship.[6]

The Sri Lankan apparel sector's specialization and niche production were distinct from the usual strategy in Bangladesh, India, Nepal and Pakistan of producing for mass-scale retailers, which these countries have pursued with mixed results (Ruwanpura and Hughes 2016; Mezzadri 2017; Shakya 2018). Hence, by the time the MFA ended in 2005, the country's apparel sector had alternatives in place to withstand the likely economic impacts (Kelegama

2009; Athukorala and Ekanayake 2018). The feared death knell was deftly avoided by the Sri Lankan apparel sector because it chose a path less well trodden. The value upgrading outlined by Gereffi, Humphrey and Sturgeon (2005) might resonate for Sri Lanka. Yet what about the role of labour in this transformation? What social conditions and institutions facilitated this upgrading process?

Value Upgrading to Valued Labour?

As we have seen before, the Sri Lankan apparel sector's ability to withstand the initial global challenge following the expiry of the MFA in 2005 was partly due to the path of value-added niche production it had pursued, coupled with the position it had crafted for itself in the global imaginary as an ethical sourcing destination, as has already been traced in the scholarship (Kelegama 2009; Athukorala and Ekanayake 2018). Within this context, it is pertinent to inquire the following: Did industrial upgrading translate into valued labour? Equally, did labour have a role? I will return to these questions in more detail in *Chapters Five* and *Six*, with the latter chapter also probing whether ethical branding led to the transmutation of the lives of labourers.

The expiration of the MFA, in Sri Lanka, did not lead to the rapid cull witnessed elsewhere (Plankey-Videla 2012; Kim 2013; Shakya 2018). While some smaller producers did fold, the larger firms consolidated, and others found buyers or started to subcontract for the consolidated firms (Saxena 2014; Athukorala and Ekanayake 2018). My management interviewees not only noted how the value-added niche production path that was pursued helped firms withstand this initial global challenge, but also went on to say that upholding work conditions within the factories was important in easing the sector along this path (Ruwanpura and Wrigley 2011).

So, by the time the UK-based ETI was formed in 1998 by tripartite constituents, spanning the state, employers and union movements, with faith in collective action (Blowfield 1999, 2007; Hughes 2001; Hughes, Buttle and Wrigley 2007), the Sri Lankan apparel sector was already ahead of the curve. The Sri Lankan state had given clear directives to the apparel sector industrialists by the 1980s that required adherence to minimum standards.[7] Managers repeatedly mentioned how, by the time ethical codes were adopted globally as a form of corporate governance in the mid-1990s to late 1990s, the Sri Lankan apparel sector was already well placed. Some managers indicated that the Sri Lankan apparel sector was a cut above the rest and in the global vanguard. They attributed this favourable position to state directives that had come into place by the late 1980s – at least a good decade before ethical governance regimes gained traction globally. These decrees ranged from minimum wages and zero tolerance on child labour to the provision of locker rooms for workers and appropriate toilet ratios, all of which was monitored by three bodies – the Board of Investment (BOI), labour department and zonal authorities. They noted that these basics appeared to be appreciated by their Western buyers and it became '*kind of like inherent in the industrial mindset*' (Ruwanpura and Wrigley 2011: 1037, original emphasis). Adhering to and improving on compliance was part of the package deal offered by Sri Lankan garment firms in producing value-added apparel.

Transformational leadership by the state and select industrialists is how the managers accounted for the sector's branding as an ethical producer. They capture how the Sri Lankan apparel sector's strategic shift was not only about moving into higher-value-added production, but also about creating a niche position in the global supply chain as an ethical producer. This chronicling, however, may ignore the labour struggles that were just as important in facilitating value creation (Women's Centre 2006). Yet, even as a partial rendering, management narratives nevertheless offer an important lens through which to appreciate the industry position on manufacturing GWG.

The industry mission statement on the JAAF's web archive, for instance, is appealing, as it claims to aspire to improve the workers' quality of life by adhering to Sri Lanka's strong legislative framework (JAAF 2011). The JAAF (2019) explicitly draws upon the legal and social institutions that matter for doing business ethically. Adopting ethical business credentials was important and played out favourably for Sri Lankan apparel firms (Kelegama 2009; Goger 2014; Athukorala and Ekanayake 2018). Yet so were the social institutions and legal frameworks within the country that not only provided an educated labour force, but also helped protect them. Being conscious of scales of state intervention within global production, globalization and uneven development is pivotal to redressing the blissful ignorance that assumes that the state does not matter in a neoliberal age (Sunley 1999; Waller 2006; Tewari 2008; Selwyn 2012b; Kim 2013; Chang 2014; Smith 2015a, 2015b; Werner 2016, 2020; Silver 2019; Hughes, Morrison and Ruwanpura 2019).

This upgrading strategy is viewed by management as an initiative driven by corporate leaders with a transformative vision, with scholarship stressing this view, as if it was simply a capital-driven strategy (Kelegama 2009; Athukorala 2018, 2019; Athukorala and Ekanayake 2018). Even though this literature emphasizes that non-price factors aided the successes of Sri Lankan apparel firms, with educated labour playing a role, the lion's share of praise is accorded to various management-led initiatives. I do not want to negate this storyline entirely, as reading and conversing with management and workers alike about where the sector was at and where it is now confirmed that, undoubtedly, management vision was important. Yet, in the interviews with management, workers were often a hidden element. Frequently, I had to press managers to respond on whether labour was an important constituent, or whether the drive and vision came only from the connections with retailers, buyers and industrial contacts. When management contemplated their workers' role in the upgrading initiatives, they routinely referred to the fact that Sri Lankan workers were unlike those in neighbouring countries. Sri Lankan labourers, they said, were highly educated, there were higher social development levels within the country and the baseline was different. The following reflections by a middle manager capture this spirit:

> Sri Lanka, social development was quite important – like universal franchise was here before Britain had it. So, in that sense ... our people would have required, they would have wanted to be treated differently ... And labour regulations are quite stiff here, which is both a positive and a negative.

Yet buried within this view, he was involuntarily also revealing that, although visionary and transformative industrial leadership may have been important, it was also a response to labour voice and collective agency.

Management perspectives that emphasize the value of workers need to be juxtaposed with previous findings of stigmatized young women workers, where garment work was defamed socially and culturally and poverty wages did not relieve workers' material conditions (Lynch 2007; Hewamanne 2008). This shift signals the likely place that the industry finds itself in, where jobs may be shunned rather than sought by potential workers. I did not realize the magnitude of this challenge for the industry until I started being located at the two factory sites, where recruitment rounds to rural areas – far from the factory sites – were organized by the

HR and operations staff. Managers with whom I was familiar and who had been in the industry since its inception spoke frankly about the difficulties in recruiting and retaining workers. It was an unanticipated outcome for the industry. Workers no longer sought the sector; the factories instead had to seek workers. Often too, I came across handbills and posters circulated around the local area or amongst workers in an effort to encourage them to entice their family, kin or friends (Image 4.2).

Likewise, JAAF officials conceded that they needed to produce promotional television dramas representing the value of workers to their families, the industry and even the nation. Attracting workers and removing any blemish linked to factory work by using tropes of family, industry and nation are telling of how industrialists coupled cultural and material symbols to ensure viability (MAS 2020). While our conversations particularly emphasized the challenges faced by factories within designated FTZs in Sri Lanka, my production sites outside FTZs and in semi-rural areas faced similar recruitment and retention issues, suggesting a more endemic difficulty. The representation of valued workers using tropes of home, industry and the nation was in accordance with findings for other countries (Ruwanpura and Hughes 2016; Shakya 2018; Zaki-Chakravarti

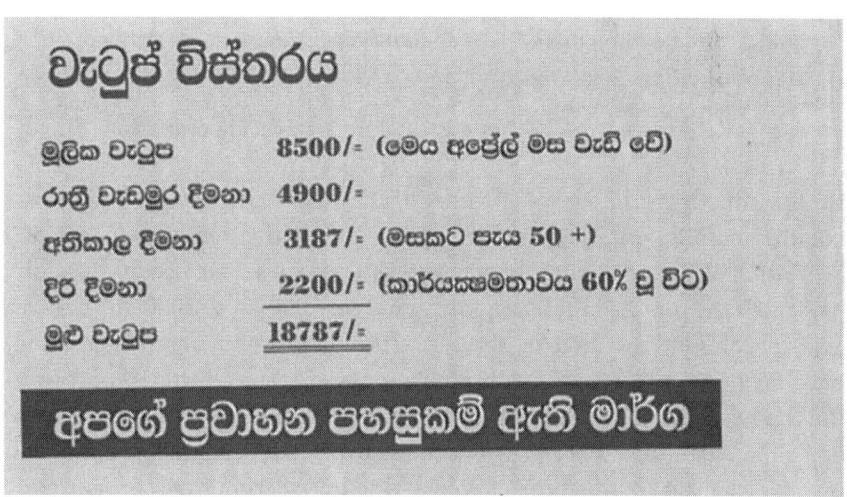

Image 4.2 In this excerpt of a leaflet, the factory details the wage breakdown and goes on to detail the public transportation routes. To maintain confidentiality – as the bus routes would possibly reveal the factory and location – I provide a shorter version of the original flier.
Source: Author's own photo.

2019). It was also, however, as Goger (2013a) remarks, no longer about portraying workers as disposable but about re-articulating the sector as one that empowered women workers. This shift of gears and dis/articulation, as feminist scholars argue, were reflective of social hierarchies and legacies of inequality that shaped upgrading processes and value creation and not just of economic logic alone (Bair and Werner 2011; Goger 2013a; Werner 2016; McGrath 2018). Goger's call, amongst that of other feminist scholars, for us to be perceptive about management interpolations is useful to understand the post-2008 Sri Lankan context (Salzinger 2003; Wright 2006; Bair and Werner 2011). In what ways does the articulation of valued labour coincide with the global downturn of 2008, the ending of a protracted war in Sri Lanka, along with any other external factors that may have required an attuned management position? Was 2008 a stimulus or a setback for the Sri Lankan apparel sector?

2008: Catalyst of *Efficiencies, Effectiveness and Excellence?*

Let us innovate constantly to reduce all waste from our processes. Let us all add value in everything we do. Let us compete on efficiencies and effectiveness, and not on being the cheapest source, let us make great products and work with the most demanding of customers, so that we will constantly be driven to achieve excellence.

—CEO of a leading Sri Lankan apparel firm (2011)

By the time my ethnographic research located at the two field sites was coming to an end, the position as articulated by this senior manager of a leading Sri Lankan apparel firm suggests that the sector had successfully navigated the rough global economic winds of 2008. Post-2008, Sri Lankan apparel firms were fixated on competing not on price but on value creation, efficiency and effectiveness. It is a position that stands in stark contrast to the themes found when I began my fieldwork in late 2008, when the global economic downturn was rapidly spreading worldwide. Then, one of the first interviews I did on this project was with a friend from my teenage years, who was now the head of the country office of a global apparel brand. We had not met for well over fifteen years. Yet our close friendship during our teenage years and into our early twenties meant it was easy to revive contact through mutual friends and have a long-extended discussion about the apparel industry. We spoke at different stages of my research. When we met after a long hiatus, the opening statement he made was: 'You have come to do your research at a challenging period for the industry; these are difficult times for us with a global recession in tow.' Similar views were echoed by several of my interviewees. Yet through my initial fieldwork, when the recession was most severe, I witnessed how Sri Lankan apparel firms skilfully manoeuvred through the global apparel production landscape. It was apparent that the economic depression in the West was not the only factor to dictate the fortunes of the Sri Lankan apparel industry. The adaptability and malleability of capital were made evident during my time and thereafter, as Table 4.1 captures.

Table 4.1 illustrates that, despite the number of firms within the apparel industry initially recording a fall by 2008, in the post-2008 phase and especially after 2012 most indicators suggest that the industry is thriving. As Athukorala (2018) has noted, the consolidation of larger apparel firms and the strengthening of their positions explain this oddity. Accounting for winners and losers, then, is central to understanding the Sri Lankan apparel industry, as it helps us appreciate the complexities of the global supply chain. It is also important because, as Kumar (2019) astutely reads, using the case of Arvind Garments in Bangalore (India), this consolidation of supplier power is also about forming monopoly firms.[8] My ongoing research and conversations with management personnel offered diverse prognoses for the industry's future. Some forecasts were optimistic, while others were pessimistic (see also Goger 2013a; Perry et al. 2014). These varying views are likely to reflect the challenging global pressures within which the industry operated; yet the fact that it continues to thrive needs closer analysis.

The benchmark of 2008–2009 is important for Sri Lankan apparels for multiple reasons. Firstly, it helps us appreciate how the industry has evolved and transformed during a time of global economic crisis. Secondly, turning away from the global picture, 2009 also witnessed the violent culmination of a three-decade bloody ethnic conflict in a tragic and gory war (Thiranagama 2014). Afterwards, the North and the East Provinces, which had been effectively disconnected from the incursion of industrial capital previously, were open for business. This period was therefore a momentous time for the apparel industry to transform and envisage its own future in a distinctly post-war local, and economically volatile global, landscape. All of these shifts were compounded by the fact that, by 2011, post-war Sri Lanka had

Table 4.1 An overall profile of the apparel industry of Sri Lanka

Category	2006	2008	2010	2012	2014	2016	2018
Size of the industry – export value (Rs. Mn.)	320,829	376,990	379,185	508,607	643,688	710,768	865,975
Number of workers in the industry	476,125	340,103	271,701	266,405	474,060	691,461	n/a
% of working men in the industry	23	23	26	24	25	31	n/a
% of working women in the industry	76	76	74	76	75	69	n/a
*Contribution to the nation's GDP – as a %	10.92	8.55	6.77	6.71	6.58	6.00	5.99
Number of firms with at least 50 employees [In brackets = number of firms with 50 or fewer employees]	1,122 [1,123]	475 [1,376]	452 [1,036]	428 [47]	1,059 [2,455]	1,478 [2,256]	n/a

Source: Athukorala and Ekanayake (2014), Central Bank of Sri Lanka, *Annual Reports and Economic and Social Statistics Reports* (2006–2018) and Sri Lanka Department of Census and Statistics Annual Survey of Industry Reports (2006–2017). *Contribution to GDP calculated using export value (Rs) and GDP at market value.

also lost its Generalized Scheme of Preferences Plus (GSP+) preferential access to the European Union (EU) against the backdrop of the war and charges of war crimes. On the one hand, the timing of my initial entry was turbulent for the industry. On the other hand, along with the challenges came unanticipated changes that safeguarded against dramatic downward dips.

During my initial ethnographic phase, factory closures were being reported, including by the national newspapers. In one instance, I visited a factory that had recently closed, and the owner/manager was willing to share with me his experiences, including showing me a wall of grief left behind by the workers. This wall contained posters and relevant memorabilia pinned up to show appreciation for the management, the factory and the owner. In another case, after contacting the journalist of a news report, we visited a factory and met workers who were striking outside the factory premises because of an unannounced overnight closure and non-payment of wages (keep aside severance). The effects on factories and workers were palpable (Plankey-Videla 2012; Shakya 2018). Even for those factories still in operation, managers repeatedly spoke of the difficulties they faced. At the two factories in which I was based, doing short runs for smaller orders (in quantity) for survival was the norm.

Alarmist practices too were widespread. For instance, in some factories, including where I did my research, biopics of factory closures at FTZ-based factories were shown. Batches of workers were shown these documentaries, with the purpose of making them recognize the stresses the apparel sector was undergoing. I was told:

> We did interviews with laid-off workers and documented it in the zone .... Sinotex had about 3,000 plus workers, was well established and solid. There were no apparent reasons for it to go under, but the management decided to close up shop and they left. We showed this video to the workers because we wanted them to know how real the threat of the recession is.[9]

It was not only that there was palpable uncertainty amongst managers and management, but making workers aware of the effects on them was also part of the armoury. Image 4.3 of a CEO of a leading apparel firm's New Year message for 2009, shared with the workers, encapsulates the foreboding.

Yet, within this message, a tinge of possibility, hope and the likely opportunities a crisis may bring is inscribed, at least to management. In

This is going to be a year in which we will have to perform at a very high level to ensure that we survive as an organization. As always difficult times also bring opportunity to those who are willing to make the sacrifices required and put in the hard yards, encouragely for us the organization is strong and we have no debt to service. If we execute well and build a lean organization by eliminating our waste, deliver top quality goods in time and do this while making sure that we spend only on absolute essentials and plan well ahead to ensure that things do not have to be redone we will emerge from this crisis a stronger and better organization.

Image 4.3 Excerpt from New Year message to workers at the start of 2009
Source: Author's own photo.

his statement to workers, he calls for further efficiencies and introducing lean organizing. We need to recognize that economic crises are also moments for capitalism to introduce new production systems to further extract value. I witnessed the intensification of the labour process and attempts at initiating lean manufacturing in other factories (see also Bair and Werner 2011; Plankey-Videla 2012; Goger 2013a; Kim 2013). For the Sri Lankan apparel sector, there were other factors at play, however. A 30-year conflict and the accompanying war were firmly behind it. For Sri Lankan apparel firms, 'the turmoil and uncertainties of the world financial crisis ... are behind us, as we look towards 2010 with renewed hope and expectation', said the same CEO to herald 2010. Hence, by 2010, the Sri Lankan apparel sector had withstood the challenge and difficulties it faced with the onset of the global recession. While the rest of the world, including the West, was still reeling from the financial crisis and gloom, how was the Sri Lankan apparel sector able to steer from this phase?

Table 4.1 underlines how, in the immediate aftermath of the global economic recession, the number of firms active in the apparel sector declined. However, by 2012, the fortunes of the sector had started to change – although it is not in the same place as it was before the recession. At the start of my research, my interviewees often read a list of companies that had collapsed or were running down, and they indicated this as a sign of a dwindling industry. Did it augur a dying industry? Or, instead could one read this as another opportunity for the consolidation of an industry, a process in which some fall by the wayside but others strengthen their position? In Ruwanpura and Wrigley (2011), I documented the fears and anxieties of management in the context of a global economic downturn. Such fears reinforced Smith's (2015b) observation that a few stronger firms consolidating via successful strategies of economic upgrading might have knock-on effects on smaller firms and 'marginalization ... lower down the clothing value chain' (Smith 2015b: 350; Kumar 2019). The fact that these views get airplay during an economic recession in particular should come as no surprise. Consequently, it seems that in Sri Lanka these shifts manifested in terms of firms exiting the industry altogether, with this getting read as a sign of a weakening of the apparel sector despite other evidence of a healthy industry.

Table 4.2 confirms that, despite a slump, Sri Lankan industrialists did not shy away from investing in manufacturing apparel in the post-2008 period, with an upswing post-2014. While foreign investment had seen a decline from the period before 2008, nevertheless a little over 50 per cent of investment in Sri Lankan apparel continues to come from overseas. Athukorala (2018) notes that these foreign investments increasingly take the form of collaborations with local capital, and we need to read the data here in this light.

Table 4.2 Local and foreign investment in the apparel sector of Sri Lanka

Year	Foreign investment (Rs. Mn.)	Local investment (Rs. Mn.)	Total investment (Rs. Mn.)
2006	36,970 (66.3%)	18,797 (33.7%)	55,767 (100%)
2008	47,629 (67.3%)	23,092 (32.7%)	70,721 (100%)
2010	53,778 (66.6%)	27,008 (33.4%)	80,786 (100%)
2012	65,608 (67.2%)	31,983 (32.8%)	97,591 (100%)
2014	79,070 (61.2%)	49,758 (38.8%)	128,828 (100%)
2016	87,640 (60.2%)	57,957 (39.8%)	145,597 (100%)
2018	113,709 (53.4%)	99,137 (46.6%)	212,846 (100%)

Source: Central Bank of Sri Lanka Annual Reports (2006–2018).

Note: This table shows the percentage of investment (foreign versus local) in the Sri Lankan apparel industry.

If we read total investment in the apparel sector as showing healthy growth and collaborations as the industrial norm, then Sri Lankan apparel firms continue to bolster their position within the industry (Athukorala 2018, 2019). Domestically, opening up the North and the East of Sri Lanka in the post-war period, with various tax incentives and concessions offered by the Sri Lankan state might help explain the continued flourishing of the garment industry. Nonetheless, as Figure 4.1 captures, the investment arc for the apparel industry is upward – through a multitude of challenges.

Along with this internal shift in the economic environment, other vagaries pulled and pushed Sri Lankan apparel firms in different directions. Many managers had feared the negative effect of the withdrawal of the GSP+ concessions, for instance.[10] Yet, by the end of 2011, senior managers were able to speak of *adding value* and competing not on cost but on *efficiency, excellence* and *effectiveness*. The external trading environment was also favourable: the rise of real wages in China and labour struggles in Bangladesh over wages were making these countries less reliable destinations for sourcing. When procurement from Bangladesh was tarnished by numerous factory collapses, including Rana Plaza, Sri Lanka turned out to be the safer location for ethical and quality sourcing. The *value creation* of ethical sourcing appeared to be paying off.

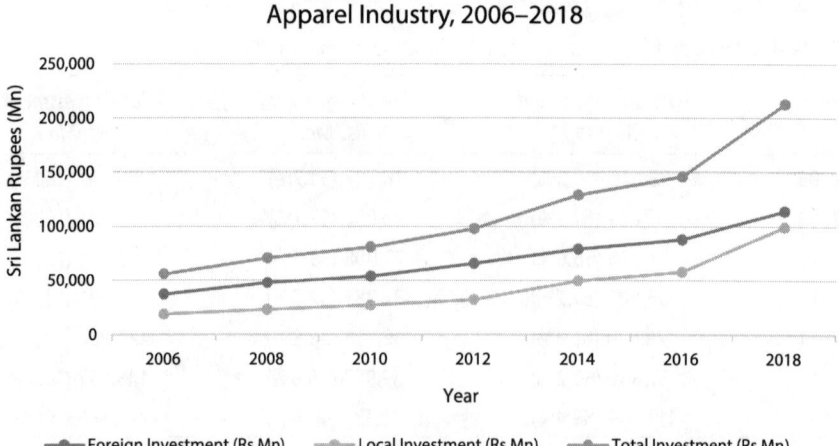

Figure 4.1 Investment trajectory in the post-2006 period for the apparel sector
Source: Central Bank of Sri Lanka (2006–2018).

The Labour Question: Recruitment and Retention

Employers mentioned their difficulties in recruiting and retaining workers. Their efforts to lure labour engaged sociocultural spheres, from the influence of TV dramas to enticing current workers to recruit their kin and friends to the factory fold. How economic factors might also influence the decision-making of potential workers was never really explored, although the handbills created for circulating usually included the wage potential of the most productive workers (a minority) rather than that of the average worker. A point of conversation between managers and myself was how new workers were likely to find these leaflets misleading, and how disappointment and frustration were likely to beset new workers, which might work against retention. Managers had divergent views on this. Some insisted that workers could indeed earn these wages, through a combination of incentives, allowances and basic wages, while a few others conceded that these handbills and posters might be misleading, especially for workers with average productivity.

In contrast, when I inquired into the living wage and its non-payment, the issue was either gingerly avoided or lengthy justifications were given for how it was unlikely to support industrial viability. I will return to questions around living wages in *Chapter Five*, as part of the discussion of the ethical code regimes. However, examining the strength of the industry more through its value creation strategy is worthwhile. It permits the raising of pertinent queries on whether the industry might be in a place to more effectively redistribute captured gains to the workers.

Using Sri Lankan Customs data, Athukorala and Ekanayake (2018) traced how the top three firms netted an increasing share of the export market. My management interviewees agreed that there was consolidation amongst top-tier Sri Lankan apparel firms. There are advantages and disadvantages to a few firms positioning themselves as forerunners. Oligopolistic consolidation may appear attractive, especially as it bolsters confidence in placing Sri Lankan apparel firms in a formidable place in the global imaginary. Yet are there risks to this path? The managers of medium and smaller production facilities spoke to me about the difficulties they sometimes faced initially in their efforts to enter the market – 'the entry costs can be tremendous'. This view was shared by a medium-sized apparel producer who moved away from a larger apparel-producing firm; others shared similar sentiments. When small firms are producing manufacturing basics, they may not necessarily benefit from the path created by the leading firms, possibly even creating a landscape of uneven economic insecurity, in which healthy competition within the sector in the country falters (see also Kumar 2019). Athukorala (2018, 2019), however, noted that this trajectory has helped the industry navigate a successful path. The increasing dominance of a few larger and strategically successful firms and the dwindling of medium and smaller firms, however, may be interpreted as being cautious because the Sri Lankan apparel sector is working within a challenging environment (Ruwanpura and Wrigley 2011). Yet what is more likely to be the situation is the limitation identified and investigated by Smith (2015b). He shows how the uneven political economy of economic security/insecurity associated with the 'exportist' model 'predicated on … geographically uneven development' also needs to be accounted for in discussions of economic upgrading/downgrading as well as the possibility of monopsony capitalism (Smith 2015b: 446; Kumar 2019). While upgrading/downgrading within an uneven development terrain might have evident implications for small- and medium-sized enterprises, situating labour within these processes also needs to be assessed.

The Sri Lankan apparel sector does not simply lure retailers on the basis of ethical sourcing, but also makes much of its educated and healthy labour force. *Quality, reliability* and *delivery,* along with sophisticated lean operations, however, are feasible largely because of the workers. When the top three producers set the standard for work conditions within plants, there is some level of compulsion for medium and smaller production sites to follow suit to attract and retain workers. Yet there is trepidation amongst labour unionists and activists that a continual refusal to pay living wages to workers by the industry front runners can also deflect others from doing so. Alternatively, managers of the leading firms also said that paying a living wage might mean pushing small- and medium-sized enterprises out of business. Corporate solidarity was at stake; living wages for labour was less of an issue. Any pressure to implement living wages lessened with the opening up of the North and the East, through which the bottleneck around labour recruitment was tackled.

Tax incentives and inducements to take manufacturing to these regions were an added bonus. The view was that the end of the war necessitated employment creation, especially for the large swathes of young people. Low wages and a ready labour pool, coupled with tax incentives and subsidies, meant a bonanza for industrial capital. The answers to the labour shortages faced by the apparel sector came with other inducements: subsidies, tax incentives, funded training programmes and infrastructure creation to tap into cheap and underemployed labour in the region. In post-war Sri Lanka, state support extended beyond the pecuniary. The military too was on standby to support the apparel industry set up these initial production sites, to renovate derelict buildings into factory premises and to ensure that the infrastructure was in place to transport workers and freight. Military fiscalism, à la Venugopal (2018), had taken a different guise in a post-war country where military forces were crucial to paving the way for the industrial class, including the apparel sector, to enter, set up and potentially flourish (Kadirgamar 2013; Goger and Ruwanpura 2014; Ruwanpura 2018).

The state then was crucial, yet again, for supporting the Sri Lankan apparel sector's capacity to evolve and prosper via tax incentives and other mechanisms (see also Waller 2006; Sunley 2008; Chang 2014; Sunley and Pinch 2014; Smith 2015a). The state was clearly aligned with the interests of the apparel sector's industrial capital. During interviews with senior managers from the apparel sector at the end of 2013 and in mid-2014, they referred to the multiple changes taking place within the industry. Some were increasingly making improvements so that more of their production plants would become eco-friendly and environmentally sustainable – because this was seen as the future for apparel production (Fernando et al. 2019). Despite initial difficulties around labour recruitment in post-war areas and having to mobilize the support of the military to enlist workers, the factories that had located in the region saw it as a long-term strategy. None of the managers I interviewed saw any contradiction in getting the support of the military to recruit workers. There was no awareness of how deploying the military in this manner may be violating the ethical code that governs forced labour, as I discuss more in *Chapter Seven*. The militarization of Sri Lankan society had permeated well into the social fabric (de Mel 2007; Kadirgamar 2013). So, the fear and intimidation that communities from war-affected regions might feel was not considered, because the sector was bringing jobs to the area.

All these factors were therefore important in ensuring momentum and an upward path for apparel exports. The disaggregated graph here on Sri Lanka's world share for its top five exports shows this ascendant path, especially for lingerie and even with a global recession (Figure 4.2). Towards the tail end of my located ethnographic phase (2011), when I inquired of a manager at one of my sites that exclusively produced lingerie

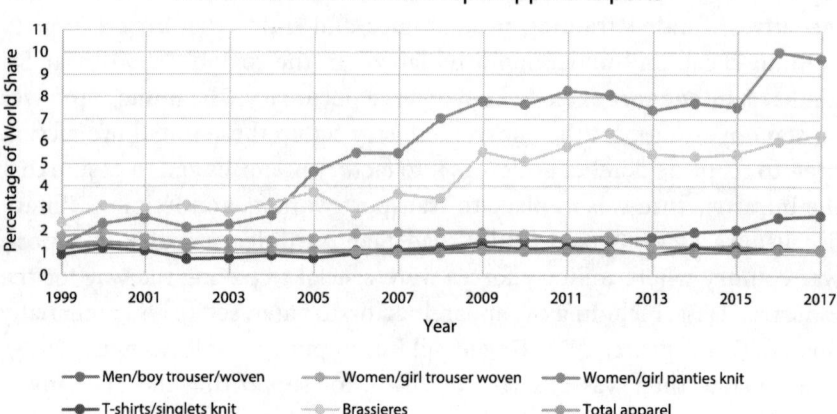

Figure 4.2 World share of Sri Lanka's top five exports

Source: Athukorala and Ekanayake (2018); UN Comtrade (2019).

Note: Only two years were taken from Athukorala and Ekanayake (2018); the rest were calculated from UN Comtrade. In these calculations by Peter Rowe, we found that the STIC codes did not match exactly; however, the text descriptions of the codes and the results they produced were very similar.

how orders were holding up, he said that they were doing very well. At the start of my fieldwork this same manager, amongst others, was apprehensive and had mentioned the possibility of turbulent times for the industry, and I reminded him of this. In response, he said, 'Women always need underwear, I guess.' Lingerie production has hence continued to increase, even in a post-recessionary context, helping the overall world share of Sri Lanka's apparel exports to remain steady over the years.

The Sri Lankan apparel sector's ability to mobilize its advantages as a niche and ethical producer was also because global and regional dynamics – from worker turbulence and factory fires and collapses in Bangladesh and Pakistan to rising wages in China – all aided, however indirectly, the ascendancy or bolstering of the Sri Lankan apparel sector. I was told by another senior manager: 'It is tragic and horrific for Bangladesh, but when buyers turn to us, they know this risk of factory fires and collapses is not associated with Sri Lankan apparel firms.' This difference has a simple explanation: I never visited a factory in the country that was more than two stories high; often they were on one level. From a health and safety viewpoint, they were relatively risk-free environments. When looking at the data then, despite the vagaries of the immediate post-recession years, the Sri Lankan apparel sector is in a strong place. Yet how do the workers fare?

Capturing and Redistributing the Gains?

Almost all managers, as if part of the same choir, pointed to the low productivity of labourers or how productivity levels do not reach their potential. This is frequently reinforced in published works by economists, although without data verification or recognition of management responsibility (Kelegama 2009; Athukorala 2018). Another constant management refrain was the high per capita cost of Sri Lankan labour vis-à-vis its competitors; again, this is repeated in published works (Athukorala 2018). Union and labour rights groups challenged this assessment by underlining how it would not have been possible for the sector to be strong and dynamic, if this were the case. None, however, shared data to back these viewpoints – instead making vague references to various studies.

In an earlier intervention, Knutsen (2003: 237), in contrast, describes Sri Lankan labourers' productivity levels as second only to those of Singapore; she also ranks Sri Lanka '31st of 40 countries in a list of hourly labour costs'. A more recent study by the Overseas Development Institute (ODI) on the manufacturing sector of Sri Lanka illustrates both how labour productivity is on the rise and how 'output per worker has also grown quickly, above that of other countries in the region, demonstrating productivity growth' (ODI 2015: 20). The graphical representation of this inquiry in the same report for selected Asian countries for the 1992–2012 period suggests that Sri Lankan workers' output was second only to that of Thailand (ODI 2015: 18).[11] Along similar lines, and more recently, Selwyn (2019) offers further support for the view that labour productivity levels of workers in the Global South are higher than those in the Global North.

These discrepancies prodded me to question the veracity of views expressed during my various fieldwork phases, especially as there was no supporting data to show that labour costs for workers were high or the highest in the region. Equally, workers seldom made a living wage, and the increments of the Wages Ordinance Board (WOB) rarely kept pace with the inflation rate (Ruwanpura 2012). The lack of a living wage was a concern of workers and featured amongst various campaigns, regionally and nationally. The Asia Floor Wage campaign and ALaRM (Action for

Labour Rights Movement) frequently raised this concern (Asia Floor Wage 2013, 2014). While wages for apparel sector workers were sometimes above the norm within the country, they still fell well short of a living wage. It was a repeated grouse of workers, with reason, as our more recent data tabulations reveal in Figure 4.3.

The academic or policy work done around the living wage campaign highlights that wages are not an exorbitant input cost for the final garment, and paying workers a living wage through committed action by the retailers and buyers is feasible (Palpaucer 2008; Miller and Williams 2009). Selwyn (2019: 78) pursues this line further by contending through a detailed analysis that 'surplus value extracted ... is captured by lead firms', with poverty wages abounding in the industry. From the perspective of industrial capital, managers talked about how difficult global conditions coupled with productivity issues prevented them from providing a living wage. Moreover,

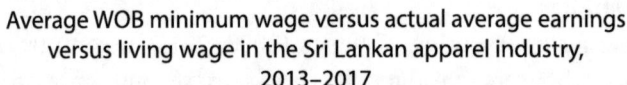

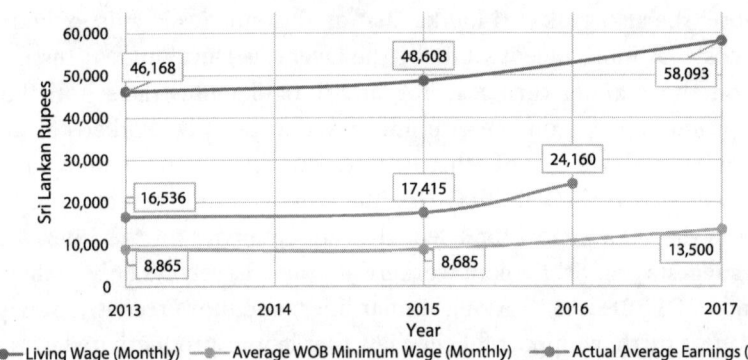

Figure 4.3 Average WOB minimum wage versus actual average earnings versus living wage in the Sri Lankan apparel industry, 2013–2017

Source: Sri Lanka Department of Labour (2013, 2015, 2016), Asia Floor Wage (2019), Global Press Journal (2017).

Notes: Data from the Asia Floor Wage is only available for 2013, 2015 and 2017, hence the limited presentation; average WOB minimum wage (monthly) represents the average minimum wage (as set by the Government of Sri Lanka Wage Ordinance Board) for each year listed across all employee grade levels (i.e., Grades I A–V); relatedly, actual average earnings (monthly) represents the actual monthly earnings (for each year listed) for all employee grade levels.

in the various corporate codes of conduct, there is no clarity that employers should pay living wages, with most referring to national minimum wages. On minimum wages, the Sri Lankan apparel sector is on safe ground. It has not only paid minimum wages but more usually paid an average wage packet above the minimum stipulated – although still well below a living wage, as Figure 4.3 reveals.[12]

Given the labour shortages and retention issues that the sector faces, it might have to pay workers above the national minimum in order to attract the labour required. Yet it falls shy of compensating workers with a living wage. When I presented my research findings at a workshop in Sri Lanka in 2012, the unionists present at the event were critical of my findings, because my study aimed at a nuanced narrative. A manager from one of my study locations took the extraordinary step of meeting me a few days later to share the wage sheets with me – albeit on his laptop. This was rare for me. While I had good access to the shop floor, unlike other scholars, I did not seek nor was I provided with access to factory documentation throughout my located ethnography (Plankey-Videla 2012; Kim 2013). I realized through the workshop and the subsequent one-to-one meeting that I may have struck a sore point – with both the unions and management. For the unions, my research did not give any credence to a black-and-white storyline that they might find useful for campaigning;[13] for management, raising concerns around living wages was sensitive. From that management meeting, I again gathered that the supposed low productivity of workers was a deciding factor.

How pressing an issue is per unit labour costs and productivity for Sri Lanka? It was only during a return fieldwork phase in 2014 that managers started to concede that there might have been improvements in productivity or that this was less of a pressing concern. However, they would quickly point out that further improvements were always possible. The various productivity-enhancing measures identified by Goger (2013a) in response to mounting labour shortages were likely to have resulted in beneficial effects for the industry. In sharp contrast to the frequent discourse on the need to improve worker productivity in the sector (Ruwanpura and Wrigley 2011), Table 4.3 reveals that labour productivity for Sri Lanka is second only to that of Malaysia in the region. While this data is for the country overall, it would be difficult to suggest that workers in the apparel sector were less productive than the national average (see also Selwyn 2019).

Table 4.3 Labour productivity by country: output per hours worked in USD, adjusted for 2018

Country	2006	2008	2010	2012	2014	2016	2018
Bangladesh	3	3	3	3	4	4	4
Cambodia	2	2	2	2	2	3	3
India	4	5	6	7	7	8	9
Indonesia	9	10	10	11	12	13	14
Malaysia	24	26	25	26	27	29	31
Pakistan	7	7	7	7	8	8	9
Sri Lanka	*12*	*12*	*13*	*15*	*17*	*18*	*18*
Thailand	11	11	11	12	13	14	16
Vietnam	3	3	4	4	5	5	6

Source: The Conference Board (2019).
Note: All output values here are for 2018 (USD).

The same theme holds true with regard to average labour costs for the region, although, again, I am hampered by the data being for the nation rather than the apparel sector alone. The data in Table 4.4 reveals that the average cost of labour per hour is higher only than that in Bangladesh and certainly much lower than that in most of East Asia.

For a range of reasons, including active state support at various critical junctures, the apparel sector has dexterously pursued an upgrading and value-adding strategy; those labouring for the industry, however, have not captured the redistributive gains. The business strategy the industry has pursued has helped it to continue to be dynamic, and its visions for the future are admirable. Leading industrialists have carved out a role for Sri Lanka as a regional and global hub, in which not just production, but also designing and product promotion are integrated (Goger 2013b; Athukorala 2018, 2019). So, whether it is offering buyers designs that use recycled or waste apparels or creative clothing lines, the Sri Lankan apparel sector sees design as necessary for adding value. Incorporating design to achieve business innovation and market growth signals that the Sri Lankan apparel sector is marking its territory in the global supply chain for the long haul and sees design as a key to delivering a competitive edge for the sector (Gopura, Payne and Buys 2019).

Table 4.4 Average cost of labour (USD/hour) in various Asian countries

Country	2006	2008	2014	2018
Vietnam	0.26	0.38	0.56	0.79
Indonesia	0.27	0.44	0.68	1.19
Cambodia	0.33	0.33	0.63	0.92
India	0.38	0.51	0.92	n/a
Bangladesh	0.39	0.22	0.36	0.4
Pakistan	0.41	0.37	1.23	0.6
Sri Lanka	*0.34*	*0.43*	*0.27–0.33*	*0.41*
China	0.78	0.87	1.04	1.7

Source: Athukorala and Ekanayake (2018); Korrakoon (2015).

Note: The data is mainly the cost of labour in general in the aforementioned countries and is not specific to the apparel sector in each country. However, it is representative of the overall trend of wages in each country.

Conclusion

Even though my fieldwork in Sri Lanka began with the onset of a recession and in a challenging post-war context, I have been able to illustrate that the sector sustained growth with more than a little help from the state. Contrary to Athukorala's (2012) assessment of the return of state *dirigisme* under the Rajapaksa regime of 2005–2015, my assertion is that the state was an inalienable ally for apparel industrialists from the beginning. Taking a cue from Polanyian understandings of market economies as historical constructs, created through political action and formal institutions, the state's transformative role in shaping and re-regulating economic trajectories of the sector specifically needs acknowledgement (Polanyi 1957). This is a headline that chimes with the work of Chang (2003, 2014) and others that the state is an institution that has shaped the current global political economy, as it has done in the past (Wood 1981; Standing 1997; Waller 2006; Sunley 2008, 2011; Smith 2015a; Werner 2020).

Post-2008 was also the time for securing the North and the East of Sri Lanka through a bloody war. It meant that the then ruling regime (2009), re-elected in 2019, took on the task of nation-building with gusto, with an emphasis on economic dividend rather than political settlement (Hagar

2012). A nexus of large-scale infrastructure development, job creation and trickle-down economics meant barely addressing the political violence and everyday insecurities experienced by the people (Thaheer, Peiris and Pathiraja 2013; Thiranagama 2014; Lingam 2019). The economic dividends were meant to address the everyday violence that the minorities who had experienced protracted conflict and trauma had lived through; they conveniently allowed the state to avoid redressing political grievances and nationalist chauvinism.

Apparel industrialists were included in the state's plans for the North and the East by being offered financial and tax incentives or funded training programmes (Hagar 2012). Hence, firstly, their role in abetting a militarized capitalist culture and nation-building was rarely reflected upon (Kadirgamar 2013; Goger and Ruwanpura 2014; Ruwanpura 2018). Secondly, given the labour shortages the apparel sector was facing in other parts of Sri Lanka, it was hoped that moving to the North and the East would offer the industry the chance to regain its position of attracting labour – given the dearth of jobs in the region. The start of my research also coincided with Sri Lanka's top three apparel producers opening eco-friendly production facilities, because they saw the future value of green production and the sustainability agenda (Goger 2013b; Fernando et al. 2019).

How Sri Lankan labour has benefitted materially from this export-oriented route is, however, less clear (Palpaucer 2008; Smith 2015b; Selwyn 2019). In this chapter, I have outlined how the dynamism of the apparel sector was feasible, partly because of the dynamic role of the state – in many ways reminiscent of the state intervention that Chang (2003, 2014) and others have argued to be the bedrock of development in East Asia and the West (Standing 1997; Waller 2006; Smith 2015a). There is clear historical evidence of state support towards capital; yet when it comes to living wages, labour has been neglected by all governments, irrespective of political hue, since 1977. The role of the state has also appeared to be contradictory. On the one hand, the state helped to set strong standards for safety and health and nurtured the industry through several challenges. However, on the other hand, through incentives and tax holidays it has helped the industry to evade labour shortages, while simultaneously sidestepping the issue of living wages. These paradoxes facilitate understanding of the state–labour–capital dynamic in our next chapters vis-à-vis ethical code governance. The skewed ethicality of the Sri Lankan apparel sector means that the state, through its background role, facilitated benefits for capital while leaving labour behind.

As Kadirgamar's (2019) astute remarks on the political fallout of the 2019 elections underline, this neglect of class inequality may well be the beast that keeps raising its ugly head in the form of ethno-nationalism in the country. It is to the constituent of labour that my following chapters turn.

Notes

1. Some tables and figures I use initially appeared in Athukorala and Ekanayake (2018) but are updated for my purposes. I gratefully acknowledge Prema-Chandra Athukorala's generosity in letting me use this data and thank Peter Rowe for his meticulous research assistance in both gathering and updating many of the tables used in this chapter.

2. An omission that I hope to address in *Chapter Five*, by bringing neglected labour struggles and histories into the account of the successes of Sri Lankan apparel firms.

3. Basics are mass-manufactured simple garments, while fashion-basics usually have additional intricate work done, such as embroidery in lingerie, and are considered value-added products.

4. All three companies, along with a few others, have apparel production sites in much of South Asia, parts of East Asia and even in the African continent. Their expansion from local to global capitalists in the garment sector is worthy of further research and evaluation.

5. In the schema of ethnic markers, Sri Lankans are often categorized into Sinhala, Tamil, Muslim and Burgher. This narrow typology alone, however, does not capture those born of intermarriages or offspring of cross-marriages between not only notable majorities, but also Malays, Chinese, Sindhis or Parsis and other ethnic communities (Silva 2001). Hybrid Sri Lankans reflect the melange communities of the country – including of those that identify themselves as belonging to one or another ethnicity but possibly have buried histories of intermarriage across ethnic and religious lines (Guneratne 2001).

6. Please see Appendix A for a table of Sri Lankan apparel exports to key countries and regions for the period 2009–2017. It gives a sense of the need to be ethical, given the markets that Sri Lankan apparel firms were catering to (my thanks to Doug Miller for suggesting the inclusion of this data and Peter Rowe for his assistance in tabulating it).

7. I will discuss the history and backdrop that led to state directives on conditions of work and the implementation of existing laws in *Chapter Five*.

8. Monopoly firms are also monopsonies when it comes to hiring labour; and so, for Sri Lanka, there is scope for further research on this angle and to assess implications for the labour market, power and agency.

9. Sinotex Lanka Limited was part of the Hong Kong–based Crystal-Martin Group that closed down after 27 years in Sri Lanka in 2009 and made 2,250 workers redundant with severance pay, although the relevant trade union disputed that the compensation followed Sri Lankan labour laws (Samaraweera 2009).

10. Union and labour rights organizations, however, used to say that workers never gained the subsidies that came with GSP+ and the EU was never concerned with the various labour rights violations that were brought to its attention prior to 2009. It later transpired that the assessment of unionists and labour activists may have been correct, as the removal of GSP+ did not cause the industrial meltdown described by policymakers, the industry and the media. (Alternatively, the suggestion by unions and labour activists was that GSP+ needed to be restructured so that the subsidy went into the hands of the workers – and not to augment further the profit margins of management and industrial capital.)

11. Macro level proxy for labour productivity of apparel sector workers is provided in Appendix A that captures sectoral employment over a period vis-à-vis volume/value exports trends or output. These tabulations suggest that labour productivity for the sector is robust.

12. Doug Miller has noted in a personal communication that this variation is because, in some countries, 'living wage' is still a non-concept amongst employers and policymakers. Most noise is made in the consumer countries, and the charge is laid at the buyers' feet, who are supposed to pay a living wage. As non-employers, however, they can only cost for a living wage but not enforce suppliers to pay that to the labourers.

13. This sense was verified when one of the stronger unions got a journalist to attack my research in demeaning ways through a national newspaper (Perera 2012; see also Chandrasekera-Edirimuni 2012).

5

Neglected Labour Histories

The Sri Lankan State Responds to Labour

There is, after all, no subject on which it is so important (for capitalism) that the truth should be hidden.

—Paul Sweezy (in Braverman (1974): x)

Introduction

Sri Lankan labourers in the apparel sector are amongst the most educated workers in the global industry. Sri Lanka's human development achievements, however, came through decades of state intervention in the social welfare of its people, especially through investment in public education and health. The highly educated nature of Sri Lankan workers has played an important role in the apparel sector, cultivating an image in which 'quality, reliability, and punctuality', as management repeatedly informed me, are givens. As I noted in Chapter Four, it is an image that, according to suppliers, imbues buyers with the confidence to source from Sri Lanka.

The workforce that Sri Lankan apparel firms make proud proclamations about in their websites is then the product of previous state actions in response to labour agitation during the late colonial and pre-1977 periods (Jayawardena 1971, 1972; Kearney 1971). However, the critical role collective labour struggles played and how the state had to respond to them rarely get the attention or acknowledgement they deserve. They need to be taken account of in order to acknowledge how labour too shapes the state and industrial development (see also Chang 2003; Featherstone and Griffin 2016; Silver 2019; Palpacuer 2020). Chang (2003, 2014) makes this and other related points about the pivotal role of the state in industrial development in several places. He stresses its importance not just for East Asia, but also for most Western nations – including the USA, where protecting infant industries was key in the industrial development trajectory.[1] While it may be that this level of mediation to secure a good quality of life for Sri Lankan citizens was a pre-1977 preoccupation, Sri Lankan apparel firms did not do it alone in the post-neoliberal landscape either. As I outline here, labour struggles were crucial for how the ethical sourcing strategy was secured for the apparel sector. In this chapter, I hone in on three such pivotal moments for post-liberalized Sri Lanka, with a particular emphasis on the post-recessionary phase (circa 2008 onwards).

In the sections to follow, I start by revisiting accounts by labour scholars and historians to allow me to place collective labour struggles in the chronicle of the country's political economy. These narratives underline how such struggles shaped Sri Lanka's legislative framework for labour, statutes that are currently under review. It is these labour laws that enabled workers employed in the first FTZ to agitate and to charge the state to fulfil its constitutional and statutory duties towards labour. This is the first event I capture: the voices of early agitators at the inception of an open economy. During the early 1980s, labourers highlighted the exploitative nature of their jobs and championed better work conditions. This meant that the state was pressed to respond, and it did. In this way, the foundations were laid for industrial capital to take on the mantle of ethical sourcing a decade later, in line with changes in the global governance discourse. In other words, solidarity action and early labour struggles were the harbingers of Sri Lanka's ethical sourcing credentials. My second illustration is the 2011 state reversal in response to labour protests. When the government attempted to alter the pension pot of workers, labourers in the apparel sector – especially from the FTZ – led massive protests to quash the bill. One worker tragically died, while others sustained serious injuries in struggling for justice, for both themselves and their peers. The third moment concerns the labour reforms currently under consideration, which purport to streamline a complex legal inheritance but are rightly contested by labour collectives.[2]

I use these examples to puncture dominant narratives, including those in the media, which tend to attribute the Sri Lankan apparel sector's ethical credentials solely to the foresight of capital and to value upgrading (Karp 1999; O'Leary 2009). Victoria's little secret, alluded to by Karp (1999) in the Wall Street Journal (Image 6.1 in Chapter Six), is then a story of labour, as much as it is of capital and the state – and it is to these neglected and entangled labour–capital–state histories that I now turn.

Transitions: From Democratic Socialism to an Open Economy

Sri Lanka's transition from a country that prioritized democratic socialist principles to one that promoted market-oriented policies came from a political decision that reverberated in class dynamics and ethnic relations alike (Gunasinghe 1996; Dunham and Jayasuriya 2000). This political-economic shift, in which capitalist consolidation took centre stage, placed economic concerns over the welfare of people. In many ways, Sri Lanka's political establishment was keeping in tune with the neoliberal impulses that had started to gain ascendency on a global scale throughout the 1970s (Harvey 2005; Selwyn 2012b; Silver 2019). Hence, 1977 was a watershed year for many reasons, including the effects it would have on labouring groups, effects which continue to resonate.

Prior to 1977, the trajectory of Sri Lanka's political economy was marked by a commitment to social democratic principles of some kind or other. These priorities and pledges were a response to collective action by labouring communities that started during the latter part of the colonial period and continued during the immediate post-independence years (Jayawardena 1971, 1972; Kearney 1971). The agitation against exploitative labour conditions led to legislation to protect workers and their health, well-being and welfare (Kearney 1971); in other words, it created a social state (Supiot 2003, 2013).[3] The gains made during this period also percolated through to ensure the paramountcy of the social welfare of the country's citizens and had a positive resonance for Sri Lanka's development policy priorities too (A. Sen 1981; Humphries 1993; Klasen 1993).

While Sri Lanka's early economic growth route placed it at the threshold of a developing nation, its high social development was considered a virtue. Development economists used the country, along with Kerala in India, for instance, as a paradigmatic case study of people-centred development, where gender parity in human development indices had been achieved (A. Sen 1981; Humphries 1993; Neethi 2016). In the decades from independence until 1977, for instance, the Sri Lankan state allocated 20–25 per cent of its annual budget to social welfare – a comparatively higher level than its neighbours in South Asia (Herring 1987, cited in Biyanwila 2011). This investment in the social welfare of people was pivotal in producing the highly educated and healthy workforce that industrial capital not only drew upon, but also boasted about to make the country an attractive supplier to the global garment industry.[4] In other words, the high literacy rates and longevity of Sri Lankan workers came about through a prioritization that attempted to regard all citizens on an equal basis – and in which social concerns were less likely to be brushed aside.

This was a different time.[5] It was also a time in which unions, and especially public sector unions, had a strong presence in the national economy (Kearney 1971; Biyanwila 2011). Since 1977, however, workers' rights have been under attack. The advent of open economic policies in Sri Lanka – which was the first country in South Asia to embrace a free-market system – also resulted in a growing economic polarization that transmuted into ethnic schisms and social conflict (Gunasinghe 1996; Dunham and Jayasuriya 2000). The ethnic violence and war that plagued the country for three decades began in 1983, six years into the economic liberalization. For the two decades following 1983, the country was marred not just by an ethnic war, but also by political violence that took the form of a resurgent youth uprising; in other words, almost all parts of Sri Lanka were engulfed in political violence. Accounts of the rise of Sinhala–Buddhist chauvinism and its violent effects on the sociality and polity of Sri Lanka underline the fragmentation and trauma endured by all of its communities (Tambiah 1992; Ismail and Jeganathan 1995; Thiranagama 2014; Jegathesan 2019; Maunaguru 2019). What is important for my purposes is the documentation by Biyanwila (2011) of the perpetration of violence towards the labouring classes. According to him, these decades were also a period in which unions were not only under frequent assault, legislatively and politically, but also reconstituted. The narrow version of employee councils promoted at that time within firms and enterprises resulted in workers and unions getting subsumed 'under a paternalist rule of employers' (Biyanwila 2011: 77). He also notes how there was an intensification of the rivalry between party-political unions that weakened the labour movement, although Kearney (1971) traces such inter-party union rivalries to the immediate post-independence years.

Changes in political regimes by the mid-1990s (1994) led to a relaxation in union repression, with attempts at strengthening worker rights via a charter (Biyanwila 2011).[6] Yet, by this time and in the decades to follow, as Venugopal (2018) notes, each subsequent government remained firmly committed to a market economy; re-regulating legislation to suit the needs of capitalism was the priority. Moreover, for four decades, ethno-nationalist forces had a stranglehold on the political terrain, and with that came not just political volatility, but also repeated efforts at labour repression. It also meant that party unions were closely aligned with Sinhala–Buddhist nationalism, and the space for cross-community labour solidarity was non-existent. Equally, many leadership positions within unions were the domain of men, despite women predominating in the relevant sectors (see also Kabeer 2008; Jayawardena 2017).[7]

Nonetheless, during the same period there were pivotal moments when labour and women labourers in the apparel sector exerted their agency. These instances have deviated from previously celebrated union politics and have sometimes taken the form of building alliances via new social movements (Gunawardana 2007; Biyanwila 2011; Neethi 2016; Nowak 2016a). They have, however, arisen even against multiple odds. Taking a cue from labour geographers, this chapter aims to unpack 'the making of ... capitalism through the eyes of labour' (Herod 2001: 18), while also scrutinizing, à la Thompson, 'the ways in which new antagonisms and articulations of political community and agency were shaped and generated' (Featherstone and Griffin 2016: 380; see also Wood 1981; Wills 1996; Gidwani 2004; S. Sen 2008; Neethi 2016). However, in a variation from existing scholarship, I want to argue that the ability of labourers to exert agency has as much to do with their education and knowledge as it has with their unwillingness to be exploited. So, while workers need jobs, a closer look at these vital events suggests a refusal to be mistreated and abused, because their higher education level is also a factor that enables them to rebuff work place indignity. Worker histories within the apparel sector in the post-1977 period suggest that they will collectively rise and struggle, with these moments of resistance forcing the state to uphold labour rights, some of which are inscribed in the Sri Lankan constitution. They have compelled the addressing of conditions of work within factories, by bringing these issues to the forefront and, hence, have shaped the terrain of capitalist evolution within the apparel sector. The Sri Lankan apparel sector, in other words, would have been unlikely to have gone ethical without the push that came from important labour struggles within the garment sector in the early 1980s.

1980 and 1982: Strength of Striking

In Padmini Weerasooriya's reflections on the 1982 Polytex strike, she notes that the '1982 strike became a strength for us to rise against exploitation of labour while it worked as a bar against maltreatment of any worker'

(Women's Centre 2006: 43). It also led to cross-class solidarity that included the involvement of middle-class feminist activists, which in turn significantly strengthened the women's movement in Sri Lanka (Rosa 1989; Abeyasekera 1990, cited in de Alwis 2002). The oral testimonies of striking women gathered in this publication by the Women's Centre highlight the feminist consciousness and the risks that workers, especially women workers, were taking against a backdrop of political violence.

The 1980s were a stage in Sri Lanka's political history in which political violence, terror and state repression were acute and intense. Emergency powers intended to curb political violence were unabashedly used by the ruling regime to curb strike activity, with employers too eradicating and suppressing workers perceived to be a threat (Women's Centre 2006: 90). In a decade in which many workers and those supporting the rights of workers were murdered and intimidated, to engage in collective protests was particularly valiant. Moreover, when the initial Polytex strike of 1980 began, workers were collectively resisting against a recent background (1980) of emergency powers meant to curb political violence being used to break a general strike. Yet these early agitators were willing to gamble their lives and safety to advocate for better work conditions.

By the time of the Polytex Garments strike in 1982, Biyanwila (2011: 72) remarks that the United National Party (UNP) had already 'decisively altered trade union militancy and the labour movement in Sri Lanka' during the July 1980 general strike.[8] It was a violent chapter in Sri Lanka's post-liberalization labour history because of state repression of striking workers and transformed industrial relations, and the early signs of security forces colluding with national and state governments increased. Nevertheless, women labourers working for Polytex Garments within the FTZ took to protesting about their work conditions and the failure of employers to uphold their side of the bargain – to ensure wage increases for raising production targets.

When the workers of Polytex Garments initially walked out in 1980, they did so to protest about the 'inhuman exploitation by the administration', because it had transpired that the employers were to pay new recruits more than the existing cadre, who were on salaries below that prescribed by the WOB (Women's Centre 2006: 21). This news irritated workers, who were prevented from taking leave, had to meet high hourly targets, were curtailed from using toilet facilities and had to work overtime at short notice. They walked out, in a manner reminiscent of women workers calling it quits in locations as diverse as Mexico or China, when they were of the view that management and workers do not belong to the same 'community of fate' (Plankey-Videla 2012: 135; see also Kim 2013; Ahuja 2019). In response, the day after the stoppage, 'management closed the factory gates and threw the workers on the streets' and brought in police to exert the power of management and capital (Women's Centre 2006: 21).

It is partly this heavy-handed response that led to the unionization of Polytex Garments. The striking workers contacted the Ceylon Mercantile Union (CMU) and went on strike between 20 and 28 March 1980, until management recognized the CMU branch within the factory.[9] Through this strike, the workers had many of their demands met. These included the reinstatement of dismissed workers, a lunch interval of an hour, a higher annual bonus, an increase in the number of toilets (initially there had been four toilets for 800 workers), permission to use the toilet more regularly and more holiday pay (Women's Centre 2006: 22–23).

Two years later (1982), a larger strike took place at Polytex Garments, in which all workers were involved in a work stoppage, as they objected to the suspension of the union branch secretary and two women workers. On this occasion, when women workers gathered in Ekala, an area adjacent to the FTZ in Katunayake, to discuss and converse on solidarity action, they were attacked by police officers. While the women workers were unarmed, the police officers were 'carrying clubs, cudgels, bludgeons, batons and frond heads' (Women's Centre 2006: 15). It was not just the sheer use of brute force by the police against unarmed workers that was a concern, but also the fact that the police officers were sent from the Ja-Ela police station – which at the time (1982) was under the control of Sri Lanka's first elected President (J. R. Jayawardena). The Women's Centre's (2006) chronicling of these events also documents the close and personal relationship that existed between the owner of Polytex Garments and the then president. By detailing personal relations between the person holding the highest political office in Sri Lanka and the chair of Polytex Garments, the collusion between the government and employers was revealed.

During the 1980s, the bravery of these women workers was an inspiration to workers in other factories within the FTZ. Others began to agitate and protest when their work conditions dictated this. This period, 1989 in particular, is recorded as a time of 'terror, corruption, injustice and thuggery', with several workers from the industrial zone sacrificing their lives for labour rights (Women's Centre 2006: 89). The state regime provided an unwritten licence to employers to use the prevailing emergency legislation to eliminate (i.e., kill) workers who agitated. The open economic policies of Sri Lanka, then, came with state-orchestrated violence, not only against ethnic minorities, but also against the working classes, the backbone of the new economic system (Biyanwila 2011).

Hence, it is with a certain pride that workers involved in the Polytex Garments strike recount their courage and assuredly take credit for the work conditions currently available to other cadres of workers. In the words of Mallika Senarathna, 'We won the Polytex battle. If today's worker comrades enjoy some privileges, our blood, sweat and tears are mixed in it' (Women's Centre 2006: 19). When Senarathna voices these sentiments, she is not just asserting workers' agency, but also taking ownership of a narrative that has tended to negate the role of labour in Sri Lanka's shift to an ethical sourcing destination. She is reminding us that it is because of their constant agitation, amidst difficult and challenging political conditions, that the apparel industry is able to rest on its ethical credentials. In other words, Mallika Senarathna joins a long list of labour agitators and a history of the labour movement in the country that have helped shape work conditions (Kearney 1971; Jayawardena 1972). She is also reminding us that women workers too have been part of this labour history in Sri Lanka; she thus disrupts a narrative that has seldom credited women workers. More importantly, in more recent times, when the role of workers in shaping the ethical credentials of the apparel industry is rarely acknowledged, she is calling for attention to and acknowledgement of their equal contribution.

These struggles were pivotal to the state introducing thresholds around minimum wages and the provision of toilet amenities, lighting, windows, fire safety standards, and so forth. When the late R. Premadasa announced the need to protect workers within the FTZ, it may have been a populist response – which the former prime minister and then president were frequently identified with (Venugopal 2018). Less remarked is the fact that he was also responding to labour struggles that highlighted the exploitative work conditions that came with an open economy. By getting the state to respond, labour was also shaping the evolution of capital and the trajectory of capitalist investment in the apparel sector. With Premadasa's intervention came the gradual exit of foreign investors in the sector, often perceived to be in it for a quick buck (Ruwanpura and Wrigley 2011; Athukorala 2018).[10] The ascendance of local investors and the initial space for, and the strategy of creating, a value-added investment trajectory emerged during this period. Their feasibility for capital was not simply due to the vision of niche marketing, but also because the educated workers had struggled to make themselves heard and for it to be known that they would not settle for work conditions that trampled on their rights. Workers' agency also had an unacknowledged role in the way in which the apparel sector evolved in Sri Lanka into niche production, ethical sourcing and value-added production. It is because their role goes largely unacknowledged by capital, employers and the state alike that, fast forward to three decades later, in 2011, the state attempted to override their precious pension fund. Yet again, however, workers resisted, although again not without loss of life and suffering violence.

Taming Post-War Hubris via Labour Defiance

Two years after the end of a bloody ethnic war, the chutzpah of an authoritarian government was put to the test by the rallying working classes. Three decades on from the politically turbulent 1980s, Sri Lankan labourers were reminded that their own government would not hesitate to use political force and violence against them too.[11] This is the second moment of solidarity, which captures the energy of labour struggles and their agency under an open economy. I delineate how this united labour force pushed the state back and, by doing so, signalled their strength to employers.

In May 2011, I was in Sri Lanka to hold a workshop and disseminate my research findings. Repeated coverage of the impending Private Sector Pension Reform Bill (PSPRB) dominated the airwaves and print media during this time. My awareness of it, however, had been raised during a previous visit in December 2010, when I had had to reschedule a meeting with an older worker I knew from my previous research stays. According to my fieldnotes, Lata was one of the first workers who mentioned to me how she had visited the Department of Labour to obtain the relevant forms to claim her gratuity and employee provident fund (EPF)/Employer Trust Fund (ETF) savings. She wanted to do this before any possible changes to the pension system were proposed (Ruwanpura 2014b). During this return research phase, it became a topic of discussion with many other workers too, as it was with the managers I continued to interact and converse with. At this point, it did not occur to me that worker distress was so strong that they would take to the streets en masse; my inability to take the pulse may possibly also be due to the fact that my field sites were not within the FTZ, where the public protests took place.

Running on the high of post-war victory, the Sri Lankan state proposed a pension bill that purported to benefit private sector workers. However, as details of the legislation emerged, it became clear to unionists and labour activists that neither the relevant minister nor the secretary to the Ministry of Labour was entirely clued in. The PSPRB was more an attempt by the state to access the lucrative EPF savings and meet the privatizing impetus of the World Bank. Specifically, Sunil (2011, unpaginated) notes that 'the purpose of the legislation is not to provide decent pensions for private sector workers, but to introduce a form of compulsory saving, designed to inject money into the stock market and other forms of private investment'. The pro-market stimulus of the proposed bill and the role of the International Monetary Fund (IMF) and the World Bank were patent (Biyanwila 2011; Women's Centre 2011).[12] Once unions, labour rights activists and worker organizations got the hint that the proposed bill was less about the state benevolently acting in the interests of workers and more about accessing resources in the EPF, their organizing began.

The publications by the Women's Centre document the steps they and the unions took to get the government to reflect on and reconsider the proposed policy reforms. These ranged from a petition with the signatures of 15,000 FTZ workers, to co-signed protest letters written to the President, to formal objections by unions at the National Labour Consultative Council on 5 April 2011. In their view, the 'opposition of workers was being levelled from all quarters against' the proposed act (Women's Centre 2011: 22). The neglect, disregard and deceptive interpretations by the government made unions and labour activists increase the education, organizing and eventual mass mobilization of workers.

I was in Sri Lanka at the start and peak of worker protests during May and June 2011. Yet, because my fieldwork was not located within the FTZ area, I relied mostly on news media, information shared by labour rights activists and other contacts to gain an insight into the machinations around the organizing. Fortuitously, as I was also arranging a dissemination and outreach workshop for workers around my research results, various opportunities arose to discuss and learn about worker concerns and their struggles. As tends to be the case, there were multiple and even conflicting reports trickling through the various sources. Indeed, in trying to make sense of and reflect upon these media reports, my own writings and fieldnotes reveal both the controversies and the audacity of the workers.

According to media reports, it was the Free Trade Zones and General Services Employees Union (FTZ&GSEU) that was at the forefront of worker education campaigns. As the *Sunday Times* reported on 5 June 2011, they began by distributing leaflets to workers, which 'was followed by picket meetings outside factories and even boarding houses' (10). However, this partial and gendered coverage attributes the success of the worker mobilization primarily and largely to one trade unionist, characteristically a man (see also Biyanwila 2011). It leaves out how women labour rights activists may also have been mobilizing workers, especially women workers, within the FTZs. Deviating from national media reports, the Women's Centre's (2011) account shows how their mass movement approach and connections with women workers over years and generations were also key to effective strategizing and building momentum. Organizations, such as the Women's Centre, Da Bindu (Drops of Sweat), Kalape Api (We, in the Zone) and the National Workers Congress, infused by feminist values, initially started locally and changed their organizational strategies over time. Through everyday working and living experiences, they both made women workers aware of the interconnected spatial politics, namely work place and domestic issues, and drew out energies and built different cadres of working women leaders via temporal struggles. Current women workers develop generational leadership, both through their experiences and by immersing themselves in contact with existing women worker leaders (Women's Centre 2006, 2011; Biyanwila 2011). In other words, as Gunawardana (2008) has already noted, these groups foregrounded gender inequality concerns overlooked by traditional unions in the country.

The mainstream media line that the organizing was done primarily by the FTZ&GSEU conveniently negates the organizing by women's labour rights movements and activists and displaces the underlying inconvenient gender inequities that plague industrial women workers, and those working in the FTZ in particular (see also Kabeer 2008). Moreover, the reporting sums up worker education as 'winding them up', when the truth of the matter was that in areas distant from the FTZ, where I was doing my fieldwork, workers had been fretful about the opaque bill as early as December 2010. By the time of the May Day rally on the first of the month, the Joint Trade Union Alliance (JTUA), unions and labour activists began to invest their energies in educating and raising awareness around the proposed bill.[13]

Between the start of the month and 24 May 2011, worker seminars were also held for FTZ workers. The initial protests, starting as early as 16 May, sometimes had one union or another taking the lead.[14]

These initial protest days were relatively small in scale and, perhaps consequently, the state miscalculated the force of feeling. By 24 May 2011, when tens of thousands of workers met in what was supposed to be an hour-and-a-half meeting before work began (between 6.30 am and 8.00 am), even those organizing the meeting did not anticipate the scale of what would happen. The Women's Centre's (2011: 24) astonishment at the pouring in of workers is recorded when an hour and a half of strike activity took much longer: '24 May, on which an hour and half was stretched to a whole day.' They remark how the camaraderie from the morning hours led to work stoppages by those working or the finishing of overnight shifts to join the assembly of workers, which eventually became a rally, because of the 'sea of workers' uniting (Women's Centre 2011: 25).

The workers moved along the Colombo Airport Road until 4.00 pm. This led to road closures through the day, disrupting 'normalcy' and successfully exposing and discrediting the government's miscalculation of the level of opposition. However, it was not until the rallying workers were disbanding that the police brutality began. The workers' agitation resulted in 'important political consequences, both intended and unintended' that came about through rallies and strikes (Kearney 1971: 138; Sirilal 2011; Women's Centre 2011; Werner 2020), and there were growing cracks in the pugnaciousness of the government. To illustrate, Gamini Lokuge, the minister of labour, held talks on 28 May 2011 with relevant unions, activists and women worker representatives, with the meeting concluding with a signal to ensure that 'action will not be taken to bring in the Act without the consent of FTZ workers' (Women's Centre 2011: 29). However, the very next day (29 May), there were attempts at fake news under former authoritarian president Mahinda Rajapaksa, with leaflets approving the proposed bill getting circulated to cause confusion amongst workers.

Provoking workers in this way led to another impromptu and peaceful gathering on 30 May 2011, this time without either unions or social movements providing the lead, which also led to the witnessing of the full force of state violence against workers (Sunil 2011; Sunil and Liyanage 2011; Dias 2017). The presence of anti-riot police outside the FTZ main entrance activated workers to stage a protest within the zone itself. When the workers neared the entrance gates, the police issued warnings to workers not to depart from the FTZ; workers defied these, partly because their continued gathering could not be contained within zone premises. The various, and sometimes conflicting, accounts note how the ensuing police brutality took place both within and outside the zone; to illustrate, police officers went into factory premises assaulting workers with physical and sometimes even sexual violence (Women's Centre 2011). The upshot of the day was that the use of violence against protesting workers led not just to the death and injury of workers, but also to a resolve amongst the workers that did not abate (see Image 5.1).

Roshen Chanaka Ratnasekera, a 22-year-old young man working at the FTZ and with just four months' work experience, was shot in the leg during the chaotic scenes. As he was not taken for immediate medical treatment, he eventually succumbed to his injuries (*Sunday Times* 2011; Women's Centre 2011). While President Mahinda Rajapaksa announced that FTZ workers would be exempt from the proposed bill, the gesture was clumsy as it was not only late, but also ineffective. Specifically, how would the exemption treat similar workers, such as apparel sector workers for instance, who worked both within and outside the FTZ? The agitations did

Image 5.1 An image of workers protesting the Pension Reform Bill in 2011
Source: With thanks to Vikalpa.

not stop, and when Roshen Chanaka died in hospital, that mobilized over 40,000 FTZ workers, all the way from the FTZ in Katunayake to Colombo, 27 kilometres to the South. On their march, women workers also boldly brought down a huge cut-out of President Mahinda Rajapaksa, which had been tactically placed by a vainglorious government on the Colombo–Negombo Road from/to the airport. They directly assaulted a symbol of an authoritarian patriarch, asserting their agency, as working women and labourers, to bring down the proposed bill.

When the household economy is under duress, low and underpaid workers will not flinch from solidarity action. Women across the life-cycle collectively mobilized to protect their hard-earned gains for distinctly gendered reasons: the risk that their savings for a dowry, house loan or meagre pension pot were likely to be depleted were these reforms to take place. Their action and agitation were shaped by gendered concerns, inclusive of social reproduction (Ruwanpura 2014b; Rai et al. 2019). Alongside this, the concealed role of the World Bank in the PSPRB has been remarked upon to highlight how 'restraining social protection ... and privatizing public goods' was also on the agenda (Biyanwila 2011: 14). Speaking specifically to the temporal political climate in Sri Lanka, other commentators noted how the reform initiative was symbolic of a state trying to act with impunity, only to find its grand ambitions severely curtailed (Gunasekara 2011).

The analysis around the politics of this remarkable resistance, however, has not examined how this particular collective labour struggle was also another juncture in Sri Lanka's labour history, which was stalling state–capital's incursion into and erosion of worker rights. Supporting this stance, women workers record and celebrate their outcome thus: *'However, the battle, which is written in the history as the first one in which the whole of the Free Trade Zone fought for the rights of all workers is the massive struggle waged against the proposed pension for workers ... introduced with a view to looting the money belonging to workers deposited in the Employees' Provident Fund'* (Weerasooriya 2011, in Women's Centre 2011: 4, original emphasis). With her words, Padmini Weerasooriya shares her staunch sentiments emotively, revealing the two reasons why labour rebellion was significant.[15] On the one hand, the indignity of workers having to contend with uneven economic and political geographies is given voice, with workers effectively stalling government robbery and looting couched as pension policy reform. On the other hand, she also marks the significance of this particular moment of labour defiance within Sri Lankan working-class history. Her emphatic words are a reminder that labour collectives will impede the rewriting and eroding of their precious rights.

Take Two: State Amnesia and Labour Reform

It has barely been a decade since this large-scale labour protest, and yet another government has been working towards reforming labour legislation in its entirety. This is the business of government, to look into existing legislation and initiate reforms where necessary. However, the fact that governments that try to do so seemingly suffer from amnesia is worthy of some examination – partly because locking out the participation of the very constituencies that may be affected by such reform is unlikely to lead to an effective outcome.

Post-war, Sri Lanka's political regimes have changed more than anticipated by those in power. The calling of the 2015 presidential and then general elections and their results were to some degree unanticipated by almost all political commentators (Venugopal 2018). The presidential elections in 2019 and the ousting of the previous government, however, were more predictable, given the uneasy coalition between the former president Maithripala Sirisena and the parliamentary government, led by former prime minister Ranil Wickremesinghe. It meant at best being at loggerheads over various policies and at worst facilitating conditions for a tragic Easter bombing that took Sri Lankans off guard. The government in power during 2015–2019, led by the UNP, was nakedly more wedded to an open economy, where neoliberal policies are embraced without reserve. This necessarily comes with close relations with the bastions and institutions that promote neoliberalism – in particular, the World Bank, the IMF and the USAID (Harvey 2005). Yet 2011 ought to serve as a reminder to governments that the working masses will stand together if labour rights are trodden down. Nevertheless, the UNP was itself so entwined with these global institutions that the evidence suggests it had been working in cahoots with USAID over the previous 18 months towards reforming labour legislation in its entirety (IDG 2016). While it may seem a footnote in Sri Lanka's politically volatile context, the political fallout for the UNP government ought not to be disconnected from labour politics in the country.

Labour politics is often neglected by political analysts and commentators, who can be preoccupied with Sri Lanka's ethnic politics, as if they are divorced from class inequality and the growing precarity of labour: identity politics without recognizing its interconnections with material inequities.[16] When I was in Sri Lanka during July 2019 for fieldwork, the news media was again picking up initiatives and protests by unions and comments by the relevant employer representative organizations on reforming existing labour legislation. Trying to be a good detective, as effective researchers ought to be, as Barrientos (2002) reminds us, I decided to follow the labour reform story, although it was not the purpose of my initial fieldwork, which was much more to do research on workers in the post-war regions of the country. By trailing an unfolding initiative, I was able to glean information, in this instance, on early efforts by unions and labour activists to resist labour reforms. They were recording their concerns, because a process that was not embedded in the tripartite mechanisms had begun – and yet again with external actors advocating these changes.

The gist is that the Sri Lankan state had initiated the drafting of a labour legislation bill that purported to consolidate the multifarious labour laws because their complexity was proving to be ineffective. A cabinet decision press briefing issued on 5 June 2018, as per Image 5.2, noted that, given 'several discrepancies ... found between certain service conditions in these Acts, it has been proposed to make a single Act ... without prejudice to the existing labour rights'. The statement then went on to outline four pieces of legislation to be merged into one act that was going to give employers and employees the ability to define the terms and conditions of employment.

In one of the interviews I did in July 2019, I was handed a hard copy of the draft act and a print out of the above web page by a unionist. He was sharing both documents with me to accentuate the timelines and the lack of process. We had the following exchange:

KNR: I saw; this is the draft Act.

MS: It has a date of 6 July 2019. It was handed over to us on 9 July 2019 at the National Labour Advisory Council by the Commissioner General of Labour.

KNR: And none of you all were consulted before?

MS: No.

KNR: What about the ILO?

MS: The ILO has nothing to do with this.

He noted how the cabinet decision was allegedly made in June 2018 and there had been a year's time lag before the draft of the proposed legislation

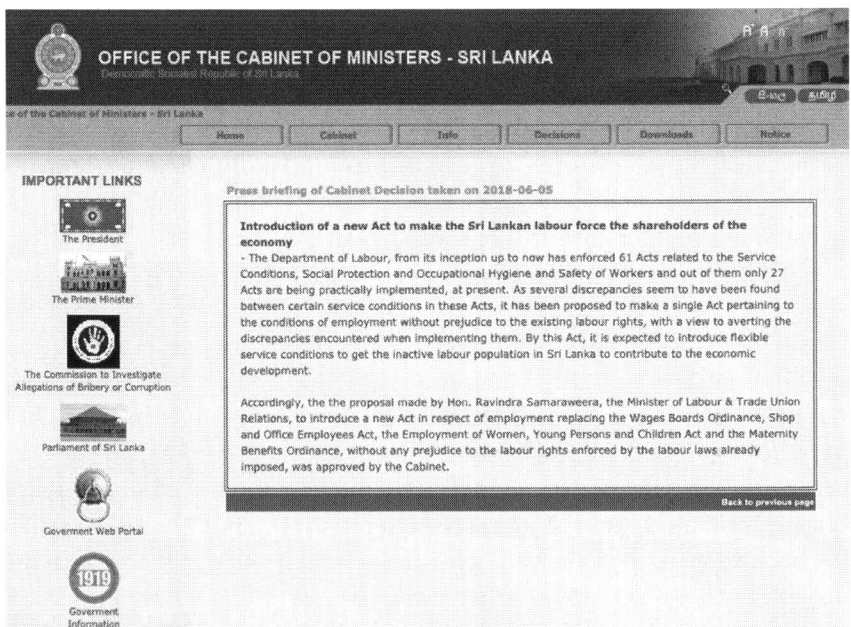

Image 5.2 Screenshot taken by the author in July 2019 from the Sri Lankan government's cabinet office website

Source: Office of the Cabinet of Ministers – Sri Lanka (2018).

actually made it to the relevant tripartite constituency. Our entire interview was more productive than usual, as MS was willing to share various documents with me to verify and validate his concerns about the way in which the Sri Lankan government had proceeded. In doing so, he was able to establish that the drafting of the legislation had not involved the relevant tripartite constituents within the country – namely, the related state department, employer and union organizations; it had not even involved the local ILO office. It was USAID that was involved in consolidating the existing legislation and drafting the new labour laws for the country, with the backing of the World Bank and the IMF. According to MS and many other unionists, state officials and labour rights activists, this was an affront; the slight was not just because due process had not been followed, but also because it was an insult to the civil servants that regularly boast of the country having a highly educated populace.

It was not a lack of capacity within state institutions that made the government circumvent the tripartite processes, as both my interviewees and the documents I perused revealed. The briefing paper by the International Development Group (IDG) LLC, the consultancy group charged with the task, notes that 'IDG is providing advice aimed at introducing a new, unified labour law that will ... better safeguard workers without onerously burdening companies' (IDG 2016, unpaginated). While this same document goes on to say that it will consult the various tripartite constituents, with the exception of the employer organization, this transpired not to be the case. This IDG brief, however, acknowledges that the 'Employers' Federation is the main civil society advocate for labour reforms' (IDG 2016, unpaginated). What was revealed during my multiple interviews was that despite the cabinet announcement that the proposal was made by the relevant minister (Minister of Labour and Trade Union Relations), most state officials were not involved in drafting the legislation. Instead, state officials and unions were asked to comment on the draft legislation. Moreover, the input to, support of and advocacy for the new legislation did not come from the related Ministry of Labour and Trade Union Relations; rather, it came from the now defunct Ministry of Development, Strategic Investment and Trade (MODSIT) – which was then ministered by Malik Samarawickrama, a close ally of the former prime minister Ranil Wickremesinghe.

The oddity of MODSIT's involvement was repeatedly brought to my attention by many of my interviewees, including the employer representative. In fact, he shared what he told the consultants spearheading the labour reform legislation: 'I advised them. I told them "look why don't you all immediately through that Ministry contact this Ministry?" ... I said that if you want, I can even get them to meet you, facilitate the meeting.' The two ministries being referred to are MODSIT and the Ministry of Labour and Trade Union Relations. MODSIT's interest frames the entire labour reform initiative: to ensure that Sri Lanka's investment-friendly ethos is deepened, with a more flexible labour regime. Adhering to process had become less of a concern for a government that had come in on a mandate of yahapalanaya (good governance), something endorsed by the World Bank and USAID but not carried through in practice. It is also instructive that, when considering the mechanics of the everyday state and the government, working towards a coherent agenda is not a given (Gupta 2012); doing so is undertaken by a cast of functionaries, bureaucrats and politicians, often at odds with each other, and without attention to procedure by politicians.

Process, or the lack thereof, was the pivot for registering disquiet about the labour reform process amongst all of my interviewees. An ILO officer elaborated:

> To my knowledge, the ideal process from the perspective of trade unions, at least, and I think I am fair in saying, for the ILO too, is that the idea for the proposal for any amendment, reform, repeal of any law, of any labour law, should first be tabled at the National Labour Advisory Council. Why? Because it is a tripartite body. Based upon a consensus ... of the different constituents, then we would anticipate that the Ministry of Labour submits a cabinet paper to that effect, gains cabinet approval for this exercise and, thereafter, the ILO, as you know, makes itself available to offer its technical assistance in that process.

None of this occurred. Process and governance were left by the wayside and, with state amnesia about the 2011 labour resistance, a labour rights activist remarked: 'If this government or any future government tries to push through this draft labour law, 2011 would be a small moment in our history. We will come out in larger numbers – and we are already educating our workers all over the country.' She said this and shared the leafleting they had begun in both Sinhala and Tamil.

Every other labour rights movement cadre I interviewed voiced similar sentiments and let me have their leaflets, newsletters and early campaigning efforts. State officials who made time for me likewise disclosed the draft act, with their comments and questions on the draft legislation. I was only permitted to make notes and not record the interview with one official, who said, 'We are taking the draft legislation apart paragraph by paragraph (*eka vaganthiyan, anith vaganthiyata*)', and shared a hard copy of the draft legislation with questions and queries noted, using the comments function. The state official was using process and procedure to jettison a draft bill, which, in his view, had been disingenuously taken over by another ministry. That ministry was then trying to enforce it through the official's own ministry, the relevant one. Thus, these state officials were not just enlivening the document with their views and concerns, but also exposing a willingness to cull it and stop it in its tracks.

The state officials interviewed not only felt for workers that were likely to be given short shrift through the erosion of labour rights, but also felt a sense of indignity that a qualified and knowledgeable state cadre was entirely removed from the process. On that day, when I walked into the scorching outdoors from an interview at the end of the work day, I was baffled both by the timing – an impending presidential election within six months – and by the arrogance of a government trying to push through legislation that was not just ill-timed, but also likely to lead to a political fallout. Come early December, these fleeting thoughts turned out to be prophetic.

Conclusion

In my correspondence with various contacts in the field, I have learned that the draft labour legislation hangs suspended at the time of writing. One unionist let me know in July 2019 that they were confident that if there was a change of government, this bill would not come to pass. I, however, reminded him that the record of the previous government, if we take the pension reform debacle alone, was no better than that of the current regime. An ILO press statement about a speech made by the former president Mahinda Rajapaksa (now holding office as prime minister) to the ILO General Assembly was passed on to me, in which he said, 'With Mahinda, we know he is fully committed to the tripartite mechanisms. You can read this statement and make up your own mind.' He left it at that. It was an assertion that seemed to be based on ideological affiliation rather than the patchy records of both leading political parties in Sri Lanka (Kearney 1971; Biyanwila 2011).

Nonetheless, this third moment makes it patent that where the government and foreign institutions work on behalf of capital, resistance can come both from within the state and from labour collectives, whether recognized unions, labour movement organizers or labour activists. It is illustrative of 'agentic spatial practices', where space is used to 'produce and sustain agency' (Featherstone and Griffin 2016: 386; Jayawardena 2017; Ahuja 2019), with labour mobilizing and working in league with sympathetic state and ILO officials to disrupt a tendency that is weakening their rights. Equally, employer organizations that have to work within the tripartite mechanism are fully aware that there are risks associated with non-cooperation with unions and union representatives or in bypassing the relevant state bodies. It is particularly telling that, despite Sri Lanka being a signatory to numerous relevant ILO conventions, not upholding the tripartite consultative mechanism suggests not simply a neglect of governance, but also a moment in which the state–capital nexus acts at its own peril for ideological reasons – and in doing so leaves the ideological terrain wide open to be struggled over, contested and negotiated by labour and state officials alike.

The attempt to intensify an open economy in the case of Sri Lanka shows how it hinges both on active government intervention and on (faulty) mediation. Consequently, government reforms get rolled back, because contending with labour agitation and contestations within the state remind Sri Lankan political regimes that an educated labour force still has considerable autonomy. Making Sri Lanka even more investor friendly at the cost of degrading labour rights exposes their priorities and an inability to recognize how safeguarding labour rights too is pivotal to equitable development processes.

In contrast to the labour geographies that have tended to regard labour agency at a local scale (Hensman 2011; de Neve 2014; Ruwanpura 2013b, 2015; Neethi 2016), Sri Lanka offers evidence that 'labour's spatial fix' also occurs at a national scale. This labour power is not determined merely by the 'worker's relationship to the means of production' (Herod 2001: 35), but its agency is also co-constituted by particular spatial practices and the modes of production (Featherstone and Griffin 2016). For Sri Lankan labour, intersections between educational and legislative apparatuses matter but need accentuating. This is not just because these facets have tended to be underplayed in contemporary debates, but also because doing so resuscitates valuable and yet neglected historical contestations (S. Sen 2008; Supiot 2013; Neethi 2016; Srivastava 2018), with Ahuja outlining how these facets shape 'horizons of expectation that continue to inform labour struggle' (Ahuja 2019: 207; see also Supiot 2003, 2013). These public goods and valuable attributes of the social state, acceding to Supiot (2013), are critical then, not just because they mould labour agency, but also because they facilitate the shaping of the nature of capitalism itself. Moreover, Sri Lankan labour's voice reminds us that this is not just about workers' agency, but also about the essential and positive contributions they make to process and the economy (Kearney 1971; see also Supiot 2003; Kucera and Sarna 2006; Silver 2019).

Returning to the case of the Sri Lankan apparel sector, while 'the upgrading analytic ... renders the social relations that mediate the production of exploitable workers and the conditions of their exploitation marginal to the analysis' (Werner 2012: 407; Hoskins 2014), a reorientation of attention to social and spatial relations is illuminating for multiple reasons – and I pick two here. Firstly, this is because it denotes not just that institutionalization of exploitative relations may be attempted, but also how labour and its allies within the state will exert themselves to shape the conditions and geographies of capitalism. Secondly, as Chapter Seven outlines, the attempt at governmentalizing value through codes of conduct, traced by scholars, such as Gidwani and Chari (2004), Freidberg (2004) and Dunn (2007), who show how these codes are implemented, practised and struggled over on the shop floor, is also shaped by the social state, which both enables and disables their (uneven) application.

Notes

1. I cite only a few of Chang's latest books here, although he has made this point through various outputs, ranging from academic material to books for lay audiences.

2. This evaluation is all the more important because, in the CoVID-19 context, some employers are agitating for the suspension of existing labour laws in Sri Lanka (Amerasinghe 2020), while in India, and in the region, a pausing of labour laws without consulting the tripartite mechanism has already begun (Gaur 2020; *Scroll.In* 2020).

3. Supiot (2003, 2013) explores the underlying impetus for a social state, with others exploring similar worker discourses in neighbouring India on efforts to reallocate resources and enhance the productive and reproductive capacities of labour (S. Sen 2008; Srivastava 2018; Ahuja 2019).

4. These investments, however, have tumbled in the past decades and have led to university academic and student protests in Sri Lanka (Witharana 2015; Abeyasekera 2020).

5. Yet, it is worth recalling in a CoVID-19 context. With humanity and our environment facing existential threats, the rupture caused by this moment is likely to require the advocating of a political vision that at a minimum is about re-investing in public goods and a social democratic polity.

6. Kearney (1971: 17) records how 1956 witnessed 'governmental tolerance and permissiveness' alongside 'a generally more egalitarian and political environment' towards unions, which provided impetus for the growth of unions a decade after. It is important to observe that both 1956 and 1994 were overseen by the same dynastic political family: the head of state (prime minister) in 1956 was S. W. R. D. Bandaranaike (father), while, in

1994, the president was Chandrika Kumaratunga (daughter). Both aspired to create an egalitarian country, but in the end failed to address the class and ethnic fissures that divided the nation.

7. Strong patriarchal personalities and fiefdom mentalities often frustrate the possibilities of building bridges and shaping strategies to mobilize workers towards collective action – and are relics from bygone years (Kearney 1971; Biyanwila 2011). Consequently, membership of FTZ&GSEU is a mere 14,000 across 22 branches throughout Sri Lanka, and – despite 60 per cent of union members being women – men unabashedly head the union leadership (History of the FTZU-GSWEU, http://ftzunionlanka.com/history/, accessed 15 June 2015).

8. Polytex Garments has since 2018 been fully acquired and renamed as Esquel Sri Lanka Limited.

9. Kearney (1971) traces how the CMU, which was formed in 1928, went from representing white-collar workers to representing all grades, levels and sectors by 1969. As one of the most powerful labour organizations and seen as an inspiring leader, under the stewardship of Bala Tampoe, it actively eschewed communal politics and emphasized solidarity across working classes (Gunawardana 2008).

10. We, however, know through ethnographic research elsewhere that social relations between foreign management and local workers are more textured and layered than this crude representation suggests (Plankey-Videla 2012; Kim 2013).

11. In Sri Lanka's complex political landscape, where alignments and realignments have become a frequent feature, the Sri Lanka Freedom Party (SLFP) and the People's Alliance (an alliance of allegedly left-wing parties) are seen to be the champions of the working classes, the petite bourgeoisie and the rural people (Kearney 1971; Venugopal 2018). Recent events suggest that more research needs to be done to understand the shifting political and ideological threads of various political parties in Sri Lanka.

12. Ruwanpura (2013b) details key features of the proposed bill and its attempt to transform the meagre savings of workers. Workers, and women workers in particular, hold the EPF and gratuity payments dear, because of the intricate connections between work (productive) and household (reproductive) economies (Rai, Brown and Ruwanpura 2019). As my purpose in this chapter is more about the nature of labour agitation, my narration highlights these aspects.

13. The JTUA is an umbrella organization consisting of 26 trade unions from the health, port, transport and education sectors. It joined the resistance campaign begun by the FTZ&GSEU.

14. For instance, Ada Derana, a broadcast news media organisation in Sri Lanka, reports how the Inter-Company Employee Union registered its protest outside the Department of Labour on 16 May 2011 (Ada Derana 2011).

15. Where workers, labour rights activists, unionists or employers have made public pronouncements, I use their actual names, because these outputs are publicly available and the attributions made to persons concerned. In this instance, the actual name – rather than a pseudonym – is used.

16. Kearney (1971), for instance, captures the complex politics between the demotion of working-class interests at the national party level and early signs of communal divides in the mid-1960s, and their effects on formal trade unions, whether party-sponsored or otherwise (1971: 90–91 and 111–119).

6

Ethicality with a Blind Eye?

Ethical Code Practices at Production Sites

India, Pakistan, Sri Lanka and Bangladesh
have similar labour laws – which stem from the
British colonial period. With the exception of Sri Lanka,
what we have witnessed in the other countries in the past decade
is a process of circumventing these laws and a
greater informalization of the labour market.
Sri Lanka has been an exception because the human and
social development levels have been high and have a greater voice,
which comes along with strong human and social development

—Senior officer, UNDP regional office

Introduction

Commentators often portray the Sri Lankan apparel industry as visionary, giving industrialists credit for pursuing an ethical and niche-market production strategy. In *Chapter Five*, I attempted to puncture this storyline to reveal its partiality – since the rendering ignores how labourers have held the state culpable for violating their rights. Early collective struggles led to general legislative frameworks that continue to offer workers some recourse, and resistance by apparel sector workers in particular helped shape work conditions within that sector from the late 1980s (Kearney 1971; Jayawardena 1972; Women's Centre 2006; Biyanwila 2011; Saxena 2014). When a senior officer at the United Nations Development Programme's (UNDP) regional office shared the above sentiments, she was capturing another dimension to Sri Lankan apparel's successful ethical trajectory: that of the voice and place of labour, enabled by social and human development factors, as well as by labour legislation.

By the time ethical trade practices were promoted via global governance initiatives, the apparel sector in Sri Lanka was poised for success due to reasons beyond that of management vision. From the 1980s, workers had compelled the Sri Lankan state to respond to their concerns regarding working conditions and rights, often endangering their lives in doing so. The global move to implement voluntary codes of conduct barely caused a squeak, because Sri Lanka was already ahead of the game (Ruwanpura and Wrigley 2011). In a country and sector that had achieved this lead, and where workers had *greater voice*, what were work conditions like within production sites?

I now turn to an examination of ethical codes at production sites. I return to my located ethnography and long-term field research to tease out the nuances in the media narratives that often describe Sri Lankan factories in terms of extremes – either as idyllic spaces or as exploitative ones. The news image screenshots in Image 6.1 capture two such moments in the mainstream media in relation to the Sri Lankan apparel sector.

I want to argue – possibly to the dismay of all sides, including management, unionists, labourers and campaigners – that the way in which global governance codes are negotiated at production sites depends on local factors that are shaped by an interplay of institutional, gendered, cultural, social and political economy factors (de Neve 2009; Hensman 2011; Mezzadri 2012; Selwyn 2012b; Kim 2013; Neethi 2016). Consequently, the complex politics around ethical codes on factory floors mean that bold claims for either extreme, whether that of guilt-free garments or of outright exploitation, are difficult to sustain. The politics of production, shop-floor dynamics and labour agency mean that neither of these polar positions is tenable.[1] My purpose in this chapter is to unpick the differences between guilt-free garments at one end of the continuum and turning a blind eye at the other, and suggest that implementing ethical codes is necessarily both limited and contested.

To illustrate, there is near-complete compliance with a requirement to have no child labour. This is generally recognized and offers a seemingly sound ethical base. Yet the continuing lack of a right to freedom of association and collective bargaining, despite the country's labour union history, does not seem to raise the questions it should. Compliance with the other elements of the codes falls along this continuum. There is a need to unpack how global governance regimes might be contested on the shop floor. How does a country with generally sound labour legislation, strong social and human development and *labour voice* still manage to evade implementation

THE WALL STREET JOURNAL.

Subscribe Sign In

Home   World   U.S.   Politics   Economy   Business   Tech   Markets   Opinion   Life & Arts   Real Estate   WSJ. Magazine

SHARE

f

Sri Lanka Workers Produce Panties In Cool Comfort for Victoria's Secret

By Jonathan KarpStaff Reporter of The Wall Street Journal
Updated July 13, 1999 12:01 am ET

PRINT   TEXT

PANNALA, Sri Lanka -- Dian Gomes strides through the factory he runs on this tropical island, introducing some of his managers. Among them: a recently recruited investment banker, a mathematician with a doctorate from Yale and a physicist who measured the electromagnetic field generated by honeybees.

"And now they're making panties," giggles Mr. Gomes, managing director of Slimline Ltd., a leading supplier to Victoria's Secret. Slimline, a Sri Lankan-U.S.-British venture, produces much of the

THE WALL STREET JOURNAL.

Morning Risk Report

Daily insight on governance, risk and compliance curated for corporate executives.

READ NOW

Sponsored by   **Deloitte.**

RECOMMENDED VIDEOS

Why China's Official Coronavirus Numbers May Not Tell the Whole Picture

INDEPENDENT

Subscr

NEWS   CORONAVIRUS ADVICE   UK POLITICS   US POLITICS   2020 ELECTION   VOICES   SPORT   CULTURE   INDY/LIFE   INDYBEST   INDY100   LONG READS   VOUCHERS

Sport > Olympics

Forced labour claims dent image of London 2012

They were supposed to be the most ethical Games yet, but research in Asian factories supplying official clothing has led to allegations of sweatshop conditions

Emily Dugan | @emilydugan | Friday 29 June 2012 14:43

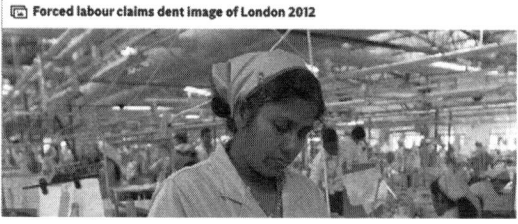

Forced labour claims dent image of London 2012

Show all 3

Image 6.1 Screenshots of news headlines on Sri Lankan apparels from broadsheet newspapers in the USA and the United Kingdom

Source: Web archives for *Wall Street Journal* and *The Independent* newspapers.

of some elements of ethical codes? And yet retain its reputation for ethical sourcing? I will explore these questions and scrutinize the evidence with regard to the context within which GWG are produced.[2]

Ethical Codes: The Bedrock of Global Labour Justice?

In *Chapter Four*, I detailed how the Sri Lankan apparel sector adopted a distinctive strategy towards apparel manufacturing. Instead of relying on mass-produced garments, like many of its regional neighbours, it decided to utilize Sri Lanka's assets, including an educated and healthy labour force, to shift strategically towards higher value-added production. This strategy was bolstered by a commitment to ethically responsible trading, which, as I outlined in *Chapter Five*, was feasible because labour exerted its collective will, making the state meet its legal commitments and sometimes even respond to calls for change.

Hence, by 2002, the Sri Lankan apparel sector had pushed to operate on the premise of ethical manufacturing and increasingly of environmental accountability (Goger 2013b, 2014; Fernando et al. 2019). The five-year GWG promotional plan emphasized quality of life for all workers, with poverty alleviation as the cornerstone of a JAAF strategy to draw in various manufacturers within the country. The intention was for all Sri Lankan garments to carry a GWG tag, which, as mentioned in *Chapter Four*, was to attract niche buyers who sought 'clean' manufacturers. Trying to draw all manufacturers under the same label proved challenging and was eventually abandoned. Yet the lobbying and campaigning did successfully attract a strong and stable retailer base, drawn to the commitment of the Sri Lankan apparel sector to facilitate an ethical supply chain. As I established in *Chapter Five*, this strategy was also the culmination of state–employer–labour struggles in the post-liberalized period. So, the Sri Lankan apparel sector was well placed to adopt ethical governance codes by the time they were introduced globally in the 1990s, whether by individual retailers or by multi-stakeholder initiatives.

Hughes et al. (2008) have traced how ethical codes vary depending on institutional structures in each nation and region. Codes have varying emphases, determined by whether they are driven by multi-stakeholder initiatives or their own corporate codes (Jenkins et al. 2002; Hale and Wills 2005; Hughes 2005; Hughes et al. 2008). The core ILO conventions are, however, their common foundation. Hence, ethical codes commonly cover nine key elements, ranging from how employment is chosen to freedom of association. Within the ETI Base Code, the coverage is as follows:[3]

1. Employment is freely chosen.
2. Freedom of association and the right to collective bargaining are respected.
3. Working conditions are safe and hygienic.
4. Child labour is not used.
5. Living wages are paid.
6. Working conditions are not excessive.
7. Discrimination is not practised.
8. Regular employment is provided.
9. No harsh or inhumane treatment is allowed.

These are seemingly simple on the face of it. Enforceability ought to be easy enough for countries with labour-friendly legislation in place, although, as Hensman (2011) notes, codes are a weak, if not an ineffective, substitute for protecting labour laws and are entangled in globally inequitable power relations (see also McIntyre 2008; de Neve 2009; Mezzadri 2012; Hoskins 2014). Sri Lankan apparel's website explicitly remarks on the (relatively speaking) strong labour legislation that facilitates ethical sourcing. The nuances of the ETI Base Code are revealed through the resources and guidance packages associated with each element (https://www.ethicaltrade.org/eti-base-code). These tools make explicit reference to the labour conventions underpinning them. Hence, ethical code observance may require more than simply putting up the notices I usually found hanging around the various factories during my fieldwork. This makes a stronger case for social and labour justice, even within global governance regimes that are often identified as having weaknesses, a neocolonial tone or uneven power dynamics (Hale and Wills 2005; de Neve 2009; Hensman 2011; Cross 2014; Dutta 2016; Tighe 2016; Raj-Reichert 2019). How Sri Lanka's exceptionalism makes a difference (or not) for workers as they negotiate the ethical code regimes shaping the shop floor and their lives is the subject of my evaluation here. In my discussion, I aim to underline an often-neglected dimension: the institutional and legislative setting. My purpose is to stress that how effectively voluntary ethical codes are followed depends on the local institutions.

Buzzing Factories, Loud Music and Code Consciousness

I still recall my initial unplanned visits to two factories, when, as outlined in *Chapter Three*, management interviews were held at factory premises. I was shown around both factories, which were serendipitously to become my long-term study sites. As I walked in, I was mesmerized by both the loud buzz and the Sinhala pop music blaring. I recall being captivated by the mass production processes, the colours and sounds. I was also attracted by the bright lights, seeming cleanliness and the labourers beavering away, deeply absorbed at their machines, busily walking from one station to another or having loud conversations. Any attention to detail was, hence, lost on me that day. I was simply super-impressed. Sri Lankan factories appeared to be clean and organized in large, open, ground-floor spaces; they were not crowded and dingy, as my initial exposure to factories in neighbouring countries had led me to expect.

Unlike on these hypnotic initial visits, minor mishaps punctured my first full day on 10 August 2009, almost nine months later, at the first factory. A small car that refused to start, then stalled midway through the journey, changing to another vehicle, getting lost, endless driving (*two hours of driving, driving*! my fieldwork notes record), smiling, smiling, smiling women operators and defensive men workers and supervisors are all snippets recorded in my field notebook. Despite this jittery start, I eventually learnt to observe and record the shop-floor and labour dynamics, with specific attention to the implementation of global governance codes at both factories.[4] Amongst these smiling women operators and defensive men supervisors or operators, I came across a young woman who was doodling. It was her lack of work, and her picking up clothing scraps and doing designs on them or unpicking them, that caught my eye. She was vivacious and friendly, possibly in her early twenties. While doodling, she spoke to me at length about her experiences, working times and breaks. When our conversation was disturbed by the lunch break call, she said I should join her and her friends at the meal; and so, I sat with her and her friends over lunch at the canteen. They deftly used forks and spoons to have their meals, which took me by surprise because this is uncommon for rural Sri Lanka. I am told that this was for *health* and *safety* reasons (Ruwanpura 2014a). They had as many questions for me as I had for them, although they were circumspect, careful and offered short responses. Then almost everyone left, and only *C* and *P* remained.[5]

P, especially, asked more details about my project and seemed aware of ethical codes, as she had worked in Jordan for three years; the audits done there had made her more informed. To *C* and others on the same bench, in contrast, I had to point to the board hanging on the canteen wall and an illustrated comic strip pinned behind a glass cabinet on the ETI Base Code. I gathered through this casual chit-chat over lunch that awareness of ethical codes amongst workers was likely to differ. My initial impressions turned out to be correct.

Over time, it became evident that age, gender, education levels, economic (in)security and length of work experiences within the sector all determined the extent of code consciousness. It was older workers, irrespective of gender, men more often than women, irrespective of age, and those with extended employment experiences in the sector who were most likely to be aware of and attentive to code practices. Women workers in their late twenties and thirties felt less inclined to assert their rights, even when they were aware of them, because of their income poverty, whilst others were strident about their rights and how they were ignored (Ruwanpura 2012). These factors appear to be more critical than education per se, reflecting Jeffrey, Jeffery and Jeffery's (2007) conclusions that education may be a necessary condition for agency but it is not sufficient. So, the *greater voice* that the UNDP officer identified at the start of this chapter, although it should not to be dismissed, needs other enabling social conditions to be realized (E. Ruwanpura 2011). In tracing worker voices, teasing out these facets is important to appreciate code consciousness and adherence.

Before situating the array of labour voices on ethical governance, I start with a general view reported by workers overall. Figures 6.1, 6.2 and 6.3 capture how workers reported which code elements were followed within their work places, not just offering us a sense of labour views on ethical codes, but also indicating that claims of ethical sourcing are likely to be contested by workers.

Figures 6.1, 6.2 and 6.3 provide a snapshot on code adherence. The visual illustrations are a useful guide to the ethnographic and qualitative data I discuss. What is important to register is that, according to the workers, while the Sri Lankan apparel sector can trumpet about upholding a ban on child labour and about providing regular employment, freedom of association and living wages were elusive for a significant proportion of workers.[7] The code elements on the latter group were not followed, while those on the

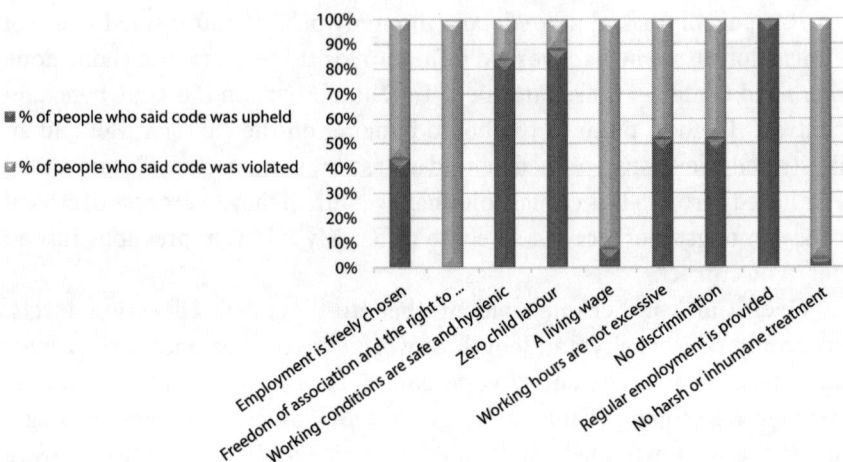

Figure 6.1 Percentage of workers who said the ETI Base Code has been upheld or violated in Factory A[6]

Source: Author's own research.

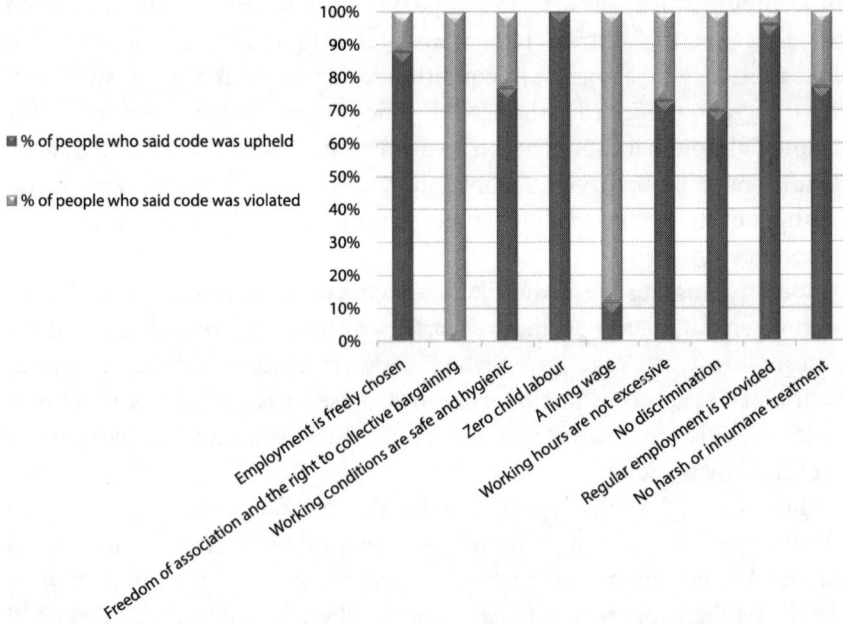

Figure 6.2 Percentage of workers who said each ETI Base Code has been upheld or violated in Factory B

Source: Author's own research.

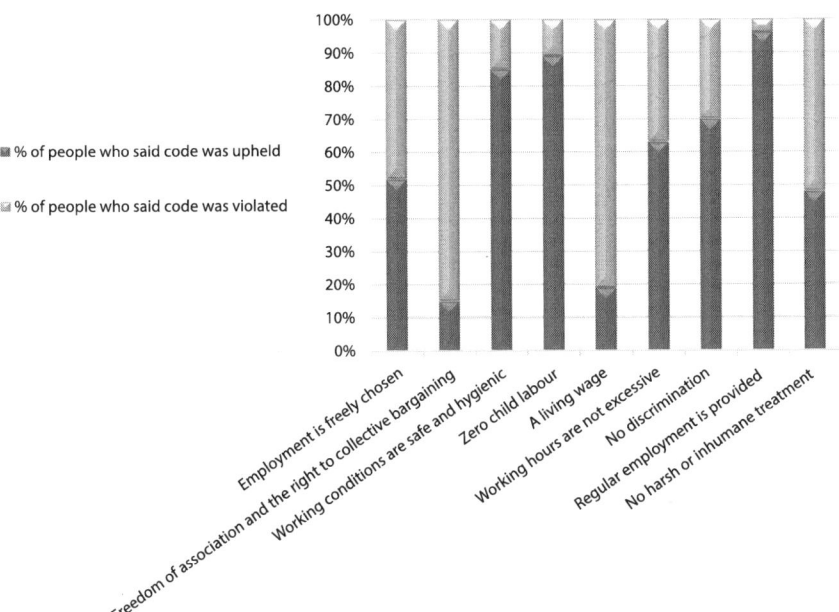

Figure 6.3 Percentage of workers who said each ETI Base Code has been upheld or violated in miscellaneous factories

Source: Author's own research.

former were fully observed. Adherence to the remaining elements of the ETI Base Code fell somewhere along that continuum.

Code Observance: Safe Factories to Code Compliance?

The buzz and colours on the production floor had me enraptured during my initial visit to the two factories in January 2009. During my ethnographic phase, I remained struck by the attention to built space. All the factories I visited during my fieldwork, although of varying sizes and standards, gave the impression that meticulous efforts had been made to create welcoming facilities for workers and visitors alike, as the collage of images in Image 6.2 captures.

The factories I was based at and visited were both impressive. Even before I started my extended stay at Factory B, one research assistant working on the project, who had already started to spend time there, told me in Sinhala: 'Kanchana, you must go to the rear of this factory and spend some time

Image 6.2 Images of different factories and workday situations I was based at or visited for my fieldwork

Source: Author's own photos.

seated there. It is a beautifully layered and landscaped area, with some huts for socializing, and it overlooks a paddy field. It is *niskalanthai* (tranquil and calm).' While I used to walk to the rear to absorb the sight, I never took the chance to sit at the huts and enjoy the tranquillity. The enthusiasm of the research assistant, however, was not misplaced; indeed, the joke amongst the workers was that the landscaped area was so perfect that it provided an ideal hideout for workers, supervisors and managers involved in romantic liaisons. With this diligent attention to buildings, facilities and scenery, management was signalling to those entering the factories that they were intent on 'creating an environment that was pleasing to come into for everyone', as one corporate manager said. In almost all the factories I visited, the built space was a striking feature. Another corporate manager who organized a factory visit in the hill country said:

> The factory you are going to visit is not of the high standard of MAS, Brandix or HG, for instance. However, we have to adhere to safety standards, ensure that there is enough natural lighting, ventilation, toilets for workers, canteen space, etc. So, don't expect fancy, but you will still visit a very good factory.

My visit to this factory confirmed his sentiments, with the factory having airy high ceilings, large windows and bright lights.

Similar opinions would be shared by workers, when they said: 'When we come in, I sometimes feel that we are entering a dream world' or 'This is a good work place; we are not overcrowded and everything is nicely kept.' Even most labour rights activists interviewed had comparable views. However, they also emphasized that the superlative factory-scape was either due to the requirements of code governance or the need to please auditors, merchandisers or retailers:

> Today some factories are like tourist hotels ... today the cleanest place may be the toilet. Now factories have dining rooms, gardens and many facilities ...; when the auditors come, they can see a nice environment. (NLR1)

> It is a way for factory owners to show that we are treating our workers very well. Our factories are like hotels ... in reality, the AC is not for the benefit of our workers. It is because the fabrics need preparation in our country's climate and to prevent machines overheating. Also, our impressive factories are used to show to buyers. (ULR1)

Visual markers are important symbols in the global apparel trade, where aesthetic sensibilities are the foundation for fashionable clothing and garments. Pleasing production facilities can impress most that enter these premises, unless the auditor, merchandiser or compliance officer has an eagle eye and is alert to any disjunct between appearance and practice. These views of labour rights activists hence strike a chord. Occasionally, too, workers would share related reactions, although usually because they had had a frustrating day at work or disagreements with their peers or supervisors.

Yet it is undeniable that while the actions of management and apparel industrialists in investing heavily in their built spaces were likely to have been motivated by multiple factors, from ticking boxes for auditing purposes to attracting merchandisers and protecting fragile fabric, the workers also gained. Older workers with long and varied experience interpreted their time in the industry along these lines, with one of the workers with whom I have been in regular touch saying: 'Our factories were not like this when I started work in the apparel sector in the early 1980s; often our working premises were sub-standard and crowded. Now our factories are of an entirely different standard; the younger workers don't realize what we have been through. Both Premadasa's directives and the codes made a difference.' She was reminding me of how state directives, in response to the worker agitation described in *Chapter Five*, had had a real effect. Creating safe and hygienic work environments was initially a response to state intervention and only subsequently to the global governance systems.

Within this recognition of generally high code compliance, all three graphs indicate a small proportion of worker discontent. During my time, labourers dealing with potentially hazardous substances or using heavy duty steaming machines and bonding would draw my attention to the possible compromising of their health, despite their protective gear and gloves. Others and I have already found that technical and auditing preoccupations with health and safety can restrict aspirations around labour justice (Mezzadri 2012; Goger 2013a; Ruwanpura 2013a, 2014a; Cross 2014; Tighe 2016). However, the extensive efforts made by JAAF in response to state pronouncements and ethical codes were undeniable. These push factors, together with an embedded management vision of investing heavily in their built spaces, have not only raised the bar within the country but have also meant that Sri Lanka was amongst the first countries to set up eco-friendly factories (Goger 2013b; Perry et al. 2014; Fernando et al. 2019). It has most certainly meant avoiding the tragic deaths associated with factory fires and collapses in other South Asian countries (Miller 2012; de Neve and Prentice 2017; Prentice et al. 2018). Compliance with building standards, purpose-built facilities and factory premises expanding horizontally should also be credited for this.[8] Labourers too appreciated these efforts, although not without critical insight into their value.

Creating aesthetically pleasing sites may be the precursor to code compliance across governance regimes. However, Figures 6.1, 6.2 and 6.3 show this to be most likely with regard to two elements: regular employment and zero child labour. What traits beyond management benevolence explain adherence to these? *Chapter Five* traced the strong position of the labour movement in the pre- and post-colonial years, with Kearney noting how a 'relatively unrestrained labour movement will not retard economic development, but can make positive – and perhaps *essential* – contribution to the process' (1971: 167, emphasis mine; see also Kucera and Sarna 2006; Supiot 2003, 2013). These struggles, continued primarily by women workers in the post-liberalized years right into the 21st century, have created a political history that safeguards labour rights (Jayawardena 2017). These undervalued foundations for upholding ethical regimes are linked to labour struggles, from yesteryear to the more recent past, with the requirement for regular employment (Code 8) complied with to a reasonably high standard because existing labour legislation necessitated this (Jayawardena 1972; Candland 2002; Ruwanpura 2016). Almost all the 90 workers interviewed confirmed that once their probation period had been completed, they were offered permanent contracts by a letter of appointment.

The noise within the graphs is because some workers who had had prolonged experiences in the sector shared how their early experiences within the industry were more chequered in this regard. Such inconsistencies, however, have tended to arise even in more recent times, with *The Independent* reporting how labourers were brought in for short periods to address bottlenecks in the production schedule for the London Olympics (Dugan 2012). The media picked up this story in mid-2012, after my extended fieldwork was completed. However, because both a number of workers from this factory were interviewed and one of my long-term worker and management contacts was from this factory, I was able to verify this news item. Two managers and the worker confirmed this report, with the worker stressing that these were temporary Tamil workers brought in from the North Central Province of Sri Lanka. She also noted the work tensions this created amongst the permanent cadre, given that they tended to be from the dominant community (see also Women's Centre 2013).[9]

Formal and secure employment is construed as an appropriate condition for both social upgrading and enforcing enabling rights, with Barrientos, Gereffi and Rossi (2011: 329) mentioning how 'greater security of employment may increase their ability to participate in work place–based trade union organizations and reduce their fear of reprisals'. *Chapter Five* has shown that even relatively strong labour legislation does not prevent apparel sector industrial capital, such as JAAF and the Employers Federation of Ceylon, with government collusion, from trying to dent labour rights by setting up worker councils within factories rather than recognizing national unions. This is the general drift nationally within the apparel sector. However, to assume that worker councils or work place–based unions, as advocated by Barrientos et al. (2011), are an appropriate substitute to facilitate social upgrading runs counter not only to ethical codes, but also to the relevant ILO core convention (see also McIntyre 2008). Moreover, as I show in the section on 'Blind-Eyed Ethical Sourcing' (later) with regard to the relevant ETI Base Code on freedom of association and collective bargaining (along with ILO core conventions 87 and 98), it is also at best debatable and an area where the industry turns a blind eye (Ruwanpura 2015; see also Miller and Williams 2009; Miller et al. 2009). The Sri Lankan apparel firms' perceived magnanimity towards workers then needs to be appreciated as a response to labour legislation and an educated labour force. Both were wrestled over historically – with labour agitating and, as Kearney (1971) notes, a state with a social democratic vision responding, including by investing in public education (A. Sen 1981; see also Neethi 2016 for the Kerala experience). Ethical apparels then are a result of social compromise and relations between forces, including global factors, which do not place all elements of ethical codes on an equal footing. This is shown in Sri Lanka, despite its long formal union history and collective solidarity struggles.

These struggles of yesteryear have also aided compliance with zero child labour. The JAAF website, which has an evolving representation of Sri Lankan apparel firms, boasts of an educated labour force. It acknowledges that extensive investment in public education has produced a competent, intelligent and trainable workforce. It has the most literate population in South Asia, with an average of 92.2 per cent (91.1 per cent and 93.5 per cent, respectively, for women and men), not only one of the highest in the developing world, but also comparable to most countries in the developed

Image 6.2 Screenshot from JAAF – Sri Lanka's older website
Source: http://archive.jaafsl.com/about-us, accessed 26 March 2020.

world. All of this, its website brags, means that workers are comfortable with high-tech production. Older iterations of JAAF's Garments without Guilt website, now archived, boldly claimed: 'In Sri Lanka, children belong to school not in our business' (see Image 6.2, screenshot):

There is, of course, a connection between investing in public education, having a literate and educated labour force and having no child labour. The linking filament has to do with historical investments in public goods – education in this instance, where universal free education was a right guaranteed by the state and education was compulsory until the age of 16 (E. Ruwanpura 2011; Abeyasekera 2020). Education is a public good that the corporate sector benefits from; so, it ticks a number of ethical requirements with relative ease. The Sri Lankan apparel sector's ability to do ethical business is then also due to social institutions and public sector investments, especially those of the past, that created an enabling context to ensure that there was no or negligible use of child labour.

I did not encounter workers in factories who were under 16 years of age. During my fieldwork, I used to gravitate towards young-looking workers, curious to ascertain the age threshold under Sri Lankan labour laws. Since workers had to wear badges around their necks, which usually carried their national identity number, beginning with the year of birth, establishing their age while talking to them was usually simple. Sometimes, workers would willingly raise their badge and show it to me. Others would be unwilling or reticent, skirt around the request or simply decline, share their details verbally or say, either jokingly or rudely, depending on temperament, 'Miss,

you don't need know those details, do you?' or 'Why do you need to know?'
This evasiveness was not always easy to assess, although it was their right
to decline my inquiries; through time, however, the reason for their refusal
became evident.

Most management interviewees made me aware that company policy
was not to hire workers under 18 because Sri Lankan labour laws do not
permit the use of young people for night work. If they did have underage
workers, meaning those aged 17 and 18, it made planning overtime shifts
challenging; from a management viewpoint, it was simpler to recruit
workers in the appropriate age group. While this may have been the stated
aspiration in both factories I was at, it later came to my attention that
exceptions did occur. I came across no child labourers; yet, as the three
graphs earlier (Figures 6.1–6.3) suggest, a tiny fraction of respondents
implied that there might be incongruities worth probing. Sometimes,
older workers mentioned that while child labour did not prevail in the
industry, it did exist when the sector began in the late 1970s. In fact, some
of the older workers themselves had started in the garment sector as soon
as they became 16, left at marriage and then returned to the same industry.
When I inquired whether this was typical, I was told: 'Miss, during those
early days, they were not so stringent. It was under Premadasa that factory
management became stricter' or 'Why should they? Nobody was checking
on these practices' or 'Some workers used to lie about their age; they did
not always check our birth certificates or identity cards then. If we looked
older than 18 years, we could get away with it.' They would chuckle in
remembering their bravado or deliberate avoidance of the rules.

Through my research I learnt that exceptions were not just a throwback
to the past. Unexpectedly, labourers brought to my attention their or
management's transgressions, with the latter usually taking place around
the use of labourers aged 17 or 18 on night shifts, contrary to various laws.
Workers brought forward these contraventions via their diaries or by
repeating rumours, which were verified by speaking to different workers or
sometimes the younger workers themselves (Ruwanpura 2014b). Instances
like these, as atypical as they might be, also reflected the fact that, despite
public investment in education (and health), Sri Lanka is not devoid of
poverty or persistent and steadily rising relative income inequality, as the
data on the Gini coefficient reveals (Table 6.1).[10]

Where poverty and relative inequality persist, variation captured by the
graphs and worker testimonies of their willing transgressions will puncture

Table 6.1 Inequality in Sri Lanka by year (various years, 2009–2018)

Year	2009	2012	2016	2017	2018
Gini coefficient	.364	.392	.398	.573	.577

Source: World Bank (2020a); Knoema (2020).

the Sri Lankan apparel sector's efforts to ensure zero tolerance of child labour. Persistent poverty and relative inequality explain why labourers also give variable responses to other elements of the codes, namely those around the free choosing of employment (forced labour), excessive working hours, no harsh and inhumane treatment, and no discrimination. In other words, the graphs capture how code adherence might be patchy within the Sri Lankan apparel sector.

Contested Codes? The Continuum of Compliance

Evolving Code Compliance: From Then to Now

Older workers, both (the few) men and the women, endlessly emphasized the need for a view over time to appreciate the evolution of the apparel sector. *M* had worked within the apparel sector in various roles throughout his adult life. I got to know him initially by visiting his spouse *D* at their home and learnt that both worked within the same sector but at different factories. They belong to the coterie of workers I keep in touch with and by now have retired, although after a short spell *D* returned to her previous employer on a contract basis, both because the factory requested this and because she wanted to keep herself occupied. When I had obtained preliminary graphs, I would share these with some of the workers I had a good rapport with and draw on their further insights. They pressed me to return to my open-ended interviews and try to understand how there might be a mixed response to ETI Base Code 1 (employment is freely chosen).

One reason was that the ending of the practice of factories withholding documents, such as birth and school-leaving certificates, from workers who wished to leave only came about in the 1980s and was rigorously enforced only in the 1990s through the governance codes. The other reason is best captured by a frequent sentiment shared with me: 'Miss, it is ok for you to visit our house. However, we are poor people, ok, so don't take our living conditions amiss. If we were not poor, we would not be doing this kind of work' or 'I would not take on this kind of job, if our family was not poor; so, I would say I am compelled to take on this kind of work.' This sentiment was frequent amongst a section of younger workers. It pointed to underlying structural conditions that forced them to do this type of work (see also Neethi 2016; Mezzadri 2017; Selwyn 2019). By interpreting the code more broadly, these workers were drawing out what scholars had already remarked upon: education per se does not bring development freedoms (Jeffrey et al. 2007; Lynch 2007; E. Ruwanpura 2011). Within the context of global governance regimes that were trying to ensure no incidents of forced labour, they emphasized the lack of broader freedom and employment opportunities that compelled them into the sector: the lack of freedom to decide on the nature of their employment. These labour views then provided a twist that stressed that the labour justice championed by the ethical codes was too narrowly defined. In other words, it was not possible to ignore social and material factors in considering legal relations and global governance around ethical codes.

Slip Sliding: Overtime, Covering and Inhumane Treatment

The material paucity in labouring lives was most apparent with regard to the code on working hours. All three graphs reveal that this was barely complied with. This code, however, was contravened, through overtime being frequently stipulated, the regular practice of covering for non-working holidays and sometimes punitive measures imposed when workers refused (Ruwanpura 2016). Although when I started my fieldwork I found workers doodling, chit-chatting or reading at their sewing station because of slow or non-existent work due to the global recession; the pace picked up. Labourers started to speak more recurrently of overtime and covering, with disdain and delight in equal measure: disdain, as it was tiring and exhausting for many workers; delight, since workers were able to take home a higher wage packet. I knew *R*, a worker, from the inception. She was formally interviewed, and, during our two years of interaction, we used to speak on the phone as well as on site and at her home. Once, at Factory A, she told me that her daughters, who had recently completed their A levels and O levels, respectively, had now started working at the same factory because there was no other work and the factory was busy. She went on to say:

> Finally, I am taking home a good pay packet through a combination of incentive payments and overtime. This long hours or Sunday or *poya* (full

moon) day work is hard; but, miss, I am not complaining because it was not too long ago that my wage packet barely helped make ends meet for our family.

The overtime, while welcome, was also linked to low wages associated with labouring for Sri Lankan garment firms, a point I will return to in the next section. Wage poverty then compelled workers to accept overtime, albeit begrudgingly, although global production schedules also had a bearing:

The nightshift is an exhausting business because by the end of the week, I feel like a rag doll. (H)

Aiyyo (Oh), Miss, work, work, work. We don't have time to breathe or rest. Overtime is the constant; we need the work Miss – otherwise, how to live? (N)

Similar sentiments were repeatedly shared, sometimes to justify inability to make an appointment or meeting over the weekend or why one worker or another could not stop their work to speak to me in more detail. 'It would be great, if we could speak more, but not today. Too much work; too much pressure – we may have overtime.' My field notes from 29 January 2009 note the following:

I had a ring-cut from R this morning. Quite early in the day – 6.40 am, and so I returned the call about two hours later. By this time, she happened to be asleep, as she had returned from work – and then when I apologized for calling and waking her, she began her litany of complaints, including doing overtime on a POYA (her emphasis) day – she said this was unprecedented in the history of the factory's work ethics. In any event, she was not a happy camper, as she narrated her complaints.

Inequities embedded in the global production process require us to reorient and inspect global–local interactions because they expose how management–labour relations were framed by the broader social setting (Neethi 2016; Selwyn 2019). R's reactions to me over a phone call highlight not just her annoyance, but also how wage poverty pushed workers to accept overtime and covering. The venting was always around fairness. The discomfiture over doing a nightshift or overtime on a *poya* (full moon) day, when normally religious rituals and observance are carried out by Buddhists, was excessive. Even if the workers did not participate in religious rituals or belonged to another religious denomination, their clear view was that a religious holiday ought to be a rest day.

Within Sri Lanka, force of circumstances then compelled overtime, because those labouring were the working poor. Although not a daily feature in their working lives, the fact that during peak demand season overtime and covering were routine resulted not just in infringement of Code 6, but also, as I have stated previously, the breaching of the forced labour code (Ruwanpura 2016: 11; see also Miller and Williams 2009; ITGLWF 2011; Selwyn 2019). More importantly, labourers found it unjust.

Occasionally, managers would coyly or begrudgingly acknowledge that complying with the code on avoiding excessive overtime during the peak season was challenging. The rhythms of global production runs were given as the explanation, but the matter was so acute that in 2012 the Sri Lanka Apparel Exporters Association (SLAE) started to advocate changes to the working week (SLAE 2012). SLAE started by calling for piloting of the 45.5-hour working week, usually spread over five and a half days (inclusive of Saturday), being reduced to five days. This was to be done by increasing working hours on weekdays without any premium being paid. The piloting was taking place at a few factories, and workers at these alerted me. Perplexingly, I was told that the relevant national-level unions were on board and the pilot factories had had discussions with their worker councils (Ruwanpura 2016). However, the workers were unconvinced. *J* told me:

> There, they have introduced some new idea that we are trying out at our factory, where we will no longer work on a Saturday – and when we do the entire Saturday will be overtime and not just half-day, as before. Our workday, however, has just got longer without any overtime payment.

She not only smelled a rat, as did many other workers, but was also commenting on the effect on their wage packet. When I queried this initiative with my management contacts, I was told that the sector wanted to be ethical in this realm too, and yet the loss to worker income – and so potentially the sector's increasing profitability – was ignored. These moments do not just lay bare the disarticulation and the poverty chains on which global production processes rest (Werner 2016; McGrath 2018; Selwyn 2019), but also how the deployment of global governance codes might end up rupturing existing protective labour regulation.[11]

Code 9 requires no harsh or inhumane treatment. With production pressures, unachievable targets and overtime work, how floor managers administered the labour process could vary from admirable to disquieting (Braverman 1974; Burawoy 1982). My fieldwork book from Factory A has copious notes of occasions where managers and workers engaged in moments of cajoling and friendly verbal exchange, designed to convince workers to be only mildly annoyed about having to meet production targets or the need for overtime. This was often in contrast to Factory B, where the management culture, in my view, often violated this code. Figure 6.2 shows that the labourers were unequivocally of this opinion too. I noted quite early on in my fieldwork:

> Noticed similarly this morning with T calling up the line to inform them of what was needed and the need to do the necessary work. Just a resoundingly different work culture and one that still presumably gets the work done. (23 September 2009)

However, management culture and tactics evolve and negotiate external pressures in unforeseen ways (Plankey-Videla 2012; Kim 2013). In Factory A, a senior manager with a military background started to cause increasing unease amongst labourers, with the introduction of regimented policies, such as shorter lunch and toilet breaks, and rules on time off for election voting and on bonus payments. By April 2010, my fieldwork notes were replete with accounts of this nature. Hence, against this background, when this manager behaved disrespectfully towards a peer in June 2010, the workers spontaneously arose, resisted, created havoc and in the end ensured that the manager was banned from work (Ruwanpura 2015). In recounting this event, my purpose is not just to highlight labour agency and its collective outpouring noted by other labour geographers (Herod 2003, 2012; Neethi 2016; Werner 2016), but also to capture the evolving shop-floor dynamics around the code on harsh and inhumane treatment.

Correspondingly, on a return visit to Factory B, a worker that I still keep in touch with said: 'Miss, I think some good has come out of your research at our factory. Now they make a real effort to speak and treat us differently.' Since in my role as a researcher, I had been asked by its corporate manager to share my findings and be candid with their production management team. I had shared the graphs and my evaluation of the positives and negatives within the site. The distinction between the three graphs on this element of the code was noticeable, and he told the rest of his team: 'We have heard this complaint before at audits. This culture starts at the top and only we can change it – and so we must make a difference. This is up to us.' The ensuing discussion was about how altercations between production-floor personnel and workers were prone to result in loss of production time, with the implication that extracting value might need more effective management practices. This might echo Burawoy's (1982: 180) appraisal – 'management initiate(d) changes ... to forestall future conflict' – but the distinctive nuance was that consent should be sought not in anticipation of a struggle but rather due to growing recognition that resistance from the floor might limit productivity gains. Moreover, instead of factory regimes being either coercive (despotic) or consenting (hegemonic) (Burawoy 1985), I found that floor dynamics evolved along a continuum and shifted due to various conditions and factors. Hence, outsider evaluations in the form of audits and critical feedback might have some clout, trivial as it may be, with the 'distinction between local and global ... puzzling(ly)' irrelevant as capital mediated across spaces (Neethi 2016: 69). What then of the realm of freedom of association and living wages (Codes 2 and 5)? The penultimate section turns to the elements of the code that fared worst.

Blind-Eyed Ethical Sourcing: Corrupted Compliance?

Almost all workers unfalteringly identified freedom of association and living wages (Codes 2 and 5) as the violated elements of the codes, as the graphs starkly capture. This section centres on these, aiding concluding thoughts on how this could happen without so much as a blinking of an eye on the part of retailers or, indeed, any blemish to the ethical sourcing reputation cultivated by industrialists. What factors facilitated the ignoring of these particular elements?

Of the 25 managers I interviewed during my first fieldwork trip, only two confirmed and discussed the presence of unions at their work place and only one mentioned an affiliation to a nationwide industrial union. Whenever managers were interviewed on their compliance around freedom of association and living wages, the responses varied from deft avoidance to incidental references. Management talked about how their factories hosted worker councils, as was stipulated by the BOI, or how, through a combination of incentive schemes, workers took home a living wage. Paying living wages to all workers or allowing national trade unions to enter factory premises was not high on their ethical agenda, and almost all management interviewees had few qualms about ignoring these and were emphatic that their factories were ethical. How did this blind-eyed ethicality go down with workers?

As the graphs revealed, labourers were emphatic that these elements were not complied with by their employers. In their view, very few allowances were made to provide living wages. On closer scrutiny of the empirical data, it could be seen that it was only highly productive workers who were able to take home a living wage. As a few of them put it: 'If we put everything together, incentives, attendance allowance, overtime, then in a good month we can take home a living wage' or 'Not always, but during peak season and occasions, I have been able to earn a wage that I would say meets our cost of living.' So, where a few workers mentioned that they had earned a living wage, it was due to a combination of allowances in the wage packet that made this possible, rather than the basic wage itself. As Salzinger (2003: 42) remarks, it is as if workers could be 'assuaged by benefits and shows of appreciation, but not by wage increases' (see also Palpaucer 2008). However, the more critically aware within this cohort or those who rarely, if ever, took home a living wage shared sentiment to the following effect:

> Miss, if we can work like machines, meet targets to earn incentive payments, work overtime regularly and not miss a day of work, then we may be able to earn a salary that covers all of our living expenses and for some savings ... We are not machines, no, miss? (L)

> Ask me how often I have taken a living wage as a monthly salary in a year! Two or three months at most, maybe sometimes four. Not more than that. How can we then say we earn a living wage? (T)

> Yes, so the months I do overtime because it is peak season and if the design is easy to figure out, then yes – so long as I also get the attendance bonus. (TH)

An entire wage packet and particularly busy periods made it possible for workers to earn a living wage, but it was not possible otherwise. Labourers across the board acknowledged they were paid the minimum wage, but all other payments were variable. Since overtime combined with incentives was a necessity for a living wage to be earned, the implication was that national regulations on overtime and Code 6 on ensuring that there were no excessive work hours might be being breached (OXFAM 2008; Ruwanpura

2016). During more candid moments on the factory floor, managers and supervisors across the ranks would tell me that the possibility of workers achieving targets was determined by standard allowed minute (SAM)/ standard vector machine (SVM), which was familiar lexicon amongst managers and supervisors. I learnt during my time on the production sites that this was determined by the quantity of the order, the price per piece, the lead time given and the design itself. Hence, a few managers acknowledged that it was not a foregone conclusion that all workers could meet their production targets and thus their incentive allowances. The ITGLWF (2011) corroborates this: management avoided paying incentives by setting impossible targets. There was low compliance with payment of a living wage, supporting Selwyn's (2019: 89) argument that global production is 'predicated upon poverty wages' and 'the moral element of workers' social reproduction costs' is neglected (see also Werner 2020; Rai et al. 2019).

Nevertheless, these varying targets are also determined by supply-chain pressures and the health of the global economy – as was the case in 2008 and as early signs of the CoVID-19 global pandemic suggest (see also Mezzadri 2012; Plankey-Videla 2012; Kim 2013; Kumar 2019). There are, however, local variations to pressures in the global economy and the supply chain. The value extraction process offers a partial reason for labourers routinely not earning a living wage, with profit margins being a preoccupation of local capital as they are of retailers (Palpaucer 2008; Mezzadri 2017; Shakya 2018; Kumar 2019; Selwyn 2019). Still, not complying with the principles on freedom of association and collective bargaining (Code 2) also mars the industry and offers a reason for the position on a living wage. Even though it is a constitutional right to associate freely, *Chapter Five* has sketched out how workers struggled to assert this. Whilst they have done so at various moments in post-liberalized Sri Lanka's labour history and thus shaped industrial capital's evolution, it is telling that this enshrined constitutional right is not guaranteed within the code regimes. In its place, management used to draw my attention to worker councils, which labourers had a derogatory attitude towards or cunningly used to advocate their personal needs rather than collective interests.

H sat on the worker council and, before I got to know her really well, she said, 'The worker council exists to fulfil some auditing purpose; nothing that really affects our welfare comes out of it.' Subsequently, I learnt that she sat on the worker council. Since I used to drop by her house on my return from Colombo on a Sunday evening, I asked why she would join an association that she derided. Her spouse, who I also got to know, laughingly said: 'Miss, it is because H can benefit from it. If she needs a day off or has to go late or come early, she knows all the managers by sitting on the Council – so they are more likely to approve it.' *H* joined in and said, 'Why else, Miss?' They then got into playful banter and offered various different instances of how the worker council was likely to be used and manipulated – none were based on the collective interests of workers at her factory. My research notebooks are replete with analogous moments (Ruwanpura 2016), with *H*'s views reinforcing that worker councils are a poor substitute for freedom of association (Hensmen 2011; Selwyn 2012b; Supiot 2013; Neethi 2016).

Not supporting freedom of association at factory settings reveal derision, fear or active fear by management and is also partly linked to reservations expressed by labourers. They frequently doubted whether unions would flex their muscles appropriately, queried their value in their everyday lives or were unsure even how to contact formal unions. Their reservations echo findings elsewhere, where 'workers reveal their deep scepticism ... of traditional unions' and yet are willing to engage in mass-scale strikes via social movement unionism (Nowak 2016a: 433). Closely examining the lives of workers helped uncover several contradictory pressures. When asked whether there was freedom of association in the factory, the graphs reveal that workers were nearly unanimous in highlighting its non-existence. Deeper conversations with labourers and the faltered initiative towards unionization within one production site used for my research, as outlined in my next paragraph, suggested that workers were willing to resist. However, their capacity to agitate was circumscribed, including by their economic insecurities.

Earlier and in Ruwanpura (2015), I outlined the context that compelled workers to agitate, where what began as a worker–manager altercation ended up in a factory-scale commotion during an overnight shift. The worker-led ruckus also resulted in an embryonic work place union. However, this fledgling initiative was gradually but surely dispersed through a combination of tactics. Worker harassment and silencing through pay outs to particular workers were the most commonly used management devices, echoing practices elsewhere (Gunawardana 2007; Hensman 2011; Neethi 2016; Nowak 2016a, 2016b). Managers also, however, cajoled frenetic workers, by pleading for dependability and reliability, both during and after the incident (Elias 2005; de Neve 2008; Prentice 2015; Zaki-Chakravarti 2019). Mostly, however, managers highlighted economic insecurities, which they said pervaded not only the everyday lives of workers, but also the very existence of the factory. Managers and supervisors across the board explained how, in their estimation, their jobs were also on the line, because the factory might become unviable if the union were to continue. Through these fears, they were able to deter and dispel a collective initiative.

The position taken by management was that to uphold freedom of association and collective bargaining could in itself be detrimental to a successful operation. The associated paradox was that the very vehicle – collective championing via unions – which might have helped dissipate labourers' economic insecurities was hampered. The approach to code governance within plants then actively drew upon labour anxieties, not to uphold ethical regimes but to query their relevance if production sites were to remain competitive, successful, and so on.

How does capital then *work place* within an architecture of global governance around ethicality, even if in contradictory ways? And, more importantly, despite this taint how does it still make such bold claims? My concluding thoughts to this chapter offer a glimpse of some possible rejoinders, before I pick this up more fully in the final chapter. Gathering further evidence from post-war Sri Lanka in *Chapter Seven* makes it possible to better appreciate how, although global governance may recompense labour in selected ways, it is also the case that the efficacy of ethical regimes is both enabled by labour legislation and limited by the sociopolitical terrain.

Conclusion

Technical and auditing priorities, varied proliferation of codes, inequitable power relations and the ignoring of local undercurrents are all associated with the architecture of global governance regimes (Hughes 2001; Dunn 2007; de Neve 2009; Mezzadri 2012; de Neve and Prentice 2017; Ruwanpura 2017, 2019). They perforate the notion that global initiatives can advance labour conditions worldwide without being rooted in the regional, national and local landscapes. This scholarship then stresses the need for analysis across these various levels, with my research emphasizing how these initiatives also have temporal dimensions that manifest differently within factories at different times. By reorienting attention towards the subtleties at ground level, it is possible to emphasize the intersections between social hierarchies and local mores and the global lexicon of ethicality (see also

Hughes 2006; Brooks 2007; de Neve 2009; Merk 2009; Mezzadri 2012; Cross 2014; Prentice 2015). Accentuating the global–local connections is a salute to the labour legislation and socio-development conditions within countries, as these too have a likely bearing on ethical code regimes. Sri Lankan apparel sector is a litmus case, because the sector boasts of its ethical sourcing credentials. As I have shown, many far-sighted initiatives usually attributed to industrial capital or global governance are also enabled by legislative frameworks, along with supportive social conditions and an educated labour force. The laws themselves are arenas that labourers from yesteryear have struggled over, resulting in, for example, the provision of permanent employment after a six-month probationary period or the non-existence of child labour.

Nevertheless, worker testimonies reveal the continued need for a pugnacious spirit, if ignoring the need for unionization or living wages is any indication. While these spheres are protected by codes, these are often not fully or even partly complied with. What does almost outright non-compliance with two notable elements of the codes say, both about global regimes and about the need to appreciate ground conditions? In Sri Lanka, my contention is that the continued and persistent relative inequality situates workers in a materially precarious position, resulting in both fear and vacillation around union politics (Ost 2005; Kim 2013; Nowak 2016a). Moreover, suspicion abounds amongst workers and labour rights activists, as amongst management, on the impetus behind ethical codes (Hughes 2006; de Neve 2009; Hensman 2011; Ruwanpura and Wrigley 2011; Ruwanpura 2016). The fact that global retailers or even the EU, in their assessments around GSP+, does not emphasize lack of action around living wages and freedom of association lends credence to the prevailing scepticism (Sarvananthan and Sanjeewanie 2008; Selwyn 2019). So, despite Sri Lanka's admirable labour history and solidarity victories (*Chapter Five*), ethical code regimes also end up acting as a cloak, under which the local state–capital nexus can cooperate with global retailers to evade compliance with the global governance architecture.

According to my research, promulgating the view that factories may collapse as business entities if there are unions within them foils opportunities to advocate for higher or living wages. Connected to this, the lack of a living wage in the sector contributes to national-level persistence of relative inequality and poverty. Subsequently, despite high education levels, the successes of the sector are built on the backs of the labouring classes. This is ethicality with a blind eye, by which the fairness that comes from ethical codes is also facilitated by labour struggles, past and present, and protective social and legislative edifices compel capital to comply with a global initiative, albeit unevenly. Partial labour justice, then? My next chapter teases out more of these uneven dynamics in the post-war region, given its politically contentious terrain.

Notes

1. This is not to deny that another set of circumstances can lead to exploitative social relations on the shop floor, as others have shown (Mezzadri 2017; Selwyn 2019).
2. The degree to which these same conditions might turn out to apply to post-war areas of the country is left in the main to the next chapter.
3. I use the ETI Base Code because I was told by most factory managers that they attempted to adhere to the highest standards and that this made compliance more practical and manageable.
4. I started my located ethnography at the second factory (Factory B) a week later and only after I had started to feel at ease at the initial base. There, while I did not have such a frazzled first day, my fieldwork notes record how I felt as if I was entering a fortress in going through the formalities to enter the premises, which I noted as strange because I had visited both factories previously.
5. C is one of the workers I have kept in touch with during the past decade, getting to know her father (her mother had passed away when she was young and she had a stepmother who I never met) and helping to sort out a complicated love-triangle between a peer and a young army officer, whom she eventually married. Since then, in keeping in touch I have witnessed her transition to motherhood (of two boys), taking time off work and then returning to the same factory, where she continues to work with a promotion. P and I kept in touch closely during the entirety of the fieldwork period. I met her family and was invited to her wedding and met her husband. After marriage, she decided to leave work – at which point we lost contact, as she eventually also did with C.
6. In these graphs, I follow a creative method adapted from Humphries (2010). I use qualitative interviews with workers and their references to the nine codes to quantify data and derive the graphs. This is an approximate quantitative representation, and my purpose is not to claim representation

as much as to offer a visual representation of how workers understood global governance regimes.

7. Lingam (2019) notes that the workers and activists she interviewed in Jaffna reported workers were not provided with contracts, with the workers reporting that they could work indefinitely with no contract. It is not an issue that I came across in the interviews done for the post-war region, although the widening practices around the use of temporary workers within to bypass labour protection legislation for workers all across Sri Lanka is also noted by Skanthakumar (2015).

8. Almost all of the factories where I did my ethnographic research were on a single floor, with one factory having an area upstairs for storing fabric, another for clerical work and the third, a small section for sewing operations. Faisal Siddiqui, a Pakistani labour lawyer, presented a paper at a workshop hosted by the University of California (Berkeley) and discussed with me how Sri Lankan industries had a similar number of incidents of fire as Pakistan but no casualties. In our conversation, he inquired about the likely reasons for this; and my response to him was that it was quite simple – Sri Lankan factories usually have only one floor, so in the case of fire mass exiting is much easier. (These remarks do not mean that workers do not have detrimental effects on their health that matter within and outwith the factory floor – see Ruwanpura [2017, 2019] and Prentice et al. [2018] for detailed discussions.)

9. In *Chapter Seven*, I pick up how ethnic cleavages between workers and worker–management relations intersect with economic shifts in contingent ways (Carswell 2013 makes similar points for India; see also Jayawardena 1972; Skanthakumar 2015).

10. The Gini index measures the extent to which the distribution of income or consumption expenditure amongst individuals or households within an economy deviates from equal distribution, where zero (0) implies perfect equality and one (1) is inequality.

11. From the labour viewpoint, the piloting was propitiously just that, although it was set in the context of the broader national-level efforts at labour reform outlined in *Chapter Five*.

7

From War to Work

Ethicality amidst Post-War Trauma?

Introduction

When I arrived at Da Bindu just before lunchtime on a Sunday in July 2019, I was not expecting to find a television crew and a small group of Tamil women workers at the premises.[1] Although it was the weekend, Chamila had suggested that I come along because they were returning from a long-distance trip and that I arrive late morning. I arrived there a bit later because a prior interview had taken longer than I had anticipated.

As I arrived late at Da Bindu, nearing lunchtime, I was hoping that the delay would not mean that I could not interview Chamila. I had contacted her because I was tracing the reactions of various groups to the employment reform bill, which I discussed in *Chapter Five*. Like all things in fieldwork, running late can fortuitously open up opportunities on the research radar that had not taken priority when setting out for the day. Following jagged little paths of research connections rather than linear and neat tracks is how I remember the month of July 2019.

As I walked into the premises of Da Bindu, four workers were seated in the garden area – and a television film crew was further into the porch area of the house-cum-office. As a native Sri Lankan (now British–Sri Lankan), I knew from the way that the workers were dressed, in colourful salwar kameez clothes and adorned with a *pottu*, that the chances were that they were Tamil workers. After smiling and greeting each other, I went into the office area, and asked for Chamila. When she came out, I apologized for my delay; she generously laughed it off, saying how they too had returned late and everything was behind schedule.

We then started our research interview, during which she explained why women workers from Northern Sri Lanka were present and outlined for me a new set of challenges faced because of management practices in the area.

According to her, 'The factories that these young women work at apparently administer birth control pills to control their periods. This way, they do not take too many breaks when they are menstruating/having their periods.' She then went on to outline both the compulsion involved in prescribing birth control pills to young women workers and the health risks because of the type of medication given. I was astonished, as I had not encountered this practice at the two production sites at which I had done my extended field research, although older interviewees had insinuated that, or commented on how, such practices were common in the Katunayake FTZ during the late 1970s and early 1980s.

During the interview with Chamila, she mentioned that I should speak to the workers directly, if I wanted to verify the details she had shared. She thought they ought to be open to speaking with me, as they were there to be interviewed and share their experiences with the *BBC* Sinhala service; thus, I learnt the identity of the television crew. With the workers' permission, I was able to converse with this group of workers, three of whom knew Sinhala. Two were fluent, one of whom was particularly gregarious.[2] I was also able to observe and make notes of the dialogue that ensued between the journalist and the respondents.

The peace, with its hallmarks of large infrastructure projects and economic stimulus to the region (Goodhand 2010; Thaheer et al. 2013; Sarvananthan 2016; Venugopal 2018), came with financial incentives for apparel investors to participate in the vision and process for post-war rebuilding. In the apparel sector, each production facility received US $1 million from the Sri Lankan government, so long as each new plant in the North and the East employed at least 100 workers and operations commenced by a given date (Goger and Ruwanpura 2014). Other incentives took the form of tax subsidies for a five-year period, including to mother plants so that cross-subsidization within the corporate entity would be possible, USAID-sponsored training programmes and fast-tracking of approvals for leases. Military support included the building of production sites, establishing electricity lines, cell and internet technologies and, finally, constructing roads connecting production facilities to the main highways.

This economic orientation sidestepped addressing political grievances, something which others have attributed to the ethno-nationalist stranglehold of the polity (Jazeel and Ruwanpura 2009; Wickramasinghe 2009; Venugopal 2018; Lingam 2019). These readings have tended to zero in on the political climate and the virulence of the nationalist tenor of the state. Although this is appropriate, there has therefore been less emphasis on the role of global institutions and the corporate sector in trying to promote peace dividends via economic inducements.

Global financial and development institutions – the World Bank, the IMF, USAID, for instance – and each government regime were singing from the same hymn sheet. There was not much reflection on the part of these institutions that sacrificing a political settlement at the altar of a liberal peace via economic stimulus might bring many problems. The most obvious of these was that the liberal peace never challenged the dominant ethno-nationalist and militarized intonations that coloured each Sri Lankan government. Hence, in 2019, when 269 Sri Lankans were tragically killed in the Easter-day bombings (*BBC News* 2019), the then prime minister Ranil Wickremesinghe in an interview given to Channel 4 afterwards offered a glib rejoinder, saying that the country had no ethnic problem and there was communal harmony (Channel Four News 2019). Fast forward ten months to November 2019, and the denial continued, with the new president Gotabaya Rajapaksa sidestepping the need for a political settlement of ethnic grievances and the bolstering of former high-ranking military personnel as state functionaries. This is unsurprising, given the president's complicity in the bloody end to the war. Without him blinking an eyelid, the ministry within which the Office of Missing Persons was housed was closed and the co-sponsorship of a resolution pertaining to reconciliation, accountability and human rights to the United Nations Human Rights Commission was withdrawn, for instance, within his initial months in office. The new government thus continued to signal the negation of political solutions and the continued militarization of the state (*Daily Mirror* Sri Lanka 2020a; Ismail 2020, Soysa 2020). Economic elements, with military backing, were to be given pre-eminence.[3]

In this chapter, I aim to explore what becomes of ethical code deployment and global governance in situations where employment is created in a post-war context. How does the Sri Lankan apparel sector's ethical record hold up to scrutiny in the region? To address these questions, the chapter considers why the apparel sector would shift to war-affected regions, how managers saw their role in writing the story of the post-war nation and how workers made sense of their experiences with existing ethical codes, highlighting both the discrepancies in governance regimes and how these uneven practices are intricately interconnected to underlying political fractures within the country. The concluding section underlines how not taking the traumatizing experiences of the Sri Lankan Tamil community into account generated specific shop-floor dynamics and interactions, which not only undermined code adherence but were also potentially risky to the wider polity.

Magnanimous Capital?

The 'economics for peace' or 'business for peace' mantra of the ceasefire period (2002–2005) under the UNP regime became mainstream thinking by the end of the war (Venugopal 2011). It was so routine that a political party, the SLFP, which claimed to be leftist, had no qualms in adopting similar or the same policies (Biyanwila 2011); with Biyanwila and others locating the impetus to global and bilateral institutions, such as the World Bank, USAID and the IMF (Biyanwila 2011; Venugopal 2018). Hence, despite the grandstanding of the post-war Sri Lankan government to imply that it stood for a sovereign nation, it was a willing party in cooperating with global institutions and China alike in extending open economic policies. The open economy approach has then continued with gusto, despite the changing colours of Sri Lankan governments since the end of the war (Biyanwila 2011; Brown, Chan and Ruwanpura 2018; Rajasingham-Senanayake 2018).

Within this milieu, a two-pronged shift was taking place that affected the apparel sector. As the war was coming to an end in May 2009, brokers, agents and dealers rapidly accessed the North and the East, aware that there might be a willing labour force looking for work. By luring a previously isolated community with 'fancy and attractive stories about jobs in the FTZ in the South', they encouraged Tamil women workers to fill vacancies in the apparel sector (Women's Centre 2013: 39). The other change was the promotion of investment and the creation of conditions conducive to attracting investors to the former war-torn regions, without paying adequate attention to the likely ethnic dimensions of a mostly Sinhala-dominated army and middle management, and largely Tamil workers in the region. Creating employment and integrating affected communities into economic life, as pictured in Image 7.1, were seen as an adequate response to 30 years of violence and war (Ridicki 2015; Sarvananthan 2015). The fact that they also fortuitously addressed the labour shortages faced by the apparel sector in the rest of the country was never mentioned (Goger and Ruwanpura 2014; Ruwanpura 2018; Lingam 2019).

Image 7.1 Screenshot image of a newly open factory

Source: Original photo taken by Priyantha Abeysundera for *The Times* newspaper in the United Kingdom, https://www.thetimes.co.uk/article/after-28-years-hope-rises-from-the-scorched-earth-in-sri-lanka-n23xvc7hwt6, accessed 5 December 2020.

After three decades of war and violence, trauma was an indelible feature of the region (Thaheer et al. 2013; Thirangama 2014; Lingam 2019). Yet, as the sector moved to work with and in communities, management interviews suggested that there was limited reflection on whether the GWG principle was being maintained. Setting up new factories in the region came with concerted efforts, often with the support of the military, to recruit a new labour force. Existing accounts of the initial years suggest that there was a willingness from those in the area to seek employment in these new factories (Ridicki 2015; Lingam 2019). However, during interviews with me, management emphasized the difficulties encountered in recruiting enough labour from the immediate vicinity. Managers were optimistic that their role in the region was essential to the rebuilding of a unified post-war nation (Goger and Ruwanpura 2014; Ruwanpura 2018). These conversations revealed the ingrained nature of majoritarian nationalism, with apparel sector capital and management no less culpable than the government in cosying up to the military.[4] In contrast, the labourers I interviewed suggested that jobs alone were unlikely to salve their sense of grievance, with the lack of a living wage compounding their concerns. This disquiet was emphasized by workers across different parts of the country, as *Chapter Six* indicated.

I sketch here the politics of management. I then turn to labour voices, as they puncture the ethical claims and record of Sri Lankan apparel firms. They also underline how infrastructure ventures, such as jobs and roads, alone will not replace the need for a political settlement.

Respect, New Futures and Economic Freedom?

> The only advice I gave my senior managers is 'treat them with respect' because this is after a war.... In a society, which, you know, is very top down, caste-ist.... It is all about treating them with respect, motivation, telling them about the new future, economic freedom, all that.... Basically, a secure job, they can earn, they can prosper in life.

Respect, new futures and economic freedoms, according to this senior corporate manager, were to be the cornerstones of reconciliation via job creation. Almost as if following the former president Mahinda Rajapaksa's vision for a renewed Sri Lanka, he passed similar views on to his junior managers as they were setting up new factories in Kilinochchi, in the north of the country. In the follow-up interviews I did with ten managers in 2014, one mentioned that 'the government was insisting' they set up factories on 'the completion of the war ... for reconciliation purposes, the only way to go forward is employment'. In sharing these beliefs, the manager was not merely reciting the government position; his tone suggested that it was an ingrained perspective. It turned out to be a widely held view, with one manager even bombastically claiming: 'We worked with the government to come here, because it was in the government's best interest for us to come and get the LTTE out of the war, so they were very supportive at that stage.' While no others openly corroborated this view, the grandiloquence of such assertions suggests active cooperation across the government, industrial capital and the military.

Often, managers stressed the need to treat their new labour force with respect, given the backdrop of the war; in return, a body of workers motivated to invest in a new future would be available. These themes, although not necessarily their undercurrents, were also picked up in Daniel

Ridicki's (2015) documentary *Being about People*, which covers MAS Holdings operations in Northern Sri Lanka. It captures the voices and reflections of various senior managers and shows the extent to which this line of thinking was entrenched and, I dare say, even genuine.

All managers were aware of the politically tumultuous terrain and the likely family and community circumstances of the new workers. However, their response tended to be located in a majoritarian nationalist project of rescuing workers from a trying 'predicament'. Often managers unreflectively told me how they had to 'Take this bias out of their minds' or 'We have to change their minds to make them think how misinformed that was. We have to act.' In referring to Tamil workers, they were unconsciously separating the country's citizenry into us and them, divided and reinforced along ethnic markers. There was, however, an urgency to instil change and to create a casteless labour force, without social hierarchy and, most importantly, without the political load of Tamil nationalism.

For predominantly Sinhala managers, as for the state, working with war-affected Tamil communities centred on focusing on 'their' biases, not the prejudices created by Sinhala nationalism, which was entrenched in the everyday of Sri Lanka – including in the state, political regimes, the people and management personnel (Ismail and Jeganathan 1995; de Mel 2007; Kadirgamar 2013; Women's Centre 2013; Rajasingham-Perera 2016; Ruwanpura 2018). The modernizing ethos identified by feminist scholars, such as Lynch (2007), Hewamanne (2008) and Goger (2013a), who were writing on Sri Lankan apparel firms, was now inflected by an explicit emphasis on cleansing workers of Tamil nationalism. Yet, as the majority Sinhala nationalism had become so normalized and naturalized in the country, there was hardly any reflection by most managers on their own prejudices.[5] When I came across reflective senior managers, they tended to be from minority communities themselves – Tamils, Muslims and other hybrid Sri Lankans. Some said that their companies had been earmarked or approached by the government and yet chose not to shift because of the contentious ideological terrain. While there were signs of awareness amongst some corporate partners and senior managers, most others took upon themselves the need to invest in the *new futures* vision for post-war Sri Lanka.

Expunging the social and ideological traces carried by Tamil workers required various management techniques and efforts that extended beyond the shop floor. Workers had to undergo pre-job training for eight weeks, often provided by USAID-funded training programmes that focused on skill development. As 'most workers had their O/Levels', the equivalent of an upper secondary education up to 16 years of age, they could be given training in factory management skills, usually with an emphasis on Japanese *lean* manufacturing processes. However, because they were seen to be lacking proficiency in personal hygiene, time management and team work, the training provided ranged from personal grooming to the culture of the work sphere, implicitly acknowledging that factory work requires more than mere efficiencies, targets and productivity levels.

On-the-job training continued for another six months, which is the standard probationary period for all workers. According to the country's labour laws, a letter of appointment (i.e., a permanent contract) should then have followed, or the temporary contract should have been terminated. Alongside this, there were also induction programmes and coaching, where management sat with workers and sometimes even invited their families to inculcate them into the ways of working and factory life (Goger and Ruwanpura 2014; Ridicki 2015; Lingam 2019). This practice in the post-war regions contrasted with the approach adopted towards Tamil women workers in FTZs in the South, where they were segregated from the Sinhala workers and association with the other group was discouraged (Women's Centre 2013). Although management interceded when there was a breakdown in relations or when derogatory remarks were made, there was no reflection on the possible detrimental effects of separating workers along ethnic lines.

Efforts at levelling the social hierarchy within the factory, however, were made in the post-war regions. To illustrate, during tea breaks, sharing 'new' cultural values, discussing the family and community conditions of Tamil workers and commiserating with their difficulties became part of the management repertoire. Management, across the ranks, used these opportunities to stress the importance of these jobs to the workers and discuss their problems so that they could also introduce conversations on absenteeism: '"What is the importance of the job? How you can manage your job, your activities [*sic*]?" so through face-to-face discussion, we had an impact, we had a result. Now, early days ... the figures were very bad. 12–13% absenteeism. Now it is 6%.' Another emphasized, 'We know that these workers are traumatized ... we have to tread carefully. We constantly make our supervisors aware of the need for sensitivity', although he went on to acknowledge, perhaps because of his hybrid ethnicity, that with production pressures and deadlines that was a difficult balancing act to achieve.

When management gives workers the sense that they have a voice on the production floor, it is never without extracting value, whether in the form of reducing absenteeism or in productivity gains (Plankey-Videla 2012; Goger 2013a; Kim 2013; Gunawardana 2014; Arslan 2019). The role of Sri Lankan apparel firms after the war was also shaped by the desire to assist in reconciliation: removing previous ethnic markers and mentalities from citizen-subjects. Hall (1980) has noted how unmarking citizen-subjects is an essential step before they can be rearticulated and reinserted as modern worker-subjects who can be a boon to industrial capital (see also Bair and Werner 2011). So, in the FTZs, there was an effort to offer Sinhala language classes, although there was never reflection on the need for Tamil language classes for the Sinhala workers. In fact, this dominant attitude meant even Tamil women workers reported a need for Sinhala language classes and assurances that time was made for them (Women's Centre 2013). In the case of post-war Sri Lanka, the dominance of ethno-nationalist perspectives resulted in a filtration process, whereby Tamil women workers also might seek to 'unmark' themselves. While some welcomed this at the initial stages, especially as it was seen to create new-found security on the factory floor (Women's Centre 2013; Indrakularasa 2019; Lingam 2019), others aired reservations, as I discuss next.

For a sector invested in ethical credentials and niche marketing, did the job-creation process aid or stretch the limits of ethical governance? On the face of it, job creation for workers with scarce employment prospects is a laudable aspiration and one which is also fostered by bilateral funding agencies and international organizations (ILO 2012; USAID 2013; Stewart 2015). Yet, were the ethical governance regimes that Sri Lankan apparel firms drew upon and made a virtue of strained? It is to these matters that I now turn.

Ethical Codes and Ethnic Markers

Forced Labour?

Almost all my management interviewees mentioned how they relied upon the military to help with the recruitment of workers; none of these managers reflected on how the communities themselves may have perceived this. Instead, I was told that the government and industrial capital made the wrong assumption that labour would be plentiful in the region: 'One of the assumptions was that there would be more than enough labour ... but this turned out to be wrong, because those places are still not highly populated.' He and others then went on to say that consequently they needed to find workers from up to 5 to 10 kilometres distance from the production site, but they knew it was still worthwhile. So instead of only resolving the labour shortfall that apparel industrialists faced in the rest of the country, the sector was able to validate its presence in the region because it was there for loftier purposes too. My reading of the sector's presence in the region then is distinct from that of Lingam (2019: 165), who reduces it to motivations that are purely profit driven: 'From a profit-oriented view, it made sense to keep them out of the workforce altogether than to amend factory policies in any significant way (there is plenty of reserve labour in Kilinochchi district, which in 2014 had the second highest unemployment level).' From my located ethnography and a decade of doing research in the sector, I have found that factory policies continually evolve, and draw upon ideological elements, because staying in business (profit-maximization) requires this. Specifically, for post-war Sri Lanka, drawing on a wider area meant drawing on the military without thinking about possible coercion, as I elucidate next.

As outsiders, to gain knowledge of villages in the vicinity, managers of factories had to rely on the knowledge of the military, which in turn used their intelligence or drew upon lists held by the *gramasevakas* (a state functionary heading the village). Some managers even used the help of the military to recruit workers from nearby villages, identifying able young people from their intelligence lists (Ridicki 2015). Bringing workers to the FTZs in the South invariably relied upon agents, brokers and manpower agencies. In doing so, there appeared to be little consideration given by factory managers to the point that using the military or the assistance of agents as brokers in recruitment efforts might breach the forced labour code.

War-traumatized communities feared the military and the Liberation Tigers of Tamil Eelam, as these bodies implied surveillance, terror, violence, fear or a combination of these factors to affected communities (D. Hughes 2013; Thaheer et al. 2013; Thiranagama 2014; Satkunanathan 2016; Lingam 2019). The lack of consideration of what the military might signal to local communities is revealing of how widespread militarization is in Sri Lankan society (de Mel 2007; D. Hughes 2013; Thiranagama 2014; Satkunanathan 2016; Ismail 2020). Senior management often deflected or sidestepped the mechanisms through which government lists of potential workers were secured. Thus, they were able to continue to make the claim that they had the 'most ethical manufacturing base'. As Hall (1980: 33) notes: 'how different ... ethnic groups (are) inserted historically into capitalist formations requires our attention because it offers a more critical lens to understanding capitalist processes'. Moreover, the close alliances between capital and the military, including the naturalization and dispersion of militarized society, are revealed when we locate capitalism within projects of militarized nationalism (see also Kadirgamar 2013; Nagaraj 2016; Ismail 2020).[6] Together, these threads reveal limits to voluntary forms of global governance that have hitherto remained unexplored.

The ILO's core conventions around forced labour – conventions 29 and 105 – partly stem from an effort to provide redress and hold accountable militarized countries, such as Myanmar, where communities were forced by the military to toil for various projects. The ETI Base Code 1 and the ILO's remit around the forced labour convention extend beyond considering the withholding of salaries, ID cards or passports or the use of prison labour, for instance. Yet there was an inability on the part of industrial capital to see that heavy involvement of the military might be breaching the ethical code on forced labour. By disregarding elements of distress, or of subtle or palpable force, pressures in recruitment drives that might have compelled or coerced young people or their families to join factories were overlooked. This raises the need to consider the degree to which the forced labour code might have been diluted.

This blindness may be due to seeping militarization and the various ways in which military presence is made use of (Ismail 2020; ITJP 2020), which have included emotionally and sexually abusive liaisons between workers and armed personnel (Hewamanne 2009). Hence, not deliberating on the global governance codes around forced labour tells of the close relations between military and capital (de Mel 2007; Kadirgamar 2013; Ruwanpura 2018), and is implicitly and increasingly conceded in Sri Lanka's wider socio-polity (Ismail 2020; ITJP 2020).

Are growing relations between the military and the apparel industry the only issue that need scrutiny with regard to ethical codes and their deployment in a post-war context? Attempting to 'heal divisions' via employment (Ridicki 2015), without adequate political awareness of the effects of three decades of ethnic violence and war, has resulted in the scars on the national psyche being overlooked. The upshot is that most Tamil women workers repeatedly raised the issue of the harsh and discriminatory terrain they had entered (FTZs in the South) and have to negotiate on the production floor.

Slippery Slope: From Verbal Abuse to Inhumane Treatment?

When workers are toiling away with difficulty, we should not be scolded in filthy words, in another language.

—A Sri Lankan-Tamil woman worker

Sri Lankan-Tamil women workers continually remarked on how they were subject to abusive language when they did not meet targets. This repeated theme was notable, given that managers had said 'respect' was to be a cornerstone of their approach in the post-war region. By 2019, within a decade of the war ending, respect appeared to be a non-priority. The Women's Centre (2013) had already highlighted concerns of Tamil women workers around the use of pejorative language and communication for those working at FTZs. When Tamil workers in the apparel sector in the North were asked what was the most pressing issue in their working lives, the misuse of language by their supervisors and middle managers was routinely raised. Workers shared the following sentiments:

'Scolding us in filthy language, in Sinhala.' (KR, 34 years old)
'Using sexually explicit language in pulling us up.' (JV, 34 years old)
'Insulting us.' (SS, 20 years old)
'They should stop rebuking workers using bad language.' (SH, 26 years old)

The use of filthy, abusive and even sexually explicit language is particularly troubling because of the angst it is likely to cause to a minority community against a backdrop of trauma, war and violence.[7] Insensitive language, when used towards a minority group, can take a tone and tenor that is tainted with ethnic prejudice. Even when that might not be the case, the inability to grasp another language (Sinhala) alone might make scolding in that language sound belittling or depreciatory. The *respect, new futures* and *economic freedom* that management interviewees promised might in reality be more difficult to deliver. I will probe this in more detail later because it has implications for various codes; however, is it only internal dynamics within production facilities that might be violating or putting pressure on ethical codes?

Workers' remarks on language issues amongst supervisors, management and workers are unsurprising because ethnicity in Sri Lanka is not only neatly tied to religion or language only, but also inflected by language: Sinhala and Tamil (Guneratne 2001; Silva 2001). Some managers mentioned in their interviews that the supervisors and production floor managers were Tamils or Tamil-speaking: 'We essentially got Tamil graduates from here, sent them for one year of training in our existing factories and then sent them North.' Another said: 'We mostly sent Tamil-speaking mid-level managers and supervisors; there are some Sinhala managers too, but we made sure that there was a good mix.' By talking about Tamil-speaking supervisors and production-floor managers, both these senior managers were signalling their awareness that the language barrier needed to be navigated sensitively. None of the senior management respondents, however, spoke of the need to train their Sinhala supervisory and production-floor management cadre in Tamil, before sending them to the North and the East.

How does one explain this contradictory evidence from senior managers and from Tamil workers? The workers I interviewed sometimes worked for the same factories as the senior managers. Tamil-speaking supervisors or trainers were rare, with most shop-floor seniors literally bussed in from Colombo on a weekly basis (Goger and Ruwanpura 2014; Ruwanpura 2018). In those cases, figuring things out on their own was considered acceptable and the ability to communicate not necessarily a requirement. This was in 2011. For 2014, Lingam (2019) corroborates these management views by offering detailed narratives from three Tamil women workers labouring for a large apparel producer. She outlines how workers, despite chronicling their arduous workdays, long travel times and exacting production schedules, felt a sense of pride, security and gladness about garment sector work: 'We are very happy working there' (Lingam 2019: 159; see also Indrakularasa 2019).

However, workers interviewed in 2019 in the North repeatedly mentioned that 'They should not separate us' (RS, 22 years old), 'We experience differentiated treatment' (S, 26 years old). They were at least hinting at their feelings of isolation or feelings of segregated management–labour relations. It is evident from the Tamil workers' testimonies that they felt mistreated. An even larger number of Tamil women workers stated that the language issue needed to be resolved, even when they did not explicitly mention scolding or berating. Thus, to be in a work place and not be able to communicate in one's mother tongue, when this is the only language one speaks, unsurprisingly caused distress. On the basis of worker suggestions, the Women's Centre report on FTZ workers recommended language training for all workers: 'It is very important that both ethnic groups in the FTZs learn each other's languages ... language training may not necessarily be targeted at improving their grammatical and writing skills, but it should be sufficient to interact with other ethnic group members' (Women's Centre 2013: 45). However, they left out the need for supervisors and production-floor managers to do the same, which is what Tamil workers in the region were emphasizing. The six-year time period since the Women's Centre's intervention heightens the urgency for labourers, supervisors and the production-floor cadre to be provided with language training. This imperative must also fall eventually on managers of all ranks who manage a labour cohort that speaks different languages, in addition to the hiring of supervisors and production floor leaders from the minority community. The lapse of time since the Women's Centre's intervention and the lack of action by the sector are reflective of the wider ethno-nationalist ethos that have been propping up and shaping factory production spaces in Sri Lanka for well over a decade (Lynch 2007; Hewamanne 2008; Goger 2013a; Ruwanpura 2018). Resolving this is imperative from the perspective of upholding ethical codes.

Eight years later, when workers are still being discouraged from communication, this management technique might be out of sync with ethical codes on harsh and inhumane treatment and be fringing on discrimination. It might well be that different production sites in post-war areas have varied practices on the shop floor, and different timelines might signal that the slackening of corporate aspirations over time reflects broader shifts in the political and ideological tenor. Factory regimes then appear to alternate between the despotic and the hegemonic, depending on time, place and space, rather than necessarily being one or the other (Burawoy 1982, 1985).

Frequent casual chats amongst workers not only frustrate productivity and efficiency, but also leave room for potential labour strategizing and make control more challenging; hence, tight management control of the shop floor is attempted. Its efficacy and nuances are, however, varied in Sri Lanka, as in other parts of the world (Lynch 2007; Hewamanne 2008; Kim 2013; Prentice 2015). However, it tends to reach its limits or fail, including through unanticipated strikes and labour withdrawal, when unilateral modes of governance are imposed without critical awareness of local situations and moral codes of conduct (Kim 2013; see also Plankey-Videla 2012; Palpaucer 2020). More specifically in the case of Sri Lanka, where apparel factories are not entirely innocent of breaking Code 9 on inhumane treatment, partly due to global production pressures and timelines, factories in the post-war regions are likely to experience evasions of the code, combined with a management tone that exacerbates underlying ethnic tensions.

Job Creation without Living Wages

Opening up employment opportunities to minority communities may appear at a perfunctory level to chime with ETI Base Code 7. When we dig deeper into the code and the core conventions underpinning it, however, it is clear that equality of treatment also requires the upholding of non-discriminatory practices. The workers I spoke to suggested that infractions occurred here most starkly. For instance, they said: 'We get treated differently' (KK, 25 years old) or 'Our voices don't get considered' (SS, 20 years old).

Equally, Sri Lankan-Tamil women workers, across a generation, brought up the issue of wages in the following ways: 'Our wages need to be improved' (AM, 33 years old), 'Our basic wages need to increase' (DA, 23 years old), 'We do not get wages that cover our living expenses' (MW, 57 years old). At each stage of the life cycle, there were hardly any Tamil woman worker who did not bring up inadequacies around their earnings; this also got raised by the respondents in Lingam's (2019) study. Comparable to the Sinhala workers I spent an extended time with during my located ethnography, wage insufficiency was a constant theme in post-war regions too. The Women's Centre (2013: 16) study reinforced this finding: Sri Lankan-Tamil women workers were seen to be underpaid, their rights to holidays curtailed, and they were separated and isolated from their peers.

Since I have already delineated in *Chapter Six* how the apparel industrialists turned a blind eye to the lack of living wages in the sector (including in relation to freedom of association and collective bargaining), thus violating two ETI Base Codes, the disquiet around wages ought not to be surprising. While this was repeatedly raised during my research and other studies support this claim, it is difficult to establish whether Tamil women workers are underpaid vis-à-vis their Sinhala counterparts. All industries, including the apparel sector, have to uphold the minimum wage stipulation of the WOB. It is possible, however, that when it comes to incentive payments, usually dictated by individual firms, workers in post-war regions, who are predominantly Tamil, get a lower level of recompense. The detailed evidence garnered by Lingam (2019) in the post-war regions suggests that there might be discrepancies in incentive structures and total wage packages in comparison with the findings for FTZ workers by others. However, this is a comparison across different times and geographical spaces and is at best indicative. Without comparative national and regional wage differential levels data by skill level, it is difficult to establish whether there were infractions of the ETI Base Code 7, specifically on wage discrimination.

Notwithstanding this caveat, it is important to emphasize that it is likely that apparel employers structure incentives differently, considering regional distinctions, including FTZ/non-FTZ, rural, semi-rural and urban. Moreover, the fact that the minimum wages stipulated by the WOB rarely keep pace with inflation levels and cost of living changes is the more critical consideration (OXFAM 2008; Ruwanpura 2012; Asia Floor Wage 2013, 2014). In other words, apparel sector workers do not get paid living wages, and that is a perpetual stain on the sector. The irony and indeed potential risk is that not paying workers a living wage undermines the prospect that job creation alone could play a conciliatory role in the post-war area. In that region, with mostly or exclusively Tamil workers, a perception of discriminatory wages might be more likely to exacerbate a feeling of disenfranchisement rather than draw these communities into a social contract for peace.

Discriminatory practices are also likely to manifest in diverse ways, where tense ethnic relations are easily aggravated. Kim (2013: 156), using his data on Han Chinese workers managed by South Koreans, notes that 'workers preferred being controlled by managerial staff with the same ethnicity' (see also Arslan 2019). Where this is absent, as is the case in some factories located in post-war regions, feelings of disenfranchisement are likely to resurface in what is an incendiary milieu. What is startling is that workers who appeared optimistic and hopeful in detailing their feelings of safety, pride and agency in 2014 (Ridicki 2015; Lingam 2019: 159–162) were now, instead, emphasizing financial strains and language differences. Intersectional identities that extend beyond the work place matter (Pearson, Sundari and McDowell 2010), with the possible effect of the displacement of the local moral order and resultant labour unrest, highlighted by others

(Plankey-Videla 2012; Kim 2013). Additionally, in post-war Sri Lanka, fears around the collapse of societal cohesion surface, along with persisting anxieties around political insecurity (see also Lingam 2019; Jegathesan 2019).[8]

Conclusion

When Sri Lankan apparel firms shifted to the post-war regions, management interviewees indicated how they tried to understand place, reflecting Herod's observation that 'capital needs to work place, if it is to be successful: it must work to embed itself locally so as to develop the economic relationships with local labour forces' (Herod 2001: 19). Ridicki's (2015) documentary especially attempted to capture the extent to which a leading industrial enterprise within the country and the sector took a measured route as it moved to an entirely new region, and attempted to *work place*.

However, the ways in which capital work place are also inflected by the ideological markers that it brings with it, which in Sri Lanka also take the form of ethnic politics. So, the apparel sector capital and its management were working place by drawing upon registers that were more likely to reflect the ethno-nationalist tenor of the country rather than to negotiate fragile ethnic relations in the area. My worker interviewees described barriers to working place because of the ethnic schisms that continued to matter, which extended beyond class antagonisms. Were these potential ethnic tensions to resurface, they are likely to have repercussions for the political terrain, because they revolve around ethnic discord. As Burawoy reminds us, 'only ... when the terrain of political and economic struggles become the object of struggle – is the capitalist labour process directly threatened. Ideological struggles take us beyond capitalism ... they are struggles over their basis in the relations of production' (Burawoy 1982: 177). Hence, without the political establishment prioritizing a political settlement, especially in light of the likely global recessionary fallout from CoVID-19, the ability of capital alone to shift the ideological terrain solely by economic stimulus is likely to be limited and even a cause of aggravation.

Sidestepping these concerns may also more immediately jeopardize the reputation for ethical credentials that industrial capital has attempted to cultivate over decades. Military assistance was imperative for the sector to move to the region, with many management interviewees underlining its importance in the early stages. Industrialists saw this relationship as essential both for *getting to know the place* and literally to *work place*. Yet this *working place* did not come with the necessary reflection as to what the military's involvement might mean for local communities who had had to endure distressing relations with the armed forces during nearly three decades of war. Moreover, how this relationship might cut across ethical codes around forced labour was barely considered. When workers persistently raised difficulties around language and being reprimanded in another tongue, an additional dimension to this lack of consideration and reflection was exposed. How another ethical code might also be fractured is revealed in this post-war region; GWG and claims of ethical sourcing appear to be being severely tested, if not undermined, by firms not being sensitive to the turbulent political and social terrain that industrial capital has entered.

Labour, in other words, never discarded its complex sociocultural registers, material conditions and ethnic belonging outside the factory floor. The inability by management to appreciate this fractured and fraught tapestry, and the need for sensitivity to complex intersections and their bearing within production sites, highlighted how *working place* could bring its own contradictions. Hence, this shift to post-war areas not only risked rupturing claims of ethical adherence and of producing 'garments without guilt' in many ways, but, if labour traces and voices continued to be neglected, might also result in an assertion of labour agency that plunged the region back to violent ethnic rifts. These are injustices that are compounded during times of distress, as the world negotiates a global pandemic and its aftermath – as traced by Asia Floor Wage (2020a, 2020b). How then does the Sri Lankan apparel sector, despite these contradictions, hold a prime place in the global imaginary as a destination that upholds ethical codes? The final chapter reflects on this question and other broader processes that underline the limits to voluntary governance.

Notes

1. The main offices of Da Bindu are located near to the FTZ in Katunayake, a good 225–300 kilometres (140–180 miles) away from the factories where these labourers were working.
2. While verbal consent was always sought from my respondents, at no point did I seek written permission or require interviewees to sign written documents granting consent. In the region, such a step might have come

across as crass and insensitive (and hence unethical), given the levels of fear and suspicion – and also the risks involved to their lives (Satkunanathan 2016). Hence, during the open-ended questions, there were instances in which some interviewees withheld their name, age and/or village but were willing to speak about their work experiences in a post-war context.

3. Although CoVID-19 may have created a dent in this economic fundamentalism, the militarized taskforce to manage the pandemic suggests business as usual (ITJP 2020).

4. Given that militarized capitalism has evaded the necessary gaze attention and scrutiny, this helps accentuate the need for more research in this troubling sphere (Kadirgamar 2013; Ruwanpura 2018).

5. There were some thoughtful managers from the Sinhala community, as captured by Ridicki's (2015) documentary. The Human Resources Director for MAS Holdings – Shakthi Ranatunga – quite frankly notes how he did not initially understand when Tamil workers spoke about safety because, as he said: 'I did not have to think about my safety when I stepped outside.' (De Silva [2018], however, recounts an incident where acknowledgement, keep aside this level of reflection, around issues of sexual harassment at the corporate level within the same firm was absent.)

6. Using brokers, agents and agencies, as the FTZ areas are increasingly doing, may likewise bring in elements of force and need further exploration.

7. There have been instances of wildcat strikes reported in social media for a combination of reasons. I have written about strong worker resistance and strike action based on my experiences at one factory, where I did my located ethnography (Ruwanpura 2015), but I refrain from drawing any inferences based on newspaper reports on worker agitation and wildcat strikes alone.

8. In the interest of space and to keep an eye on ethical codes, I do not discuss how a large proportion of these respondents spoke about the stresses to their societal make up, harking back to and drawing on war memories as a resource. Memory, Tetrault (2014: 40) reminds us, involves 'a fair amount of forgetting'; such exploration, however, is for another occasion.

8
Concluding Thoughts
Grounded Governance?

This factory runs with your courage

....

For bringing in foreign exchange to Sri Lanka
You are appreciated this way.

—Anu

Introduction

I return to the poem by Anu with which I started this book. I use the lines with which she ends her poem to reconsider the Sri Lankan apparel sector and its successes. Anu reminds us that factories run on the courage of labouring workers, emphasizing another dimension to labour agency: courage. The end of her composition, however, takes us from the factory to a different level, that of the nation; she praises the workers' contribution to the land. In her subtle way, she promotes the value creation that toiling labourers bring to two different levels, accentuating how their courage helps both the firm and the country earn hard currency. Unstated is the point that this appreciation of sweating workers does not take material form; in other words, they are not adequately remunerated and yet they are recognized. How did labourers come to be in this place? The two ends of my research trajectory may make some sense of this.

I started my research at the onset of a global recession; ironically, my writing of this concluding chapter coincides with the CoVID-19 global pandemic. Although at the time of writing it is early days in the pandemic (March–April 2020), the prognosis for the world economy is dire, with ripples in livelihoods in places far away from the current epicentres of the plague (Europe and the USA). I draw attention to the effects on the global garment industry, where reports of leading retailers cancelling orders from countries, such as Bangladesh, Cambodia, India, Myanmar and Sri Lanka, abound (Hossain 2020; Kelly 2020a, 2020b; Hoskins 2020, 2021). These accounts alert us to the large-scale cutbacks and the struggles of local activists to ensure some degree of protection and severance for redundant workers. With retail therapy adrift, many major brands have walked away from their contractual obligations. This has meant the closure of local factories or employers' inability or unwillingness to pay workers, potentially creating the prospect of mass unemployment. While labourers seek justice, retailers blame the markets and local manufacturers highlight their exposure to the vagaries of global markets. The reports from Sri Lanka are mixed and yet offer possible reasons for cautious optimism; might they also perhaps offer a glimpse into Anu's sentiment?

Like elsewhere in the world, a combination of factors has led factories producing apparel within the FTZs to close. The main union representing the sector, however, has been at the heels of the industry to ensure that monthly wages are honoured (IndustriALL 2020). Newspaper articles report how tripartite bodies within Sri Lanka are seeking state bailouts to help weather the current global turbulence and pay monthly wages (Asia Floor Wage 2020a, 2020b; IndustriALL 2020). Yet, the Facebook pages of leading labour rights organizations post video clips of workers, narrating how their promised monthly wages have not been received or only partly received. In contrast, MAS (2020) has a short promotional clip on its website and Facebook page underlining its motto 'Change is Courage' to trace how its group of factories has stepped up and shifted their production lines to personal protective equipment (Mezzadri and Ruwanpura 2020).

While verifying the truth of these inconsistent accounts during this trying global moment will require further research, this phase does seem to reveal both the painful structural inequities and the limits to voluntary ethical governance regimes within global capitalism. This global moment again magnifies the underlying strands of my argument on the need to account for structural inequities and unequal power dynamics, which resonate with those of others (Sunley 1999, 2011; Kim 2013; Smith 2015b; Zaki-Chakravarti 2019; Brydges and Hanlon 2020; Werner 2016, 2020). Proponents of ethical code regimes and industrial upgrading have championed the idea that social upgrading will follow industrial upgrading (Gereffi et al. 2005; Barrientos et al. 2011). In contrast, I posit the need for us to understand which local institutional conditions facilitate (or not) the working of industrial and social upgrading in tandem, since these outcomes are not foregone conclusions. Other scholars have rightly shown us the limits to ethical code governance, with narrow firm-centric renditions subject to critique by economic geographers and development scholars alike (Sunley 1999, 2008; Tewari 2008; Selwyn 2012a, 2013; de Neve 2014; Smith 2015a; Ruwanpura and Hughes 2016; Mezzadri 2017; Shakya 2018; Kumar 2019). Their scrutiny becomes pertinent when global cataclysms, such as CoVID-19, thrust most workers to the margins, where they struggle (*BBC News* 2020; World Bank 2020b). It is a moment, first, in which the poverty chain, the destitution of workers and the sweatshop regimes, the existence of all of which stains the apparel industry, are starkly exposed 'in all its disquieting aspects ... (as) our *industrial modernity*' (Mezzadri 2017: 188, emphasis mine; Hoskins 2014; Selwyn 2019; Brydges and Hanlon 2020). Secondly and crucially, Sri Lanka's somewhat different experience shows both that the state and that the historical institutional trajectory that determines economic relations matter; in other words, more broadly, the political economy matters (Waller 2006; Sunley 2008, 2011; Tewari 2008; Pearson 2013; Saxena 2014; Smith 2015a; Werner 2020). Critical rejoinders to dominant GVC and GPN literature have underscored the structuration of labour power (Kumar 2019; Selwyn 2019). Yet these critical mediations have shied away from interrogating the conditions that facilitate labour power, whereas I have made a modest attempt to argue for the need to privilege social institutions and the political fabric to understand how they too shape the (uneven) power of labour.

Unions and labour rights organizations are rightly pursuing employers within Sri Lanka rather than the physically and socially distant retailers. When viewed from the standpoint of labour, the capital–labour relationship is within the country, not in a dispersed globally disconnected world. The strength that contemporary labour unions draw upon in the country, however, was not conceded without historical struggles. The making of the working classes that Thompson (1966) alerted us to also took place in colonial Sri Lanka, with labour agitating for protective labour laws and a social welfare state (Jayawardena 1971, 2017; Supiot 2013). The state, in other words, was pivotal for balancing contending relations between capital and labour from the colonial period (Jayawardena 1971; Kearney 1971; Wood 1981; Herod 2003; Supiot 2013; Srivastava 2018; Ahuja 2019). And it has remained vital through the advent of open-market policies, chronicling yet again that market economies require the active involvement of the state (Standing 1997; Waller 2006; Smith 2015a; Werner 2020). For Sri Lankan labourers, the boon is that their agency during colonial times facilitated the foundational basis for universal civic rights, education and awareness – along with labour protection. The legislative frameworks and socio-development workers find now also come from the framing of their labour predecessors, signalling how they had a role in shaping their spatial environment. So, as workers continue to negotiate, rework and politicize the constraints they find today (Featherstone and Griffin 2016; Nowak 2016b; Dutta 2019), I want to accentuate that, although the labour force does not choose its conditions, following Marx's reflections, it does, however, continually play a role in creating them (Wood 1981; Herod 2001, 2003). Within an uneven global development landscape, the position of Sri Lankan labour then underlines how an educated labour force is likely to be better able to ensure that its voice is heard. When labour regulation exists, facilitating a labour spatial fix, employers are unable to abdicate their legal and political economic responsibilities entirely. Similarly, employers appeal to the Sri Lankan state rather than to faraway retailers.

It is labour's voice, buttressed by education and labour legislation, that matters in upholding the governance regimes for global ethical codes within the Sri Lankan apparel sector. Yet, despite a relatively good record, the uneven application reflects how structural hierarchies, ethnic politics, material inequities and their intersections also shape ethical regimes. Or, as Werner notes, the 'historically patterned and contingent geographies of uneven development' cannot be deflected (Werner 2016: 186; see also Hall 1980; Wood 1981). I also contend that we need to recognize that these configurations may differ within regions even in a country as small as Sri Lanka. Where war has been a marker of the country's polity, then that matters when it comes to ethical code regime practices, and a contested political terrain influences how labour experiences and expresses its agency in various factory sites in the same country. A broad blanket of global ethical governance can easily displace a fine-grained approach because of its preoccupation with cosmetic and broad brushstrokes. This emphasis on the global has value, but only so much. To actually have efficacy, global governance regimes have to heed local realities. Where they have purchase, it is mainly because local legislative frameworks, social welfare institutions and labour agency within Sri Lanka facilitate it. Where the uneven application is more pronounced, it is because the political terrain inside the country has also shaped governance outcomes at factory sites.

Scandal-Free Sri Lankan Apparel Firms?

I have established how the Sri Lankan apparel sector cultivated a desirable place in the global imaginary as an ethical sourcing destination. Not only does *Made in Sri Lanka* assure the buyer of high-quality production underpinned by reliability and punctuality, but it also usually avoids the stigma associated with exploitative labour. These achievements are in no small part, because management made a smart decision to take the high road and shift towards high-value-added apparel production. It would be difficult to deny the foresight these early capitalists had in forging a different manufacturing strategy. Also, they, unlike early foreign investors in garments, had a strategic vision of avoiding mass-scale production. This strategy was devised by local capitalists at an early stage of their investment in the apparel sector, with little or no prior experience.[1] They saw value in embedding their capital investment in the assets found within Sri Lanka, including a highly educated labour force. They were in it for the long haul. This was an admirable embryonic vision, since MAS, Brandix and HG have not only expanded in Sri Lanka but have gone global with their investments in the apparel sector.

This capital accumulation and expansion are unsurprising, since producing garments for the global market is a profitable business (Miller 2014; Kumar 2019; Selwyn 2019). However, the feasibility of having an ethical production profile is facilitated by there being an educated labour force, coupled with relatively strong labour legislation and social development within Sri Lanka.[2] It is a position that has helped the sector not just to expand globally, but also to take transformative steps towards becoming a regional hub and a design centre for apparels.

These ethical credentials, however, were possible because the Sri Lankan apparel sector did not do it alone. These landmarks were achieved with more than a little help from prevailing labour legislation, a historically strong social welfare fabric and collective labour struggles at various pivotal moments. Together, these building blocks offered the necessary foundation for the sector to succeed, although they are rarely acknowledged as such. Consequently, previous labour accomplishments were made vulnerable when pension pots were threatened with restructuring or unfavourable labour law reforms were attempted. These moments suggest that capital might be complicit in unwittingly kicking away the very ladder that helped it rise.

Historically, as Chang (2014) revealed, development in the West and the NICs required capital to work with the state and labour. State intervention and support provided the platform from which capitalists could invest. Another of Chang's conclusions is that the state was active in balancing competing interests between capital and labour, a path today often denied under the aegis of neoliberal policies (Harvey 2005; Selwyn 2012b; Supiot 2013; Nowak 2016a; Kumar 2019; Werner 2020). Nowadays, the state instead acts in consort with capital at the expense of labour (Wood 1981; Harvey 2005). The voice of labour, however, never goes away. While its capacity to respond may be under constant threat, researchers have shown that labour agency continues to shape the evolution of capitalism (Herod 2003; Pearson et al. 2010; Featherstone and Griffin 2016; Neethi 2016; Nowak 2016b). The uneven practices on the shop floor in relation to the ethical sourcing of Sri Lankan apparels are directly connected to the stability (or otherwise) of various national laws and universal social welfare provisions.

How both ethical codes and labour laws were altered by the political terrain was covered in my penultimate chapter. While the post-war regions may have been treated as a wasteland with what was perceived to be a steady stream of workers (Sanyal 2007), their experiences of war and trauma were unlikely to be erased through job creation alone (Kadirgamar 2013; Satkunanathan 2016; Lingam 2019). I have illustrated how labour does not leave its social, political and economic insecurities at the factory gates; neither does management or capital. The factory owners too do not cast aside the dominant ethno-nationalist character of Sri Lanka's polity. These contrasting realms jar against each other and influence ethical governance regimes and their practices on the shop floor. The absence of receptivity to the nuances of the ethical code on forced labour, for instance, was instructive. Military involvement was considered inescapable in expanding to the post-war areas of the country. Yet the effect of the military's connection to war-weary and traumatized communities was rarely reflected upon by either management or capital. These Colombo-centric actors, used to the epicentre of majoritarian politics, seldom pondered about the unholy alliances between capital and the military, irrespective of whether the effects were direct or indirect. A militarized state and society, which de Mel (2007) and Kadirgamar (2013) have written about, were also starting to be mirrored in militarized capital. Despite all three leading brand capitalists in the apparel sector coming from the panoply of Sri Lanka's rich and complex ethnic diversity, the militarization of capital is a potent symbol of the degree to which militarized relations have been normalized.

This naturalization of ethno-nationalism and militarized relations inhibits the apparel sector from recognizing that its ethical record increasingly rests on fragile ground. Complaints from Sri Lankan-Tamil workers that wages are inadequate or meagre get linked to labour's identity as a minority community rather than there being an awareness that living wages are absent in the entire sector and across the country. Sensitivities around discrimination are heightened by prejudiced practices. Isolating workers on the basis of ethnicity and supervisors and production floor managers often not being from the same community and/or not speaking Tamil are illustrations of this. Not only do these omissions trample on the codes on discrimination and on harsh or inhumane treatment, to name but two, but the lack of recognition of these grievances as legitimate also precludes the connection of the dots to potential political and social unrest.

I have also shown that practices around ethical regimes on the factory floor are not only unbalanced, with the provisions of some codes being adhered to more than others, but also subject to temporal changes. These shifts suggest that resting on its laurels is a luxury that the industry can ill afford. It is a gap that labour rights organizations and unions can deploy to impress on the industry that adhering to the relevant labour conditions requires continuous effort. These disparities and alterations give weight to the contention that social, cultural and political conditions all shape, and matter to, the effectiveness of ethical governance regimes. A global architecture has meaning and purchase only insofar as the local conditions facilitate these through a confluence of legislative mechanisms, social development levels, political terrain and the cultural dynamics native to the area. The social hierarchies observed on the factory floor are an interplay between cultural idioms, localized understandings, ethnic politics and universal governance norms. How labourers experience, negotiate and contest ethical codes is then not ordained by the global nature of these regimes or competitive global dynamics alone (Tewari 2008; Selwyn 2012a; Kumar 2019). I want to make the case that these possibilities also reflect the institutionalized conditions – from labour legislation and education to political (in)stabilities.

Local assertions of labour agency are important in holding capital accountable in various disparate places (Gidwani and Chari 2004; Pearson et al. 2010; Carswell and de Neve 2013; de Neve 2014; Neethi 2016; Nowak 2016b; Werner 2016). Yet, I have argued, we also need to consider the conditions that facilitate labour agency, as the power, strength and possible levels of contestation at which capitalism is challenged will vary accordingly. Relatedly, whether labour agency is exerted at the national, regional or local level will also have differentiated effects on shaping the geographies of capitalism. Sri Lankan labourers' attempts to shape the picture at the national level – to contest pension reform or labour policy amendments, for instance – are largely successful because their access to universal education has provided a platform from which to agitate or to thwart efforts to diminish their increasingly fragile rights further. As spatial politics are always open, contingent and continual, any attempt at eroding the rights of Sri Lankans, whether in the realm of protective labour legislation or in related spheres, such as universal higher education, is likely to negatively affect labour and how capitalist development evolves. To put it differently, to assume that the planned labour reform, for instance, will not impinge negatively on the ethical code regimes might turn out to be optimistic. Global governance architecture has a palpable and meaningful effect on the Sri Lankan apparel sector only because the local edifice is equally solid – not to acknowledge this is to jeopardize not just labour rights, but also the very platform that industrial capital draws upon. Otherwise, as with our neighbouring countries, sweatshop regimes, factory fires, collapses and exploitative labour constitute an easy slippery slope that Sri Lankan apparel firms may slide down. In completing writing this book, the most recent fallout from the possible culpability of Brandix over its role in the community spread of CoVID-19 in October 2020 more than hints at the unevenness of pressures inherent within global regimes (JAAF 2020; Kumarasinghe and Fernandopulle 2020; *Daily Mirror* Sri Lanka 2020b, 2020c; Hoskins et al. 2021). The association between flying workers in from its factory at Visakhapatnam, India, and the surge of over a thousand CoVID-19 cases amongst the workers in one of its branch factories in Sri Lanka represents not only a code violation around health and safety, but also the eventual community transmission of the virus in the country.[3] Ethical codes and global governance on their own have shown time and again, including in Bangladesh, India and Pakistan, that they are the capitalist emperor's new clothes.

Ethical Codes Exposed?

To understand how global governance regimes for ethical codes and voluntary corporate codes are standard bearers for labour standards and conditions, it is undoubtedly important to understand partnerships between buyers and suppliers. Sri Lankan suppliers hold a favourable place in this regard. De Neve (2009: 71) notes that the politics of compliance leads to the 'consolidation of the power of standard-setting actors by facilitating the devolution of risks, uncertainty and responsibility to the weaker "partners" in the chain'. How these collaborations play out between buyers and suppliers is shaped by an uneven global terrain that continuously confounds suppliers (Nadvi 2008; Selwyn 2012b; Lund-Thomsen 2013; Ruwanpura and Wrigley 2011; Perry et al. 2014; Kumar 2019). Yet, as McIntyre (2008: 163) notes, 'capital class interest can capture the language of human and worker rights', and evade needed scrutiny at various levels, including the national, regional and local (see also Supiot 2003). Economic geographers too have emphasized the need to give way to local expressions, permutations and variations of economic relations and networks (Smith et al. 2002; Weller 2007; Sunley 2008; Sunley and Pinch 2014; Strauss 2020; Werner 2020). Their work and mine directly challenge the upgrading and governance literature on GVCs, which notes that 'variables internal … influence the shape of governance of global values chains … regardless of the institutional context within which they are situated' (Gereffi et al. 2005: 99; see also Barrientos et al. 2011). With this broader optic, I have argued that upholding governance requires an understanding of how labour negotiates ethical governance initiatives, which in turn requires attentiveness to the state–capital–labour triad.

Often, the scholarship that critically scrutinizes the social upgrading and ethical governance regimes rightly calls attention to capital and labour relations. Selwyn (2012b: 175), for instance, argues that ministrations to time, space and place be given, because 'all of these processes are intrinsically bound up with the relations between capital and labour'. It is important to appreciate this dialectical relationship to get a sense of the global and local processes in the global production system, in which the promise of development via apparel production can be shown to be no more than a myth (Plankey-Videla 2012; Kim 2013; Werner 2016; Mezzadri 2017; Shakya 2018; Kumar 2019). Capital and labour, however, do not only intercede directly with each other. While they do of course do this, they also interact via the state, sometimes as a triumvirate and at other times bilaterally. Even where capital and labour directly interact with each other, which is what ethical code regimes attempt to bring about, this relationship hides the extent to which the state continues to arbitrate in manifold ways. Global governance regimes may have been introduced because some countries were seen as too weak to enforce their own labour laws, but multi-stakeholder initiatives on their own are also a weak and even ineffective mechanism (McIntyre 2008; Hensmen 2011; Tighe 2016). Tighe (2016), for instance, has shown how intra- and inter-firm dynamics within Bangladesh also shape global governance initiatives in a way that results in their uneven application. According to her, the weaker position of labour within the country may also offer a partial reason for this disparity.

I would, thus, argue that the extent to which corporate and ethical codes bolster, replace or complement national labour laws is shaped not simply by the extent to which these initiatives have room for 'greater worker involvement' (McIntyre 2008: 158), but also by how labour is positioned within the legislative terrain vis-à-vis the state and capital (see also Werner 2020). A political economy of labour achieved through past hardship and struggle tenuously holds on, with much unacknowledged reward for the *factory* and the *nation*. It means that both contemporary labour and capital gain within an institutional context, created in no small part by the will of collective labour, organized unions and solidarity movements alike. This resonance means that the purchase of ethical codes, from the viewpoint of labour, is shaped by the institutional fabric at the very least. However, social and cultural features within the country also matter, as they do elsewhere, and, as Shakya (2018: 126) notes, the way 'the garment industry is situated ... is neither economic nor purely cultural but rather an amalgamation and more' (see also de Neve 2005, 2008; Carswell and de Neve 2014; Miller 2014).

In Sri Lanka, the *more* also manifests in the form of turbulent sociopolitical conditions and unsettled political legacies and militarization associated with a three-decade ethnic war and conflict. Political and social insecurities intersect with material conditions such that Tamil workers' experiences are tinged with the aftermath of trauma and violence. Global governance regimes and ethicality, predictably, then take on entirely different connotations in post-war regions of the country, at least from a labour standpoint. The anxieties that workers gave voice to regarding the volatilities they face and continue to navigate are fecund ground for apparel capital to more actively advocate political resolutions to address Sri Lanka's underlying fractures. The risk, otherwise, is that parallels from the past are ignored; as other scholars have already pointed out, visible symbols of prosperity, poverty and inequality were also attributes that facilitated the ethnic pogrom of 1983 (Gunasinghe 1996; Dunham and Jayasuriya 2000). The likelihood of another political rupture along ethnic lines should never be discounted in Sri Lanka. Translating frustrations around income inequality into identity politics is already fertile ground within the country, where a festering wound has not been addressed with the relevant political perspicacity.

Ethical codes apart then, the *respect, new futures* and *economic freedom* that the apparel sector was going to provide are yet to be a tangible reality, disappointing not just Tamil workers but all workers, irrespective of ethnicity. These fissures and fault lines were never more apparent in the past decade than during the disaster unfolding with CoVID-19. The current situation has made it painfully apparent that global governance regimes alone are unlikely to make a dent in the conditions of labouring lives or hold local employers accountable. In fact, their inability to have much effect is apparent in the rapidity with which workers in the sector were rendered unemployed or unwaged in nearby countries. In Sri Lanka, it was not the global governance regimes that were invoked; rather, it was the legal edifice that provided unions with the ability to advocate for apparel sector labourers. Their intervention prevented capital from abdicating from its responsibilities, and in turn employers turned to the state to assist with wage payments for workers. Ethical codes at a globally catalytic time seem hollow, irrelevant even. This is not just because there has been no petitioning by Sri Lankan labour unions and labourers to retailers located elsewhere, but also because, even when this was the case, as in Bangladesh, it exposes the global and national fault lines that ethical codes are incapable of addressing.

Codes of reality, which are grounded in local sociopolitical dynamics, gender relations, ethnic instabilities and cultural hierarchies, illustrate how the political, economic and cultural hegemony of voluntary codes continues to short-change workers. Hence, global governance regimes are no replacement for recognizing and acknowledging the pivotal role of labour agency, both in the everyday in factory settings and in moments of collective mobilization. This in turn requires protective labour legislation.

Notes

1. As I established in *Chapter Four*, of the three big players, two were entirely new to the business of clothing and garments.
2. How else to explain Cross's (2014) finding from south India (Visakhapatnam) that BRANDIX's management was implicated in sexual violence and

coercion against women workers?* When ethical producers go global, they ought otherwise to carry the same standards across global boundaries, if Gereffi et al. (2005)'s reasoning is to hold. In a neighbouring country with a weaker labour constituency, management practices change, although the global governance architecture is the same. (*Although, as mentioned in footnote 5 in *Chapter Seven*, at senior management level, leading Sri Lankan apparel firms are not devoid of a culture of sexism and sexual harassment [de Mel 2016; de Silva 2018]).

3. Until this outbreak in early October 2020, the country and its apparel sector's handling of the CoVID-19 virus was largely commendable, insofar as community spread was limited to clusters. Initial indications, as per the Public Health Inspectors Union, are that the relevant protocols around quarantine (14 days) followed by home-isolation (another 14 days) were not followed in a final charter flight operated for/by Brandix, which carried 48 workers on 22 September 2020 (*Daily Mirror* Sri Lanka 2020c).

Appendix

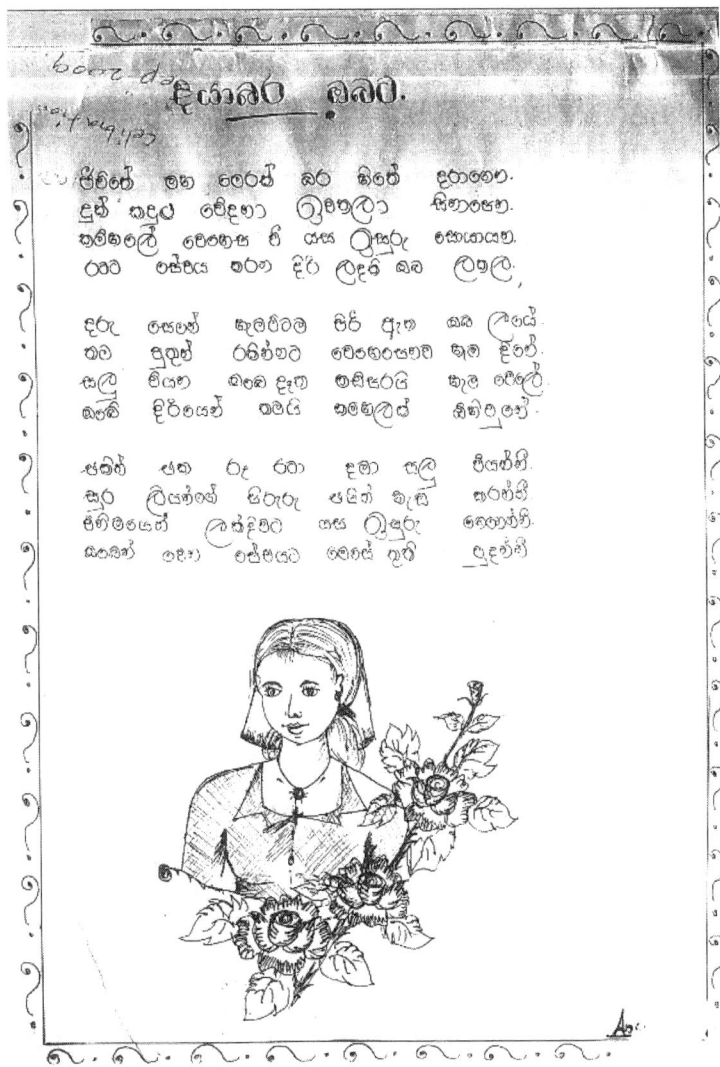

Image A.1 Poem by Anu in Sinhala

Table A.1 Sri Lankan apparel exports to key countries/regions (2009–2017). All monetary values in millions of USD.

Country/Region	2009	2010	2011	2012	2013	2014	2015	2016	2017
USA	1,325.423 (40.59%)	1,403.595 (40.20%)	1,628.362 (38.66%)	1,570.185 (39.20%)	1,886.692 (41.77%)	2,043.461 (41.54%)	2,159.441 (45.25%)	2,154.537 (44.62%)	2,196.581 (44.04%)
United Kingdom	854.433 (26.16%)	847.931 (24.28%)	934.379 (22.18%)	895.689 (22.36%)	911.687 (20.18%)	915.267 (18.60%)	824.457 (17.27%)	834.900 (17.29%)	811.518 (16.27%)
Italy	356.126 (10.90%)	368.643 (10.55%)	490.383 (11.64%)	420.354 (10.49%)	41.691 (9.23%)	50.832 (10.33%)	362.684 (7.60%)	355.599 (7.36%)	437.184 (8.76%)
Australia	12.358 (0.38%)	19.057 (0.54%)	30.400 (0.72%)	35.605 (0.88%)	38.755 (0.85%)	40.966 (0.83%)	50.971 (1.06%)	58.519 (1.21%)	71.939 (1.44%)
China	5.140 (0.15%)	5.624 (0.16%)	10.908 (0.25%)	17.398 (0.43%)	24.724 (0.54%)	37.038 (0.75%)	54.813 (1.14%)	66.147 (1.37%)	61.239 (1.22%)
India	14.805 (0.45%)	24.398 (0.69%)	37.786 (0.89%)	51.394 (1.28%)	43.859 (0.97%)	46.990 (0.95%)	41.354 (0.86%)	45.020 (0.93%)	54.070 (1.08%)
Japan	16.505 (0.50%)	24.224 (0.69%)	28.883 (0.68%)	33.232 (0.82%)	43.573 (0.96%)	53.336 (1.08%)	44.256 (0.92%)	47.732 (0.98%)	46.218 (0.92%)
Brazil	7.907 (0.24%)	13.807 (0.39%)	19.778 (0.46%)	19.762 (0.49%)	46.061 (1.01%)	29.769 (0.60%)	27.881 (0.58%)	31.285 (0.64%)	34.536 (0.69%)
Mexico	11.199 (0.34%)	11.639 (0.33%)	17.250 (0.40%)	16.446 (0.41%)	22.210 (0.49%)	25.558 (0.51%)	25.388 (0.53%)	30.844 (0.63%)	33.632 (0.67%)
North America	1,381.957 (42.32%)	1,473.860 (42.21%)	1,722.177 (40.89%)	1,669.250 (41.67%)	1,994.335 (44.15%)	2,154.101 (43.79%)	2,276.624 (47.71%)	2,288.076 (47.39%)	2,343.845 (46.98%)
European Union	836.880 (25.62%)	905.043 (25.92%)	1,180.950 (28.04%)	1,044.734 (26.08%)	1,142.323 (25.29%)	1,343.074 (27.30%)	1,156.139 (24.23%)	1,086.880 (24.14%)	1,270.188 (25.45%)

Source: UN Comtrade (2020). Calculations made using STIC Rev. 3 Code 84 (Articles of Apparel and Clothing Accessories).

Note: Figure in brackets represents the percentage of total Sri Lankan apparel exports for the given year. For example, in 2017, Sri Lankan apparel exports to the USA accounted for 44.04 per cent of all Sri Lankan apparel exports.

Table A.2 Employment and earnings (value of output) in Sri Lanka's five largest sectors (2008–2017)

EMPLOYMENT

Sector	2008	2009	2010	2011	2012	2013	2014	2015	2016	2017
Wearing Apparel	340,103	296,540	271,701	272,833	266,405	n/a	457,081	492,911	673,922	719,178
Manufacturing of Food and Beverage Products	106,950	95,875	94,142	99,002	114,746	n/a	196,511	262,168	315,693	313,297
Manufacturing of Textiles	43,779	36,432	35,419	38,547	40,616	n/a	25,013	29,911	36,248	41,485
Manufacturing of Rubber and Plastic Products	53,701	47,488	44,724	46,054	52,227	n/a	36,297	37,313	37,379	35,234
Chemical and Chemical Products	12,254	11,260	10,679	11,798	12,002	n/a	38,003	42,325	31,317	33,099

EARNINGS (Rs. Bn.)

Sector	2008	2009	2010	2011	2012	2013	2014	2015	2016	2017
Wearing Apparel	328.10	339.30	341.60	361.93	364.60	n/a	933.57	980.39	1042.99	1107.88
Manufacturing of Food and Beverage Products	332.64	378.34	384.81	532.49	522.54	n/a	1149.30	1235.30	1327.94	1407.87
Manufacturing of Textiles	78.96	73.66	74.72	82.58	91.41	n/a	110.31	104.67	130.81	153.70
Manufacturing of Rubber and Plastic Products	121.68	93.55	118.26	125.45	150.68	n/a	148.48	156.70	159.32	180.60
Chemical and Chemical Products	61.51	67.10	79.64	66.41	68.67	n/a	165.36	173.13	165.77	163.37

Source: Annual Survey of Industry Reports (2009–2018), http://www.statistics.gov.lk/Industry/StaticalInformation/AnnualSurveys.

Note: In the source, employment in the above sectors is sorted by establishments with more than 5 or 25 employees. For the data here, the employment figures are for establishments with more than 25 employees. The year 2013 has been omitted due to lack of data.

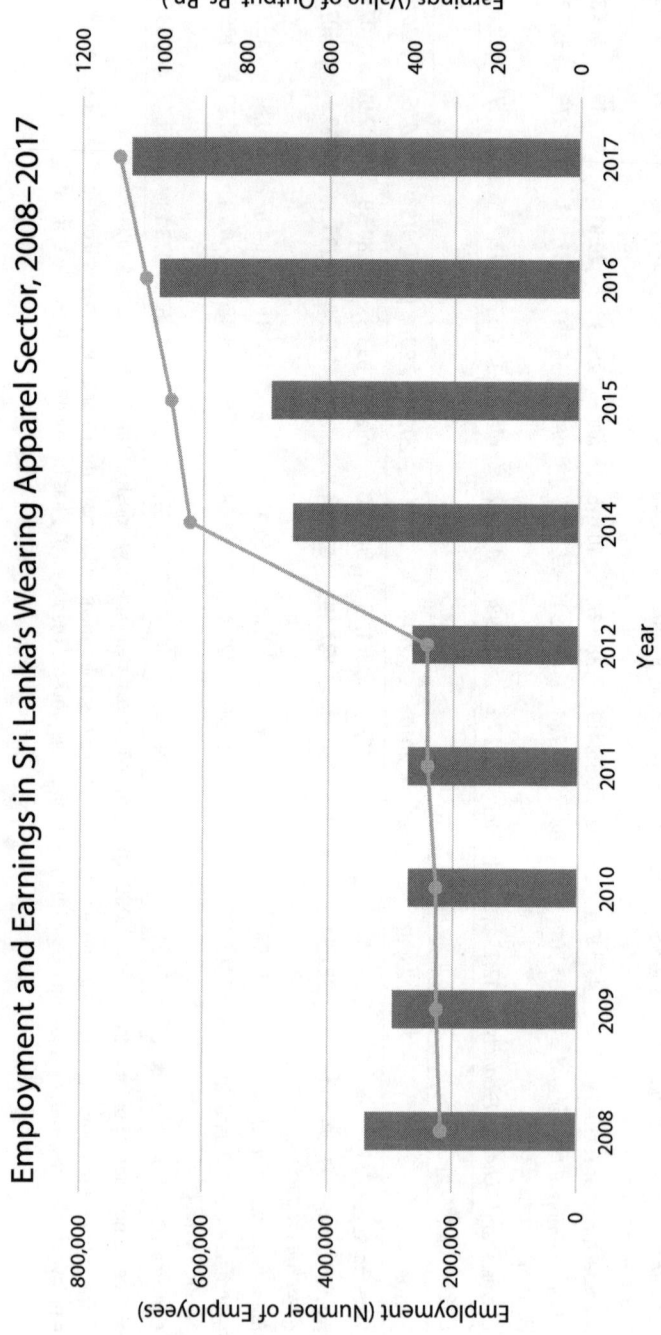

Figure A.1 Employment and earnings (gross export) in Sri Lanka's apparel sector (2008–2017)

Source. Annual Survey of Industry Reports (2009–2018), http://www.statistics.gov.lk/Industry/StaticalInformation/AnnualSurveys.

Note. Here, the bars correspond with employment figures on the **left** *y*-axis, whereas the line corresponds with earnings figures on the **right** *y*-axis. The year 2013 has been omitted due to lack of data.

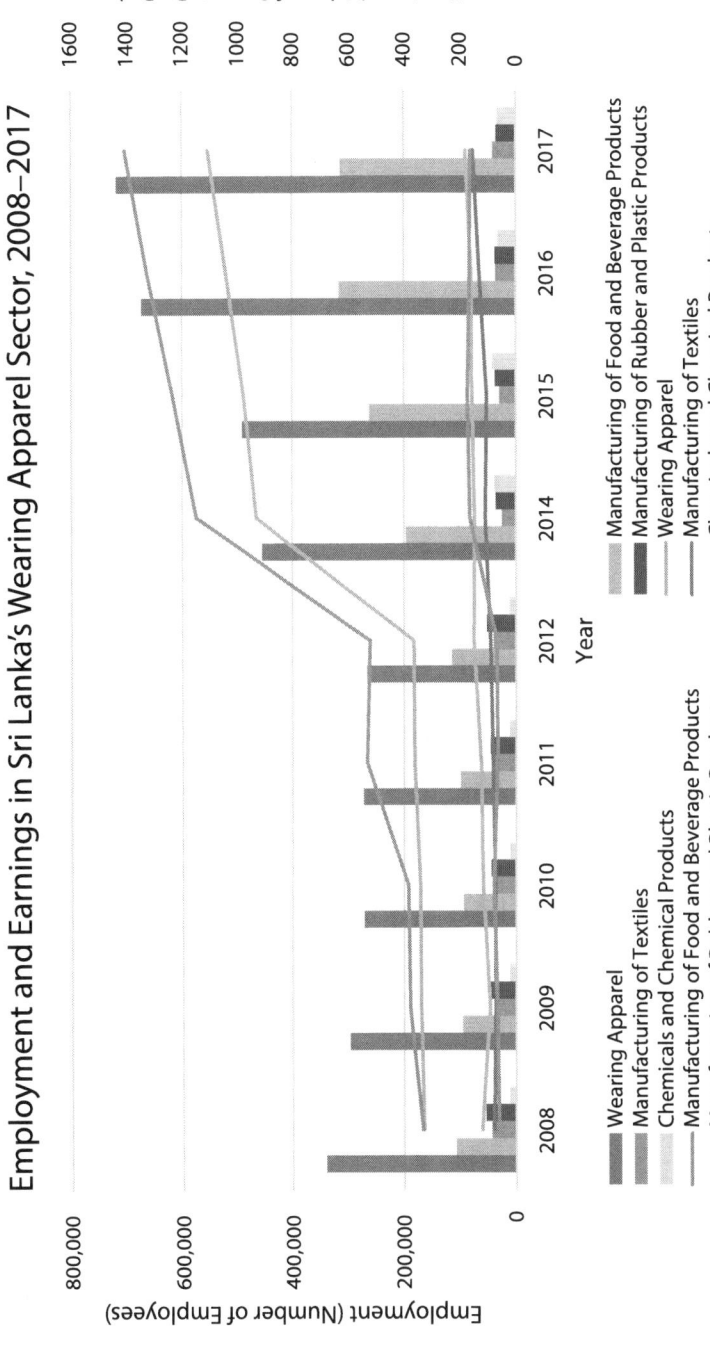

Figure A.2 Employment and earnings (gross export) in Sri Lanka's five largest sectors (2008–2017)

Source: Annual Survey of Industry Reports (2009–2018), http://www.statistics.gov.lk/Industry/StaticalInformation/AnnualSurveys.

Note: Here, the bars correspond with employment figures on the **left** y-axis, whereas the lines correspond with earnings figures on the **right** y-axis. Additionally, sectors are colour-coded. For example, the green bar and the green line both correspond with the Wearing Apparel sector. The year 2013 has been omitted due to lack of data.

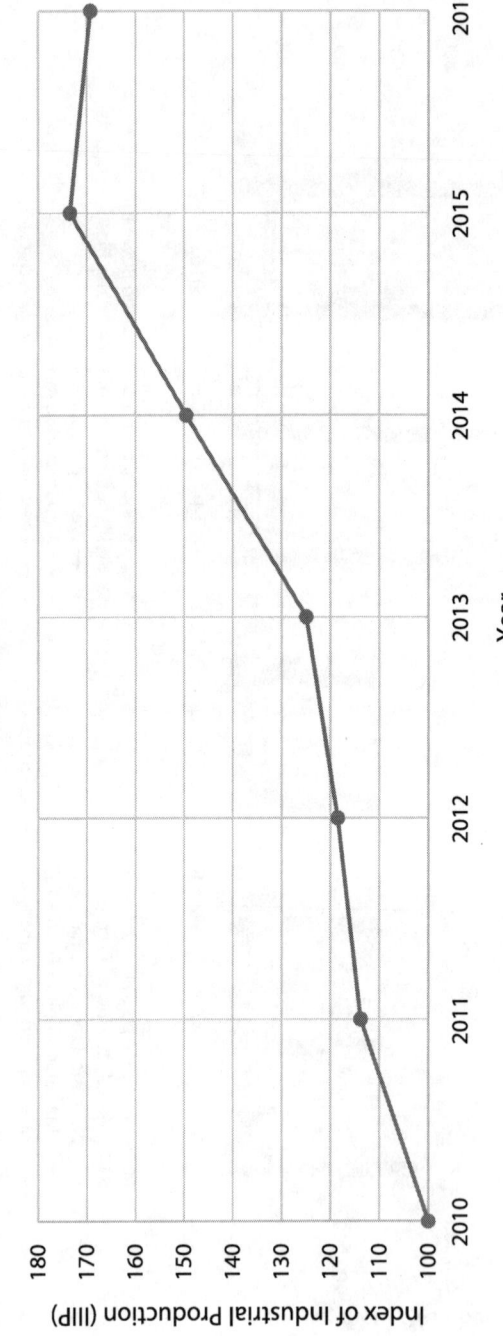

Figure A.3 Productivity of Sri Lanka's apparel sector using the Index of Industrial Production (IIP) (2010–2016)

Source: Central Bank of Sri Lanka Annual Reports, Statistical Appendix (2011–2017).

Note: The IIP shows the change in production volume of a particular good over a given period of time. In this case, the graph here displays the growth in volume output in Sri Lanka's apparel sector from 2010 to 2016, despite steady, if not declining employment in the sector over the same period.

References

Abeysekera, Asha. 2020. 'Silence and Invisibility: The Gender Dimensions of Women's Activism in Higher Education in Asia'. In *Handbook of Gender in Asia*, edited by Shirlena Huang and Kanchana N. Ruwanpura. Cheltenham, UK: Edward Elgar, 408–425.

Ahuja, Ravi. 2019. 'A Beveridge Plan for India? Social Insurance and the Making of the Formal Sector'. *International Review of Social History* 64 (2): 207–248.

Amerasinghe, Franklyn. 2020. 'Employers and Their Ability to Pay Post-COVID 19'. *Daily Mirror-Financial Times*, 17 April 2020. http://ft.lk/columns/Employers-and-their-ability-to-pay-post-COVID-19/4-698910. Accessed 19 April 2020.

Arslan, Ayşe. 2019. *Industrial Workers in the Garment Industry, Houseworkers in the Family: Women's Productive and Reproductive Labour in Izmir, Turkey*. PhD dissertation, SOAS, University of London.

Asia Floor Wage. 2013. 'General Wage Situation of Apparel Industry Workers in Sri Lanka'. http://asia.floorwage.org/wp-content/uploads/2019/10/Sri-Lanka-Wage-Report-2013.pdf. Accessed 19 November 2019.

———. 2014. 'Living Wage in Asia'. http://asia.floorwage.org/wp-content/uploads/2019/10/LW-in-Asia-AFWA-CCC.pdf. Accessed 19 November 2019.

———. 2019. 'Timeline of Revision: Asia Floor Wage 2017'. https://asia.floorwage.org/our-work/#tab-id-3. Accessed 4 November 2019.

———. 2020a. 'The Emperor Has No Clothes: Garment Supply Chains in the Time of Pandemic'. *Asia Floor Wage: Issue 1*. https://asia.floorwage.org/wp-content/uploads/2020/04/The-Emperor-Has-No-Clothes-Final1.pdf. Accessed 2 May 2020.

———. 2020b. 'The Emperor Has No Clothes: Garment Supply Chains in the Time of Pandemic'. *Asia Floor Wage: Issue II*. https://asia.floorwage.org/wp-content/uploads/2020/05/The-Emperor-Has-No-Clothes-Issue-II-May.pdf. Accessed 10 June 2020.

Athukorala, Prema-Chandra. 2012. 'Sri Lanka's Trade Policy: Reverting to Dirigisme?' *The World Economy* 35 (12): 1662–1686.

————. 2018. 'Industrial Upgrading in the Apparel Value Chain: The Sri Lanka Experience'. In *Development with Global Value Chains: Upgrading and Innovation in Asia,* edited by Dev Nathan, Meenu Tewari and Sandeep Sarkar. Cambridge: Cambridge University Press, 193–228.

————. 2019. 'Export Expansion in a Changing Global Order: Challenging Times for Post-Conflict Sri Lanka'. In *Managing Domestic and International Challenges and Opportunities in Post-Conflict Development,* edited by Dushni Weerakoon and Sisira Jayasuriya. Singapore: Springer, 151–169.

Athukorala, Prema-Chandra and Ravi Ekanayake. 2014. 'Repositioning in the Global Apparel Value Chain in the Post-MFA Era: Strategic Issues and Evidence from Sri Lanka'. Trade and development working paper 2014–12.

————. 2018. 'Repositioning in the Global Apparel Value Chain in the Post-MFA Era: Strategic Issues and Evidence from Sri Lanka'. *Development Policy Review* 36 (S1): 247–269.

Bair, Jennifer. 2010. 'On Difference and Capital: Gender and the Globalization of Production'. *SIGNS: Journal of Women in Culture and Society* 36 (1): 203–226.

Bair, Jennifer and Marion Werner. 2011. 'Commodity Chains and the Uneven Geographies of Global Capitalism: A Disarticulations Perspective'. *Environment and Planning A: Economy and Space* 43 (5): 988–997.

Barrientos, Stephanie. 2002. 'Mapping Codes through the Value Chain: From Researcher to Detective'. In *Corporate Responsibility and Labour Rights – Codes of Conduct in the Global Economy,* edited by Rhys Jenkins, Ruth Pearson and Gill Seyfang. Oxford, Oxon: Earthscan, 61–78.

Barrientos, Stephanie and Sally Smith. 2007. 'Do Workers Benefit from Ethical Trade? Assessing Codes of Labour Practice in Global Production Systems'. *Third World Quarterly* 28 (4): 713–729.

Barrientos, Stephanie, Gary Gereffi and Ariana Rossi. 2011. 'Economic and Social Upgrading in Global Production Networks: A New Paradigm for a Changing World'. *International Labour Review* 150 (3–4): 319–340.

BBC News. 2019. 'Sri Lanka Reels from Deadly Attacks'. 20 April. https://bbc.com/news/live/world-asia-48002165. Accessed 15 March 2020.

————. 2020. 'World Bank Warns South Asia's Economic Growth to Slump'. 13 April. https://bbc.com/news/business-52267117. Accessed 13 April 2020.

Bedford, Kate and Shirin M. Rai. 2010. 'Feminists Theorize International Political Economy'. *SIGNS: Journal of Women in Culture and Society* 36 (1): 1–18.

Biyanwila, Janaka S. 2011. *The Labour Movement in the Global South: Trade Unions in Sri Lanka*. London: Routledge.

Blowfield, Michael. 1999. 'Ethical Trade: A Review of Developments and Issues'. *Third World Quarterly* 20 (4): 753–770.

———. 2007. 'Reasons to Be Cheerful? What We Know about CSR's Impact'. *Third World Quarterly* 28 (4): 683–695.

Braverman, Harry. 1974. *Labour and Monopoly Capital: The Degradation of Work in the Twentieth Century*. New York: Monthly Review.

Brecht, Bertlot. 1937. 'Difficulty of Governing'. http://johnshaplin.blogspot.com/2011/12/poems-by-bertolt-brecht.html. Accessed on 15 October 2020.

Brooks, Ethel C. 2007. *Unravelling the Garment Industry: Transnational Organizing and Women's Work*. Minneapolis, MN: University of Minnesota Press.

Brown, Benjamin, Loritta Chan and Kanchana N. Ruwanpura. 2018. 'Handicapped Sovereignty: Escalating Costs of Sri Lanka's Post-War Development Vision'. *Open Democracy*, 20 October. https://open democracy.net/en/handicapped-sovereignty-escalating-costs-of-sri-lan/.

Brydges, Taylor and Mary Hanlon. 2020. 'Garment Worker Rights and Fashion Industry Response to CoVID-19'. *Dialogues in Human Geography* 10 (2): 195–198.

Burawoy, Michael. 1982. *Manufacturing Consent: Changes in the Labour Process under Monopoly Capitalism*. Chicago, IL: University of Chicago Press.

———. 1985. *The Politics of Production: Factory Regimes under Capitalism and Socialism*. London: Verso Books.

Candland, Christopher. 2002. 'The Political Element in Economic Reform: Labour Institutions and Privatization Patterns in South Asia'. In *Privatization and Labour: Responses and Consequences in Global Perspective*, edited by Masha P. Posusney and Linda J. Cook. Cheltenham, Gloucestershire: Edward Elgar, 65–82.

Carswell, Grace. 2013. 'Dalits and Local Labour Markets in Rural India: Experiences from the Tiruppur Textile Region in Tamil Nadu'. *Transactions of the Institute of British Geographers* 38 (2): 325–338.

Carswell, Grace and Geert de Neve. 2013. 'Labouring for Global Markets: Conceptualizing Labour Agency in Global Production Networks'. *Geoforum* 44 (January): 62–70.

———. 2014. 'T-Shirts and Tumblers: Caste, Dependency and Work under Neo-Liberalisation in South India'. *Contributions to Indian Sociology* 48 (1): 103–131.

Central Bank of Sri Lanka. 2006–2018. *Annual Reports and Economic and Social Statistics Reports*. Colombo: Central Bank.

Chandrasekera-Edirimuni, Duruthu. 2012. 'Patchy Record at Garment Factories on Allowing Worker Unions – Apparel Sector Study'. *Sunday Times*, 8 April. https://pressreader.com/sri-lanka/sunday-times-srilanka/20120408/282492885673438. Accessed 16 October 2020.

Chang, Ha-Joon. 2003. *Globalization, Development and the Roles of the State*. London: Zed Books.

———. 2014. *Economics: The User's Guide*. London: Penguin Books.

Chang, Ha-Joon and Antonio Andreoni. 2020. 'Industrial Policy in the 21st Century'. *Development and Change* 51 (2): 324–351.

Channel Four News. 2019. 'Sri Lanka PM's First UK Interview since Terror Attacks'. 25 April. https://youtube.com/watch?v=839fo6rzFws. Accessed 27 April 2019.

Coe, Neil M. and David Jordhus-Lier. 2011. 'Constrained Agency? Re-Evaluating the Geographies of Labour'. *Progress in Human Geography* 35 (2): 211–233.

Cross, Jamie. 2014. *Dream Zones: Anticipating Capitalism and Development in India*. London: Pluto Press.

Daily Mirror Sri Lanka. 2020a. 'Dinesh to Inform UNHRC of Decision to Withdraw from Resolution Today'. 26 February. http://dailymirror.lk/breaking_news/Dinesh-to-inform-UNHRC-of-decision-to-withdraw-from-Resolution-today/108-183769. Accessed 28 February 2020.

———. 2020b. 'Authorities Insist Brandix Returnees Didn't Break 14-Day Quarantine Rule'. 9 October. http://dailymirror.lk/breaking_news/Authorities-insist-Brandix-rIees-didnt-break-14-day-quarantine/108-197536. Accessed 9 October 2020.

———. 2020c. 'PHIs Did Not Supervise Brandix Repatriation Flights: PHI Union'. 10 October. http://dailymirror.lk/top_story/PHIs-did-not-supervise-Brandix-Repatriation-flights-PHI-Union/155-197594. Accessed 11 October 2020.

de Alwis, Malathi. 1999. 'Millennial Musings on Maternalism'. *Asian Women* 9 (12): 151–169.

———. 2002. 'Changing Role of Women in Sri Lankan Society'. *Social Research* 69 (3): 675–691.

de Mel, Amashi. 2016. 'Countering Sexual Harassment in the Workplace: Interview with Mihiri de Silva'. *Groundviews*, 25 September. https://groundviews.org/2016/09/25/countering-sexual-harassment-in-the-work-place-interview-with-mihiri-de-silva/. Accessed 7 November 2020.

de Mel, Neloufer. 2007. *Militarizing Sri Lanka: Popular Culture, Memory and Narrative in the Armed Conflict*. New Delhi: SAGE.

de Neve, Geert. 2001. 'Towards an Ethnography of the Workplace: Hierarchy, Authority and Sociability on the South Indian Textile Shop-Floor'. *South Asia Research* 21 (2): 133–160.

———. 2005. 'Weaving for IKEA in South India: Subcontracting, Labour Markets and Gender Relations in a Global Value Chain'. In *Globalizing India: Perspectives from Below*, edited by Jackie Assayag and Chris J. Fuld. London: Anthem Press, 89–115.

———. 2008. '"We Are All Sondukarar (Relatives)!" Kinship and Its Morality in Urban Industry of Tamil Nadu, South India'. *Modern Asian Studies* 42 (1): 211–246.

———. 2009. 'Power, Inequality and Corporate Social Responsibility: The Politics of Ethical Compliance in the South Indian Garment Industry'. *Economic and Political Weekly* 44 (22): 63–71.

———. 2014. 'Fordism, Flexible Specialization and CSR: How Indian Garment Workers Critique Neoliberal Labour Regimes'. *Ethnography* 15 (2): 184–207.

de Neve, Geert and Rebecca Prentice, eds. 2017. *Unmaking the Global Sweatshop*. Philadelphia, PA: University of Pennsylvania Press.

de Silva, Mihiri. 2018. 'Change Is Not Courage in a Boys Club'. *Groundviews*, 3 August. https://groundviews.org/2018/03/08/change-is-not-courage-in-a-boys-club/. Accessed 7 November 2020.

Derana, Ada. 2011. 'Employees Union Protest against the Private Sector Pension Bill'. *YouTube*. https://youtube.com/watch?v=dJNqaUHyPsI. Accessed 20 February 2020.

Dias, Keshala. 2017. 'Mother of Late Roshen Chanaka Seeks Access under Right to Information Act'. *News-First Sri Lanka*, 6 February. https://newsfirst.lk/2017/02/06/161313/. Accessed 4 March 2020.

Domosh, Mona and Joni Seager. 2001. *Putting Women in Place: Feminist Geographers Make Sense of the World*. New York: Guilford Press.

Dugan, Emily. 2012. 'Forced Labour Claims Dent Image of London 2012'. *The Independent*. https://independent.co.uk/sport/olympics/forced-labour-claims-dent-image-of-london-2012-7717615.html. Accessed 8 June 2020.

Dunham, David and Sisira Jayasuriya. 2000. 'Equity, Growth and Insurrection: Liberalization and the Welfare Debate in Contemporary Sri Lanka'. *Oxford Development Studies* 28 (1): 97–110.

Dunn, Elizabeth C. 2007. '*Escherichia coli*, Corporate Discipline and the Failure of the Sewer State'. *Space and Polity* 11 (1): 35–53.

Dutta, Madhumita. 2016. 'The Nokia SEZ Story: Economy of Disappearances'. *Economic and Political Weekly* 51 (51): 43–51.

———. 2019. 'Becoming Factory Workers: Understanding Women's Geographies of Work through Life Stories in Tamil Nadu, India'. *Gender, Place and Culture* 26 (6): 888–904.

Elias, Juanita. 2005. 'The Gendered Political Economy of Control and Resistance on the Shop Floor of the Multinational Firm: A Case Study of Malaysia'. *New Political Economy* 10 (2): 204–222.

Elson, Diane and Ruth Pearson. 1981. 'Nimble Fingers Make Cheap Workers: An Analysis of Women's Employment in Third World Export Manufacturing'. *Feminist Review* 7 (Spring): 87–107.

Enloe, Cynthia. 1989. *Bananas, Beaches and Bases: Making Feminist Sense of International Politics*. Berkeley, CA: University of California Press.

Featherstone, David and Paul Griffin. 2016. 'Spatial Relations, Histories from Below and the Makings of Agency: Reflections on *The Making of the English Working Class* at 50'. *Progress in Human Geography* 40 (3): 375–393.

Fernando, P., G. Hemakumara, P. Hewage and G. Sampath. 2019. 'Implementing the Concept of Green Space: The Case of Hidaramani Mihila CKT Apparel Factory in Agalawatte, Sri Lanka'. In *Green Behavior and Corporate Social Responsibility in Asia*, edited by Farzana Quoquab and Jihad Mohammad. Bingley, United Kingdom: Emerald Publishing, 65–71.

Freidberg, Susanne. 2004. 'The Ethical Complex of Corporate Food Power'. *Environment and Planning D: Society and Space* 22 (4): 513–531.

FTZU-CSWEU. 2015. 'History of the FTZU-CSWEU'. *FTZ Union Lanka*. http://ftzunionlanka.com/history/. Accessed 15 June 2015.

Gaur, Vatsala. 2020. 'Uttar Pradesh Brings Ordinance to Suspend Most Labour Laws for Three Years'. *India Times*, 7 May. https://economictimes.indiatimes.com/news/economy/policy/uttar-pradesh-brings-ordinance-to-suspend-most-labour-laws-for-3-years/articleshow/75609934.cms. Accessed 10 May 2020.

Gereffi, Gary, John Humphrey and Timothy Sturgeon. 2005. 'The Governance of Global Value Chains'. *Review of International Political Economy* 12 (1): 78–104.

Gidwani, Vinay. 2004. 'The Limits to Capital: Questions of Provenance and Politics'. *Antipode* 36 (3): 527–542.

Gidwani, Vinay and Sharad Chari. 2004. 'Geographies of Work'. *Environment and Planning D: Society and Space* 22 (4): 475–484.

Global Press Journal. 2017. 'Sri Lankan Garment Factories Boost Wages and Benefits as Labor Shortage Looms'. https://globalpressjournal.com/asia/sri_lanka/sri-lankan-garment-factories-boost-wages-benefits-labor-shortage-looms/. Accessed 10 November 2019.

Goger, Annelies. 2013a. 'From Disposable to Empowered: Rearticulating Labour in Sri Lankan Apparel Factories'. *Environment and Planning A* 45 (4): 2628–2645.

———. 2013b. 'The Making of a "Business Case" for Environmental Upgrading: Sri Lanka's Eco-Factories'. *Geoforum* 47 (June): 73–83.

———. 2014. 'Ethical Branding in Sri Lanka: A Case Study of Garments without Guilt'. In *Workers' Rights and Labour Compliance in Global Supply Chains*, edited by Jennifer Bair, Marsha Dickson and Doug Miller. New York: Routledge, 47–68.

Goger, Annelies and Kanchana N. Ruwanpura. 2014. 'Ethical Reconstruction? Primitive Accumulation in the Apparel Sector of Eastern Sri Lanka'. Working paper 14, Colombo, Sri Lanka, International Centre for Ethnic Studies.

Goodhand, Jonathan. 2010. 'Stabilising a Victor's Peace? Humanitarian Action and Reconstruction in Eastern Sri Lanka'. *Disasters* 34 (s3): s342–s367.

Gopura, Sumith, Alice Payne and Laurie Buys. 2019. 'The Fashion Designer's Evolving Role in the Apparel Value Chain: Perspectives from Sri Lankan Designers'. *The Journal of Design, Creative Process and the Fashion Industry* 11 (2): 175–196.

Gunasekara, Tisaranee. 2011. 'Sycophantic Gibberish of Saying Rajapaksas are Descendants of Dutu Gemunu and Relatives of Lord Buddha'. *Trans-Currents News*. http://transcurrents.com/news-views/archives/1084. Accessed 19 July 2012.

Gunasinghe, Newton. 1996. 'The Open Economy and Its Impact on Ethnic Relations'. In *Newton Gunasinghe: Selected Essays,* edited by Sasanka Perera. Colombo, Sri Lanka: Social Scientists' Association, 183–203.

Gunawardana, Samanthi. 2007. 'Struggle, Perseverance and Organization in Sri Lanka's Export Processing Zones'. In *Global Unions: Challenging Transnational Capital through Cross-border Campaigns*, edited by Kate Bronfenbrenner. Ithaca, NY: Cornell University Press, 78–98.

———. 2008. 'Meeting Bala Tampoe: A Union Leader Pursuing Social Justice'. In *Profiles in Courage: Political Actors & Ideas in Contemporary Asia*, edited by Gloria Davies, J. V. D'Cruz and Nathan Hollier. Melbourne, Victoria: Australian Scholarly Publishing, 92–105.

———. 2014. 'Reframing Employee Voice: A Case Study in Sri Lanka's Export Processing Zones'. *Work, Employment and Society* 28 (3): 1–17.

———. 2016. 'To Finish, We Must Finish: Everyday Practices of Depletion in Sri Lankan Export-Processing Zones'. *Globalizations* 13 (6): 861–875.

Gunawardana, Samanthi and Janaka Biyanwila. 2008. 'Trade Unions in Sri Lanka: Beyond Party Politics'. In *Trade Unions in Asia: Balancing Economic Competitiveness in Social Sustainability*, edited by J. Benson and Y. Zhu. London: Routledge, 177–197.

Guneratne, Arjun. 2001. 'What's in a Name? Aryans and Dravidians in the Making of Sri Lankan Identities'. In *The Hybrid Island: Culture Crossing in the Inversion of Identity in Sri Lanka*, edited by Neluka Silva. Colombo, Sri Lanka: Social Scientist Association, 20–40.

Gupta, Akhil. 2012. *Red Tape: Bureaucracy, Structural Violence, and Poverty in India*. Durham, NC: Duke University Press.

Hagar, Mark. 2012. 'Stitching the Fabric of Reconciliation'. *Joint Apparel Association Forum Sri Lanka.* http://jaafsl.com/news/788-stitching-the-fabric-of-reconciliation. Accessed 12 February 2014.

Hale, Angela and Jane Wills. 2005. *Threads of Labour: Garment Industry Supply Chains from the Workers' Perspective*. Oxford: Blackwell Publishing.

Hall, Stuart. 1980. 'Race, Articulation and Societies Structured in Dominance'. In *Sociological Theories: Race and Colonialism*, edited by UNESCO. Paris: UNESCO, 305–345.

Harvey, David. 2005. *A Brief History of Neoliberalism*. Oxford: Oxford University Press.

Hensman, Rohini. 2011. *Workers, Unions, and Global Capitalism: Lessons from India*. New York: Columbia University Press.

Herod, Andrew. 2001. *Labour Geographies: Workers and the Landscapes of Capitalism*. New York: Guildford Press.

———. 2003. 'Workers, Space, and Labour Geography'. *International Labour and Working-Class History* 64 (Fall): 112–138.

———. 2012. 'Workers as Geographical Actors'. *Labour History* 53 (3): 335–353.

Hewamanne, Sandya. 2008. *Stitching Identities in a Free Trade Zone: Gender and Politics in Sri Lanka*. Philadelphia, PA: University of Pennsylvania Press.

———. 2009. 'Duty Bound? Militarization, Romances and New Forms of Violence among Sri Lanka's Free Trade Zone Factory Workers'. *Cultural Dynamics* 21 (2): 153–184.

Hoskins, Tansy. 2014. *Stitched Up: The Anti-Capitalist Book of Fashion.* London: Pluto Press.

———. 2020. '"Thrown to the Wolves": How CoVID-19 Laws Are Being Used to Silence Garment Workers'. *The Guardian,* 26 October. https://www.theguardian.com/global-development/2020/oct/26/thrown-to-the-wolves-how-covid-19-laws-are-being-used-to-silence-garment-workers. Accessed 27 October 2020.

Hoskins, Tansy, Juan Mayorga, Dil Afrose Jahan and Nidia Bautista. 2021. 'Work and Death in Sri Lanka's Garment Industry'. *Jacobin Magazine,* 5 July. https://jacobinmag.com/2021/07/sri-lanka-free-trade-zone-ftz-colombo-garment-industry-clothing-factories-covid-pandemic. Accessed 7 July 2021.

Hossain, Akbar. 2020. 'Coronavirus: Two Million Bangladesh Jobs "at Risk" as Clothes Orders Dry Up'. *BBC,* 29 April. https://bbc.co.uk/news/world-asia-52417822. Accessed 28 April 2020.

Hughes, Alex. 2001. 'Multi-Stakeholder Approaches to Ethical Trade: Towards a Reorganization of UK Retailers' Global Supply Chains'. *Journal of Economic Geography* 1 (4): 421–437.

———. 2005. 'Corporate Strategy and the Management of Ethical Trade: The Case of UK Food and Clothing Retailers'. *Environment and Planning A* 37 (7): 1145–1163.

———. 2006. 'Learning to Trade Ethically: Knowledgeable Capitalism, Retailers and Contested Commodity Chains'. *Geoforum* 37 (6): 1008–1020.

Hughes, Alex and Suzy Reimer, eds. 2006. *Geographies of Commodity Chains.* London: Routledge.

Hughes, Alex, Eilidh Morrison and Kanchana N. Ruwanpura. 2019. 'Public Sector Procurement and Ethical Trade: Governance and Social Responsibility in Some Hidden Global Supply Chains'. *Transactions of the Institute of British Geographers* 44 (2): 242–255.

Hughes, Alex, Martin Buttle and Neil Wrigley. 2007. 'Organizational Geographies of Corporate Responsibility: A UK-US Comparison of Retailers' Ethical Trading Initiatives'. *Journal of Economic Geography* 7 (4): 491–513.

Hughes, Alex, Neil Wrigley and Martin Buttle. 2008. 'Global Production Networks, Ethical Campaigning, and the Embeddedness of Responsible Governance'. *Journal of Economic Geography* 8 (3): 345–367.

Hughes, Dhana. 2013. 'Retired Insurgents: Recreating Life after Sri Lanka's Terror'. *Contemporary South Asia* 21 (1): 62–74.

Humphries, Jane. 1993. 'Gender Inequality and Economic Development'. In *Economics in a Changing World*, edited by Dieter Bos. New York: St. Martin's Press, 218–233.

———. 2010. *Childhood and Child Labour in the British Industrial Revolution*. Cambridge: Cambridge University Press.

IDG (International Development Group LLC). 2015/2016. 'USAID Supporting Accelerated Investment in Sri Lanka (SAIL) Project'. https://internationaldevelopmentgroup.com/projects/asia/sri-lanka/usaid-supporting-accelerated-investment-in-sri-lanka-sail-project. Accessed 8 August 2019.

ILO. 2012. 'Local Economic Development and Post-onflict Recovery in Sri Lanka'. *International Labour Organization*. https://ilo.org/global/topics/employment-promotion/recovery-and-reconstruction/WCMS_181861/lang--en/index.htm. Accessed 3 May 2020.

Indrakularasa, Thayalini. 2019. 'Garment Factories Provide Sri Lankan Women with a Source of Employment – and Pride'. https://globalpressjournal.com/asia/sri_lanka/garment-factories-provide-sri-lankan-women-source-employment-pride/. Accessed 1 September 2020.

Ismail, Qadri. 2020. 'F*** You, Mr President'. *Groundviews*, 6 June. https://groundviews.org/2020/06/06/f-you-mr-president/. Accessed 6 June 2020.

Ismail, Qadri and Pradeep Jeganathan. 1995. *Unmaking the Nation: The Politics of Identity and History in Modern Sri Lanka*. Colombo: Social Scientists' Association.

IndustriALL. 2020. 'Sri Lankan Unions Protects Workers amidst CoVID-19'. *IndustriALL Global Union*, 31 March. http://www.industriall-union.org/sri-lankan-union-protects-workers-amid-covid-19. Accessed 5 April 2020.

International Textile Garment and Leather Workers' Federation (ITGLWF). 2011. *An Overview of Working Conditions in Sportswear Factories in Indonesia, Sri Lanka and the Philippines*. ITGLWF working paper, Tyneside.

ITJP (International Truth and Justice Project). 2020. 'Sri Lanka's Militarisation of COVID-19 Response'. *ITJP Press Release*. https://itjpsl.com/assets/press/English-ITJP_COVID-19-press-release-Merged-copy.pdf. Accessed 15 April 2020.

Ivy Park. 2016. 'Adidas and Beyoncé Announce Iconic Partnership'. *Ivy Park*. https://www.ivypark.com/. Accessed 13 November 2019.

JAAF. 2011. 'Sri Lanka Apparels – Garments without Guilt: About GWG'. http:// gwg. garmentswithoutguilt.com/about-gwg. Accessed 28 November 2013.

―――. 2019. 'Why Sri Lanka?' *Sri Lanka Apparel*. https://srilankaapparel. com/why-sri-lanka/. Accessed 10 October 2019.

―――. 2020. 'Sri Lanka Apparel – 13 October 2020 News'. *Sri Lanka Apparel*. https://srilankaapparel.com/sri-lanka-apparel/. Accessed 16 October 2020.

Jayawardena, Kumari. 1971. 'The Origins of the Left Movement in Sri Lanka'. *Modern Ceylon Studies* 2 (6/7): 195–221.

―――. 1972. *The Rise of the Labour Movement in Ceylon*. Durham, NC: Duke University Press.

―――. 2017. *Labour, Feminism and Ethnicity in Sri Lanka: Selected Essays*. Colombo, Sri Lanka: SailFish.

Jazeel, Tariq and Kanchana N. Ruwanpura. 2009. 'Dissent: Sri Lanka's New Minority?' *Political Geography* 28 (7): 385–387.

Jeffrey, Craig, Patricia Jeffery and Roger Jeffery. 2007. *Degrees without Freedom? Education, Masculinities, and Unemployment in North India*. Sandford, CA: Stanford University Press.

Jegathesan, Mythri. 2019. *Tea and Solidarity: Tamil Women and Work in Post-War Sri Lanka*. Seattle, WA: University of Washington Press.

Jenkins, Rhys. 2002. 'The Political Economy of Codes of Conduct'. In *Corporate Responsibility and Labour Rights: Codes of Conduct in the Global Economy*, edited by Rhys Jenkins, Ruth Pearson and Gail Seyfang. London: Earthscan, 13–30.

Jenkins, Rhys, Ruth Pearson and Gail Seyfang, eds. 2002. *Corporate Responsibility and Labour Rights: Codes of Conduct in the Global Economy*. London: Earthscan.

Kabeer, Naila. 2000. *The Power to Choose: Bangladeshi Women and Labour Market Decisions in London*. Dhaka: Verso Press.

―――. 2008. 'Globalization, Labour Standards, and Women's Rights: Dilemmas of Collective (in)action in an Interdependent World'. *Feminist Economics* 10 (1): 3–35.

Kadirgamar, Ahilan. 2013. 'The Question of Militarization in Post-War Sri Lanka'. *Economic and Political Weekly* 48 (7): 42–46.

―――. 2019. 'The Return of the Rajapaksa Regime'. *The Hindu*, 18 November. https://thehindu.com/opinion/op-ed/the-return-of-the-rajapaksa-regime/article30000527.ece. Accessed 19 November 2019.

Karp, Jonathan. 1999. 'Sri Lanka Keeps Victoria's Secret: Island Workers Produce Panties in Cool Comfort'. *Wall Street Journal*, 13 July, B1, B4.

Kearney, Robert. 1971. *Trade Unions and Politics in Ceylon*. Berkley, CA: University of California Press.

Kelegama, Saman. 2009. *Ready-Made Garment Exports from Sri Lanka*. Colombo, Sri Lanka: Institute of Policy Studies.

Kelly, Annie. 2020a. 'Garment Workers Face Destitution as CoVID-19 Closes Factories'. *The Guardian*, 19 March. https://theguardian.com/global-development/2020/mar/19/garment-workers-face-destitution-as-covid-19-closes-factories. Accessed 19 March 2020.

———. 2020b. 'Primark and Matalan among Retailers Allegedly Cancelling £2.4b Orders in "Catastrophic" Move for Bangladesh'. *The Guardian*, 2 April. https://theguardian.com/global-development/2020/apr/02/fashion-brands-cancellations-of-24bn-orders-catastrophic-for-bangladesh. Accessed 2 April 2020.

Kim, Jaesok. 2013. *Chinese Labour in a Korean Factory: Class, Ethnicity, and Productivity on the Shop Floor in Globalizing China*. Stanford, CA: Stanford University Press.

Klasen, Stephan. 1993. 'Gender Inequality and Development Strategies: Lessons from the Past and Policy Issues for the Future'. ILO Working Papers, International Labour Organisation.

Knoema. 2020. 'GINI Index by Country'. https://knoema.com/atlas/ranks/GINI-index. Accessed 16 May 2020.

Knutsen, Hege. 2003. 'Globalisation and the Garment Industry in Sri Lanka'. *Journal of Contemporary Asia* 33 (2): 225–250.

———. 2004. 'Industrial Development in Buyer-Driven Networks: The Garment Industry in Vietnam and Sri Lanka'. *Journal of Economic Geography* 4 (5): 545–564.

Korrakoon, Silaphet. 2015. 'Providing an Attractive Business Environment: The Competitiveness of Lao Garment Industry in the Global Value Chain after the Multi-fibre Arrangement Termination'. Master of Science dissertation, Ritsumeikan Asia Pacific University.

Kucera, David and Ritash Sarna. 2006. 'Trade Union Rights, Democracy, and Exports: A Gravity Model Approach'. *Review of International Economics* 14 (5): 859–882.

Kumar, Ashok. 2019. 'A Race from the Bottom? Lessons from a Worker's Struggle at a Bangalore Warehouse'. *Competition and Change* 23 (4): 346–377.

Kumarasinghe, Kalani and Sheain Fernandopulle. 2020. 'Minuwangoda Cluster 19 Expands'. *Daily Mirror*, 5 October. http://dailymirror.lk/

recomended-news/Minuwangoda-Covid-19-cluster-expands/277-197238. Accessed 6 October 2020.

Lim, Linda. 1983. 'Capitalism, Imperialism and Patriarchy: The Dilemma of Third World Women Workers in Multinational Factories'. In *Women, Men and the International Division of Labour,* edited by June Nash and Patricia Fernandez-Kelly. New York: SUNY Press, 70–91.

———. 1990. 'Women's Work in Export Factories: The Politics of a Cause'. In *Persistent Inequalities: Women and World Development,* edited by Irene Tinker. Oxford: Oxford University Press, 101–119.

Lingam, Jayanthi. 2019. 'Dispossessing Connections: Women's Working Lives in Post-War Jaffna District, Sri Lanka, 2009–2015'. PhD dissertation, SOAS, University of London.

Lund-Thomsen, Peter. 2013. 'Labour Agency in the Football Manufacturing Industry of Sialkot, Pakistan'. *Geoforum* 44 (January): 71–81.

Lynch, Caitrin. 2007. *Juki Girls, Good Girls: Gender and Cultural Politics in Sri Lanka's Global Garment Industry.* Ithaca, NY: Cornell University Press.

Marx, Karl. 1972 (1852). *The Eighteenth Brumaire of Louis Napoleon.* Moscow: Progress Publishers.

MAS. 2020. 'COVID-19: Doing the Right Thing during a Pandemic'. *MAS Holdings.* https://youtube.com/watch?v=zrHYOujdrCQ&feature=youtu. be. Accessed 28 April 2020.

Maunaguru, Sidharthan. 2019. *Marrying for a Future: Transnational Sri Lankan Tamil Marriages in a Shadow of a War.* Seattle, WA: University of Washington Press.

McGrath, Siobhan. 2018. 'Dis/Articulations and the Interrogation of Development in GPN Research'. *Progress in Human Geography* 42 (4): 509–528.

McIntyre, Richard. 2008. *Are Worker Rights Human Rights?* Ann Arbor, MI: University of Michigan Press.

Merk, Jeroen. 2009. 'Jumping scale and bridging space in the era of corporate social responsibility: Cross-border labour struggles in the global garment industry'. *Third World Quaterly* 30(3): 599–615.

Mezzadri, Alessandra. 2012. 'Reflections on Global and Labour Standards in the Indian Garment Industry: Codes of Conduct versus "Codes of Practice" Imposed by the Firm'. *Global Labour Journal* 3 (1): 40–62.

———. 2017. *The Sweatshop Regime: Labouring Bodies, Exploitation and Garments Made in India.* Cambridge: Cambridge University Press.

Mezzadri, Alessandra and Kanchana N. Ruwanpura. 2020. 'How Asia's Clothing Factories Switched to Making PPE – But Sweatshop Problems

Live On'. *The Conversation*, 29 June. https://theconversation.com/how-asias-clothing-factories-switched-to-making-ppe-but-sweatshop-problems-live-on-141396. Accessed 29 June 2020.

Miller, Doug. 2012. *Last Nightshift in Savar: The Story of the Spectrum Sweater Factory Collapse*. London: McNidder & Grace.

———. 2014. 'Regulating the "Wage Effort Bargain" in Outsourced Apparel Production: Towards a Model'. In *Towards Better Work*, edited by Arianna Rossi, Amy Luinstra and John Pickles. London: Palgrave Macmillan, 103–124.

Miller, Doug and Peter Williams. 2009. 'What Price a Living Wage? Implementation Issues in the Quest for Decent Wages in the Global Apparel Sector'. *Global Social Policy* 9 (1): 99–125.

Miller, Doug, Vaesena Nuon, Charlene Aprill and Ramon Certeza. 2009. 'Business as Usual? Governing the Supply Chain in Clothing – Post MFA Phase-Out: The Case of Cambodia'. *International Journal of Labour Research* 1 (1): 9–33.

Mullings, Beverley. 1999. 'Insider or Outsider, Both or Neither: Some Dilemmas of Interviewing in a Cross-Cultural Setting'. *Geoforum* 30 (4): 337–350.

Nadvi, Khalid. 2008. 'Global Standards, Global Governance and the Organization of Global Value Chains'. *Journal of Economic Geography* 8 (3): 323–334.

Nagaraj, Vijay. 2016. 'From Smokestacks to Luxury Condos: The Housing Rights Struggles of the Millworkers of Mayura Place, Colombo'. In *Post-War Sri Lanka: State, Capital, Labour and the Politics of Reconciliation*, edited by Kanchana N. Ruwanpura, special issue of *Contemporary South Asia* 24 (4): 429–443.

Neethi, P. 2016 *Globalization Lived Locally: A Labour Geography Perspective*. Oxford: Oxford University Press.

Nowak, Jörg. 2016a. 'Strikes and Labour Unrest in the Automobile Industry in India: The Case of Maruti Suzuki India Limited'. *Working USA* 19 (3): 419–436.

———. 2016b. 'The Spatial Patterns of Mass Strikes: A Labour Geography Approach'. *Geoforum* 75 (October): 270–273.

ODI. 2015. *Manufacturing Progress? Employment Creation in Sri Lanka*. Overseas Development Institute. https://odi.org/publications/9313-manufacturing-progress-employment-creation-sri-lanka. Accessed 10 September 2019.

Office of the Cabinet of Ministers – Sri Lanka. 2018. 'Press Briefing of Cabinet Decision Taken on 2018-06-05'. http://cabinetoffice.gov.lk/cab/index.

php?option=com_content&view=article&id=16&Itemid=49&lang=en& dID=8901. Accessed 16 July 2019.

O'Leary, Michael. 2009. 'Responsible Garment Management'. *Serendib*, 68–70.

Ong, Aiwa. 1987. *Spirits of Resistance and Capitalist Discipline: Factory Women in Malaysia*. Albany, NY: SUNY Press.

Ost, David. 2005. *The Defeat of Solidarity: Anger and Politics in Post-Communist Europe*. Ithaca, NY: Cornell University Press.

OXFAM. 2008. *Survey on Garments Manufacturing Factories in Sri Lanka – 2006*. Unpublished final report, Colombo: OXFAM-Australia.

Palpaucer, Florence. 2008. 'Bringing the Social Context Back in: Governance and Wealth Distribution in Global Commodity Chains'. *Economy and Society* 37 (3): 393–419.

———. 2020. 'Contestation and Activism in Global Value Chains'. In *Handbook on Global Value Chains*, edited by Stefan Ponte, Gary Gereffi and Gale Raj-Reichert. Cheltenham, UK: Edward Elgar, 199–213.

Pearson, Ruth. 1998. 'Nimble Fingers Revisited: Reflections on Women and Third World Industrialization in the Late Twentieth Century'. In *Feminist Visions of Development: Gender Analysis and Policy*, edited by Cecelia Jackson and Ruth Pearson. Oxford: Routledge, 171–188

———. 2013. 'Gendered Globalisation and the Reproduction of Labour: Bringing the State back in'. In *New Frontiers in Feminist Political Economy*, edited by Shirin M. Rai and Georgina Waylen. Oxford: Routledge, 19–44.

Pearson, Ruth, Anitha Sundari and Linda McDowell. 2010. 'Striking Issues: From Labour Process to Industrial Dispute at Grunwick and Gate Gourmet'. *Industrial Relations Journal* 41 (5): 408–428.

Perera, Kusal. 2012. 'Review - Reality and Rhetoric: Study on Apparel Industry'. *Sunday Times*, 22 April. Accessed 15 May 2021.

Perera, Sonali. 2018. *No Country: Working-Class Writing in the Age of Globalization*. New York: Columbia University Press.

Perry, Patsy, Steve Wood and James Fernie. 2014. 'Corporate Social Responsibility in Garment Sourcing Networks: Factory Management Perspectives on Ethical Trade in Sri Lanka'. *Journal of Business Ethics* 130 (3): 737–752.

Plankey-Videla, Nancy. 2012. *We Are in this Dance Together: Gender, Power, and Globalization at a Mexican Garment Firm*. New Brunswick, NJ: Rutgers University Press.

Polanyi, Karl. 1957. *The Great Transformation: The Political and Economic Origins of Our Time*. Boston, MA: Beacon Press.

Prentice, Rebecca. 2015. *Thiefing a Chance: Factory Work, Illicit Labour, and Neoliberal Subjectivities in Trinidad*. Boulder, CO: University Press of Colorado.

———. 2019. 'Just Compensation? The Price of Death and Injury after the Rana Plaza Garment Factory Collapse'. In *The Politics and Ethics of the Just Price: Ethnographies of Market Exchange*, edited by Peter Luetchford and Giovanno Orlando. London: Emerald Publishing, 157–178.

Prentice, Rebecca, Geert de Neve, Alessandra Mezzadri and Kanchana N. Ruwanpura. 2018. 'Health and Safety in Garment Workers' Lives: Setting a New Research Agenda'. *Geoforum* 88 (January): 157–160.

Rai, Shirin, Benjamin Brown and Kanchana N. Ruwanpura. 2019. 'SDG8: Decent Work and Economic Growth – A Gendered Analysis'. *World Development* 113 (January): 368–380.

Rajasingham-Perera, Nimanthi. 2016. 'How Bodies Matter: Working-Class Women's Theatre in a Time of War'. In *Post-War Sri Lanka: State, Capital, Labour and the Politics of Reconciliation*, edited by Kanchana N. Ruwanpura, special issue of *Contemporary South Asia* 24 (4): 374–386.

Rajasingham-Senanayake, Darini. 2018. 'A Post-War Development Disaster? Foreign Aid, Bi-Partisan Corruption and Lanka in the International Bail-Out Business'. Unpublished mimeograph.

Raj-Reichert, Gale. 2015. 'Exercising Power over Labour Governance in the Electronics Industry'. *Geoforum* 67 (December): 89–92.

———. 2019. 'The Powers of a Social Auditor in a Global Production Network: The Case of Verité and the Exposure of Forced Labour in the Electronics Industry'. *Journal of Economic Geography* 20 (3): 653–678.

Ridicki, Daniel. 2015. 'Being about People: MAS Holdings Journey to the North'. *MAS Holdings*. https://youtube.com/watch?v=bB_uU6_8eqY. Accessed 17 March 2020.

Rosa, Kumudini. 1989. 'Export-Oriented Industries and Women Workers in Sri Lanka'. In *Women, Poverty and Ideology in Asia*, edited by Haleh Afshar and Bina Agarwal. London: Palgrave Macmillan, 196–211.

Ruwanpura, Eshani. 2011. *Sex or Sensibility? The Making of Chaste Women and Promiscuous Men in a Sri Lankan University Setting*. Unpublished PhD dissertation, University of Edinburgh, November 2011.

Ruwanpura, Kanchana N. 2004. 'Female-Headship among Muslims in Eastern Sri Lanka: A Case of Changing Household Structures'. *Nivedini: A Journal of Gender Studies* 11 (1): 1–22.

———. 2006. *Matrilineal Communities, Patriarchal Realities: A Feminist Nirvana Uncovered.* Ann Arbor, MI: University of Michigan Press.

———. 2011. 'Women Workers in the Apparel Sector: A Three Decade (r)-evolution of Feminist Contributions?' *Progress in Development Studies* 11 (3): 197–209.

———. 2012. 'Ethical Codes: Reality and Rhetoric – A Study of Sri Lanka's Apparel Sector'. Working paper. Southampton: University of Southampton & ESRC.

———. 2013a. 'Scripted Performances? Local Readings of "Global" Health and Safety Standards (The Apparel Sector in Sri Lanka)'. *Global Labour Journal* 4 (2): 88–108.

———. 2013b. 'It's the (Household) Economy Stupid! Pension Reform, Collective Resistance, and the Reproductive Sphere in Sri Lanka'. In *The Global Political Economy of the Household in Asia*, edited by Juanita Elias and Samanthi J. Gunawaradana. London: Palgrave Macmillan, 145–161.

———. 2014a. 'Metal Free Factories: Straddling Workers' Rights and Consumer Safety?' *Geoforum* 51 (January): 224–232.

———. 2014b. 'Global Governance Initiatives and Garment Sector Workers: Tracing Its Gender and Development Politics'. In *Routledge Handbook of Gender in South Asia*, edited by Leela Fernandes. London: Routledge, 207–219.

———. 2015. 'The Weakest Link? Unions, Freedom of Association and Ethical Codes: A Case Study from a Factory Setting in Sri Lanka'. *Ethnography* 16 (1): 118–141.

———. 2016. 'Garments without Guilt? Uneven Labour Geographies and Ethical Trading: Sri Lankan Labour Perspectives'. *Journal of Economic Geography* 16 (2): 423–446.

———. 2017. 'Limited Leave? Clinical Provisioning and Healthy Bodies in Sri Lanka's Apparel Sector'. In *Unmaking the Global Sweatshop: Health and Safety of the World's Garment Workers*, edited by Rebecca Prentice and Geert de Neve. Philadelphia, PA: University of Pennsylvania Press, 203–225.

———. 2018. 'Militarized Capitalism? The Apparel Industry's Role in Scripting a Post-War National Identity in Sri Lanka'. *Antipode* 50 (2): 425–446.

———. 2019. 'Privatized Health Care: Sri Lanka's Story'. *Contemporary South Asia* 27 (2): 247–258.

Ruwanpura, Kanchana N. and Alex Hughes. 2016. 'Empowered Spaces? Management Articulations of Gendered Spaces in Apparel Factories in Karachi, Pakistan'. *Gender, Place and Culture* 23 (9): 1270–1285.

Ruwanpura, Kanchana N. and Neil Wrigley. 2011. 'The Costs of Compliance? Views of Sri Lankan Apparel Manufacturers in Times of Global Economic Crisis'. *Journal of Economic Geography* 11 (6): 1031–1049.

Ruwanpura, Kanchana N., Loritta Chan, Benjamin Brown and V. Kajotha. 2020. 'Unsettled Peace? The Territorial Politics of Roadbuilding in Post-War Sri Lanka'. *Political Geography* 76 (January): 1–10.

Safa, Helen. 1981. 'Runaway Shops and Female Employment: The Search for Cheap Labour'. *SIGNS: Journal of Women in Culture and Society* 7 (2): 418–433.

Salzinger, Leslie. 2003. *Genders in Production: Making Workers in Mexico's Global Factories*. Berkeley, CA: University of California Press.

Samaraweera, Dilshani. 2009. 'Sri Lanka: Garment Maker Sinotex Closes after 27 Years'. *Just Style*. https://just-style.com/news/garment-maker-sinotex-closes-after-27- years_id103054.aspx. Accessed 16 December 2019.

Sanyal, Kalyan. 2007. *Rethinking Capitalist Development: Primitive Accumulation, Governmentality and Post-Colonial Capitalism*. London: Routledge.

Sarvananthan, Muttukrishna. 2015. 'Impediments to Women in Post-Civil War Economic Growth in Sri Lanka'. *South Asian Journal of Human Resources Management* 2 (1): 12–36.

———. 2016. 'Elusive Economic Peace Dividend in Sri Lanka: All That Glitters Is Not Gold'. *GeoJournal* 81 (4): 571–596.

Sarvananthan, Muttukrishna and H. Sanjeewanie. 2008. *GSP+ and Sri Lanka: Economic, Labour and Human Rights Issues*. Colombo, Sri Lanka: Centre for Policy Alternatives & Friedrich Ebert Stiftung.

Satkunanathan, Ambika. 2016. 'Collaboration, Suspicion and Traitors: An Exploratory Study of Intracommunity Relations in Post-War Northern Sri Lanka'. In *Post-War Sri Lanka: State, Capital, Labour and the Politics of Reconciliation*, edited by Kanchana N. Ruwanpura, special issue of *Contemporary South Asia* 24 (4): 416–442.

Saxena, Sanchita. 2014. *Made in Bangladesh, Cambodia and Sri Lanka*. New York: Cambria Press.

Scroll.In. 2020. 'Covid-19: India Should Amend Labour Laws Only after Consulting Workers and Employers, Says ILO'. 14 May. https://scroll.in/latest/961977/covid-19-india-should-amend-labour-laws-only-after-consulting-workers-and-employers-says-ilo. Accessed 10 May 2020.

Selwyn, Ben. 2012a. 'Beyond Firm-Centrism: Re-Integrating Labour and Capitalism into Global Commodity Chain Analysis'. *Journal of Economic Geography* 12 (1): 205–226.

———. 2012b. *Workers, State and Development in Brazil: Powers of Labour, Chains of Value.* Manchester: Manchester University Press.

———. 2013. 'Social Upgrading and Labour in Global Production Networks: A Critique and an Alternative Conception'. *Competition and Change* 17 (1): 75–90.

———. 2019. 'Poverty Chains and Global Capitalism'. *Competition and Change* 23 (1): 71–97.

Sen, Amartya. 1981. 'Public Action and the Quality of Life in Developing Countries'. *Oxford Bulletin of Economics and Statistics* 43 (4): 287–319.

———. 1983. 'Development: Which Way Now'. *Economic Journal* 93 (372): 745–762.

Sen, Sumita. 2008. 'Gender and Class: Women in Indian Industry, 1890–1990'. *Modern Asian Studies* 42 (1): 75–116.

Shakya, Mallika. 2018. *Death of an Industry: The Cultural Politics of Garment Manufacturing during the Maoist Revolution in Nepal.* Cambridge: Cambridge University Press.

Shaw, Linda and Angela Hale. 2002. 'The Emperor's New Clothes: What Codes Mean for Workers in the Garment Industry'. In *Corporate Responsibility and Labour Rights: Codes of Conduct in the Global Economy,* edited by Rhy Jenkins, Ruth Pearson and Gail Seyfang. London: Earthscan, 101–113.

Siddiqi, Dina. 2000. 'Miracle Workers or Woman-Machine? Tracking (Trans) National Realities in Bangladeshi Factories'. *Economic and Political Weekly* 35 (21–22): L11–L17.

———. 2009. 'Do Bangladeshi Factory Workers Need Saving? Sisterhood in the Post-Sweatshop Era'. *Feminist Review* 91 (1): 154–174.

Silva, Neluka, ed. 2001. *The Hybrid Island: Culture Crossing in the Inversion of Identity in Sri Lanka.* Colombo, Sri Lanka: Social Scientist Association.

Silver, Beverley. 2019. 'Plunges into Utter Destruction and the Limits of Historical Capitalism'. In *Capitalism in Transformation Movements and Counter-Movements in the 21st Century,* edited by Roland Atzmüller et al. Cheltenham, Gloucestershire: Edward Elgar, 35–45.

Sirilal, Ranga. 2011. 'Sri Lanka Workers Strike for Fifth Day, More Unrest Feared'. *Reuters,* 3 June. https://reuters.com/article/srilanka-unions/sri-lanka-workers-strike-for-fifth-day-more-unrest-feared-idUSL3E7H30EX 20110603. Accessed 21 February 2020.

SLAE. 2012. 'Apparel Exporters Call for More Labour Reforms'. http://www.srilanka-apparel.com/news-a/143-apparel-exporters-call-for-more-labour-reforms. Accessed 10 December 2012.

Sluiter, Leisbeth. 2009. *Clean Clothes: A Global Movement to End Sweatshops*. London: Pluto Press.

Skanthakumar, B. 2015. 'Labour's Lost Agency'. In *Labour and Its Discontents*, edited by B. Skanthakumar, Weena Pun and Vrinda Marwah, special issue of *Himal South Asian* March 15: 12–34.

Smith, Adrian. 2015a. 'The State, Institutional Frameworks and the Dynamics of Capital in the Global Production Networks'. *Progress in Human Geography* 39 (3): 290–315.

———. 2015b. 'Economic (In)security and Global Value Chains: The Dynamics of Industrial and Trade Integration in the Euro-Mediterranean Macro-Region'. *Cambridge Journal of Regions, Economy and Society* 8 (3): 439–458.

Smith, Adrian, Al Rainnie, Mick Dunford, Jane Hardy, Ray Hudson and David Sadler. 2002. 'Network of Value, Commodities and Regions: Reworking Divisions of Labour in Macro-Regional Economies'. *Progress in Human Geography* 26 (1): 41–63.

Soysa, Minoli. 2020. 'Search for the Missing: A Testament to the Enduring Power of Grief'. *Groundviews*, 20 August. https://groundviews.org/2020/08/20/search-for-the-missing-a-testament-to-the-enduring-power-of-grief/. Accessed 22 August 2020.

Sri Lanka Department of Labour. 2014. 'Labour Statistics: Sri Lanka'. http://www.labourdept.gov.lk/index.php?option=com_content&view=article&id=129&Itemid=87&lang=en. Accessed 15 November 2019.

———. 2015. 'Labour Statistics: Sri Lanka'. http://www.labourdept.gov.lk/index.php?option=com_content&view=article&id=129&Itemid=87&lang=en. Accessed 15 November 2019.

———. 2016. 'Labour Statistics: Sri Lanka'. http://www.labourdept.gov.lk/index.php?option=com_content&view=article&id=129&Itemid=87&lang=en. Accessed 15 November 2019.

———. 2017. 'Labour Statistics: Sri Lanka'. http://www.labourdept.gov.lk/index.php?option=com_content&view=article&id=129&Itemid=87&lang=en. Accessed 15 November 2019.

Srivastava, Priyanka. 2018. *The Well-Being of the Labour Force in Colonial Bombay*. London: Palgrave Macmillan.

Standing, Guy. 1997. 'Globalization, Labour Flexibility and Insecurity: The Era of Market Regulation'. *European Journal of Industrial Relations* 3 (1): 7–37.

Stewart, Frances. 2015. 'Employment in Conflict and Post-Conflict Situations'. *UNDP Human Development Report Office Think Piece.* http://hdr.undp.org/sites/default/files/stewart_hdr_2015_final.pdf. Accessed 7 May 2020.

Strauss, Kendra. 2020. 'Labour Geography II: Being, Knowledge and Agency'. *Progress in Human Geography* 44 (1): 150–159.

Sunday Times. 2011. 'Workers' Crisis: Stitch in Time Would Have Saved Life'. 5 June. http://sundaytimes.lk/110605/Columns/political.html. Accessed 23 February 2020.

Sunil, W. 2011. 'Sri Lankan Government to Reintroduce Amended Pension Bill'. *World Socialist Web Site.* https://wsws.org/en/articles/2011/06/slpb-j09.html. Accessed 21 February 2020.

Sunil, W. and Ruwan Liyanage. 2011. 'Sri Lankan Court Examines Police Shooting of FTZ Worker'. *World Socialist Web Site.* https://wsws.org/en/articles/2011/06/slft-j23.html. Accessed 21 February 2020.

Sunley, Peter. 1999. 'Space for Stake-holding? Stakeholder Capitalism and Economic Geography'. *Environment and Planning A: Economy and Space* 31 (12): 2189–2205.

———. 2008. 'Relational Economic Geography: A Partial Understanding or a New Paradigm?' *Economic Geography* 84 (1): 1–26.

———. 2011. 'The Consequences of Economic Globalization'. In *The Sage Handbook of Economic Geography,* edited by Andrew Leyshon, Roger Lee, Linda McDowell and Peter Sunley. London: SAGE, 102–118.

Sunley, Peter and Steven Pinch. 2014. 'The Local Construction of Social Enterprise Markets: An Evaluation of Jens Beckert's Field Approach'. *Environment and Planning A: Economy and Space* 46 (4): 788–802.

Supiot, Alain. 2003. 'The Labyrinth of Human Rights: Credo or Common Resource?' *New Left Review* 21 (May–June) : 118–136.

———. 2006. 'Law and Labour: A World Market of Norms?' *New Left Review* 39 (May–June): 109–121.

———. 2013. 'Grandeur and Misery of the Social State'. *New Left Review* 82 (July–August): 99–113.

Tambiah, Stanley. 1992. *Buddhism Betrayed? Religion, Politics, and Violence in Sri Lanka.* Chicago, IL: University of Chicago Press.

Tewari, Meenu. 2008. 'Varieties of Global Integration: Navigating Institutional Legacies and Global Networks in India's Garment Sector'. *Competition and Change* 12 (1): 49–67.

Tetrault, Lisa. 2014. *The Myth of Seneca Falls*. Chapel Hill, NC: University of North Carolina Press.

Thaheer, Minna, Pradeep Pieris and Kasun Pathiraja. 2013. *Reconciliation in Sri Lanka: Voices from Former War Zones*. Colombo, Sri Lanka: ICES.

The Conference Board. 2019. *Labour Productivity by Country*. https://conference-board.org/ilcprogram/. Accessed 19 November 2019.

Thiranagama, Sharika. 2014. *In My Mother's House: Civil War in Sri Lanka*. Philadelphia, PA: University of Pennsylvania Press.

Thompson, E. P. 1966. *The Making of the English Working Class*. New York: Vintage Books.

Tighe, Ellie. 2016. 'Voluntary Governance in Clothing Production Networks: Management Perspectives on Multi-Stakeholder Initiatives in Dhaka'. *Environment and Planning A: Economy and Space* 48 (12): 2504–2524.

Tokatli, Nebahat. 2007a. 'Asymmetrical Power Relations and Upgrading among Suppliers of Global Clothing Brands: Hugo Boss in Turkey'. *Journal of Economic Geography* 7 (1): 67–92.

———. 2007b. 'Networks, Firms and Upgrading within the Blue-Jeans Industry: Evidence from Turkey'. *Global Networks* 7 (1): 51–68.

———. 2008. 'Global Sourcing: Insights from the Global Clothing Industry – the Case of Zara, as Fast Fashion Retailer'. *Journal of Economic Geography* 8 (1): 21–38.

UN Comtrade. 2019. 'UN Comtrade Database'. https://comtrade.un.org/data/. Accessed 11 November 2019.

USAID. 2013. 'Evaluation: USAID/Sri Lanka Eastern Garment Alliance (EGA) Project'. Washington, DC: USAID. http://pdf.usaid.gov/pdf_docs/pdacw255.pdf. Accessed 13 September 2015.

Venugopal, Rajesh. 2011. 'The Politics of Market Reform at a Time of Civil War: Military Fiscalism in Sri Lanka'. *Economic and Political Weekly* 44 (49): 67–75.

———. 2018. *Nationalism, Development and Ethnic Conflict in Sri Lanka*. Cambridge: Cambridge University Press.

Visweswaran, Kamala. 1994. *Fictions of Feminist Ethnography*. Minneapolis, MN: University of Minnesota Press.

Waller, William. 2006. 'The Political Economy of Laissez-Faire'. *Journal of Economic Issues* 40 (1): 59–74.

Weller, Sally. 2007. 'Fashion as Viscous Knowledge: Fashion's Role in Shaping Trans-National Garment Production'. *Journal of Economic Geography* 7 (1): 39–66.

Werner, Marion. 2012. 'Beyond Upgrading: Gendered Labour and the Restructuring of Firms in the Dominican Republic'. *Economic Geography* 88 (4): 403–422.

———. 2016. *Global Displacements: The Making of Uneven Development in the Caribbean*. Chichester, West Sussex: John Wiley & Sons.

———. 2020. 'Geographies of Production II: Thinking through the State'. *Progress in Human Geography* 1–12 (on-line preview).

Wickramasinghe, Nira. 2009. 'After the War: A New Patriotism in Sri Lanka?' *The Journal of Asian Studies* 68 (4): 1045–1054.

Wills, Jane. 1996. 'Geographies of Trade Unionism: Translating Traditions across Space and Time'. *Antipode* 28 (4): 352–378.

Witharana, Dileepa. 2015. 'The Story of the 6% T-Shirt: The Hundred-Day Struggle of the Federation of University Teacher's Association, Sri Lanka'. *The South Asianist Journal* 4 (1). http://www.southasianist.ed.ac.uk/article/view/1262. Accessed 25 November 1919.

Women's Centre. 2006. *We Have Arrived*. Colombo, Sri Lanka: Star Press.

———. 2011. *Uprising: Struggle against EPF Daylight Robbery*. Ja-Ela: Women's Centre.

———. 2013. *Ethnic Discrimination: The Post Armed Conflict Economic Challenges of Tamil Women*. Ja-Ela: Women's Centre of Sri Lanka.

Wood, Ellen. 1981. 'The Separation of the Economic and the Political in Capitalism'. *New Left Review* 1 (127): 66–95.

World Bank. 2020a. 'GINI Index (World Bank Estimates)'. https://data.worldbank.org/indicator/SI.POV.GINI. Accessed 16 May 2020.

———. 2020b. *South Asia Economic Focus, Spring 2020: The Cursed Blessing of Public Banks*. Washington, DC: World Bank. https://openknowledge.worldbank.org/handle/10986/33478?locale-attribute=en. Accessed 10 April 2020.

Wright, Melissa. 2006. *Disposable Women and Other Myths of Global Capitalism*. London: Routledge.

Yatawara, Ravi. 2007. 'Gender-Related Labour Transition Issues Resulting from the Expiration of the Agreement on Textiles and Clothing (ATC)'. Working paper, Institute of Policy Studies Colombo, Sri Lanka.

Zaki-Chakravarti, Leila. 2019. *Made in Egypt: Gendered Identity and Aspiration on the Globalised Shop Floor*. Oxford, Oxon: Berghahn Books.

Index